FOLK MEDICINE

A COLLECTION

Tarl Warwick
2020

COPYRIGHT AND DISCLAIMER

PREFACE

The history of medicine up until relatively recently is the history of human beings throwing everything but the kitchen sink at their maladies, pairing them with a million theories explaining sickness, and continuing to revise and re-revise their strategies going forward, utilized to heal, to standardize, and to quantify.

This fascinating topic has, of course, led to a continuously evolving and ever-expanding corpus of literature designed to allow the individual to treat themselves by various methods. Folk medicine is perhaps something we need to define, however, before we go forward: It is, at large, all medical practice and lore that deviates from whatever is conceived of in modernity as "mainstream" or "proper" medicine. I here would like to posit an interesting idea; while expanded access to "modern" medicine has denigrated the usage of folk cures, herbalism, etc, the expanded access of the public to folkloric medicine via the internet has counterbalanced this, and some of the more intriguing works and practices of homeopathy etc have actually increased in usage. Hardly an American family in the 2000s didn't at least hear about the garlic craze and the usage of that one plant as a sort of miracle cure for all ailments. Before we consider people in the pre-modern era primitive on the topic of medical science, let us remember that the usage of electrical shocks to try and stimulate the muscles was popular as recently as the late 20th century- how this deviates significantly from electroshock therapy for nervous complaints is not clear if we are being intellectually honest.

Much folk medicine is herbal in nature. The first way in which man learned to medicate was to turn to mother nature. People were licking willow trees for relief long before the active chemicals therein were pharmaceutically isolated, synthesized in a laboratory, standardized by measurement, and turned into the sometimes lifesaving pills we know today. Other than standardizing the dosage, science writ large did relatively little in this venture, no?

Let us consider briefly the ever-changing nature of medicine (especially dietary "science"!) before we consider the contents of the present work. Twenty five years ago it was broadly believed in western science that saturated fat caused heart disease and margarine was a good replacement for butter. Now, science believes the trans-fats in margarine destroy arterial health and saturated fat is, in small quantities, actually harmless. Eggs have been both the cholesterol devil and an important protein source. Wine both destroys the liver and protects the heart. Gluten sensitivity is a hoax, a common reality, and an over-diagnosed rare disorder. Mental illness is best taken care of by therapy, or by drugs, or by free range child rearing. Fat is the devil. Sugar is the devil. Salt is the devil. Coffee simultaneously manages to cause and yet prevent strokes.

Confusing, isn't it? Perhaps licking a willow tree is at least less frightfully obtuse!

The first section of this work contains, verbatim, the **Regimen Sanitatis Salernitanum**, which is one of the first comprehensive dietary and "healthy living" books ever made. Ascribed to the Salerno school of medicine, it contains a few extremely odd (and dangerous!) passages such as purporting the medicinal use of orpiment- which contains arsenic. When I first edited the book I was surprised to see that it contains what may be the first serious and potentially useful advocacy for sanitation- I have remarked at times that while medieval medical practitioners did not understand the nature of pestilence, some of their prescriptions would have had an effect- Nostradamus himself had been a plague doctor and may have used this work as a springboard when he suggested flooding out swampy or low lying areas with running water to relieve cities of disease (this would have removed the human waste in such areas which created infection via rodent hosts and insects.) I place this relatively short work in its own section because of its massive historical importance.

The second section of this present volume is about **Various Folk Remedies** and is taken from a variety of works. Such lore was especially profuse in the 19th century, when basic standardization and science ran up against expansion into colonial territories and a population used to riding horses hopped into trains and aboard steam ships and began encountering exotic people and their equally exotic medical systems. I have chosen some of the more interesting entries from all of the works referenced.

The third section deals with a few **Remedies from Alchemical Works**, which are partly overlapped with a few entries I placed in the *Alchemy Collection* published earlier this year. While some alchemists focused on making gold, finding mineral ores, or counterfeiting coins, some works of note in the tradition were provably medicinal. The ability to balance the humors definitely plays a role here; this now-outdated medical concept had alchemists providing solutions containing lead to patients, with the understanding that it was healthy that they were sweating!

Section four is a a verbatim copy of a very good work with no technical comparison that I have encountered, and is called **Medical Astrology**. It dates to 1899 and was written by F.R. White and R. Hollingsworth. I decided it was best to include this for those interested chiefly in that kind of lore.

Section five contains **Various Herbal Lore** and contains a semi-exhaustive list of some species and their medical usage. I have cast the net as widely as possible in this section, although it is absolutely the case that a great plurality of good English-language or translated works on herbalism come from the United States or Europe and this precludes a great deal of information from elsewhere, excepting India, where the former English Empire poured unfathomable resources into anthropological studies.

The sixth and final section contains various **Medical Recipes**, or receipts as they were initially called in the apothecary sense. This compiles a few basic cures from several volumes.

I have added to this present volume a short bibliography containing a few works not noted in this book, and a short section with a bit of old time medical terminology related both to diseases and to measurements (such as grains and drachms) since sometimes the remedies here use them. Any other terms the reader is unfamiliar with are easily looked up in any good reference to the subject of medical history, or on the internet at large.

~Tarl Warwick

CONTENTS

REGIMEN SANITATIS SALERNITANUM

If you want to be healthy, if you want to remain sound, take away your heavy cares, and refrain from anger.

Be sparing of undiluted wine, eat little, get up after eating fine food, avoid afternoon naps, do not retain your urine nor tightly compress your anus. Do these things well, and you shall live a long time.

Should you need physicians, these three doctors will suffice: A joyful mind, rest and a moderate diet.

In the morning, upon rising, wash your hands and face with cold water. Move around awhile and stretch your limbs. Comb your hair and brush your teeth. These things relax your brain and other parts of your body. After your bath keep warm; stand or walk around after a meal; go slowly if you are of cool temperament.

Take a short afternoon nap, or none at all, as fever, indolence, headache and chest cold may result from that nap.

Four illnesses come from gas retained in the stomach: Spasm, dropsy, colic and vertigo.

Your stomach will suffer great harm after a heavy meal. In order not to feel weighed down at night, make your evening meal light.

Do not eat a second time until your stomach has been purged and emptied of the food which you took earlier. You will be able to know for sure whether you are hungry, by judging your desire for food. The other sign is having dined lightly earlier.

Peaches, apples, pears, milk, cheese, salted meats, deer meat, rabbit, goat, and beef are melancholic and harmful to the sick.

Fresh eggs, red wines and rich gravies are recommended since they are nutritious in nature.

Wheat, milk, and fresh cheese are nourishing and fattening, as are testicles, pork meat, brain, marrow, sweet wines, good tasting foods, raw eggs, ripe figs, and fresh grapes.

Wines should be tested for smell, taste, brightness, and color. If you want good wines, these five things should be tested in them: How strong, brilliant, fragrant, cool, and fresh they are.

Most nutritious are the heavy white wines.

If too much red wine is drunk, it causes constipation and raucousness of the voice.

Garlic, nuts, rue, pears, radishes, and theriaca are antidotes for deadly poison.

The air must be pure, habitable, and bright, it should be neither contaminated nor smell of the sewer.

If you develop a hangover from drinking at night, drink again in the morning; it will be your best medicine.

The best wine engenders the best humors. If wine is dark, it renders your body indolent; wine should be clear, aged, subtle, ripe, well diluted, zesty, and taken in moderation.

Beer should not be sour but clear. It should be brewed from healthy grains, and sufficiently fermented and aged.

Your stomach will not weighed down from drinking

beer.

Take a moderate quantity of food in the springtime. Summer's heat is also harmful to those who eat immoderately. In autumn beware that fruits do not become cause for mourning. Eat as much as you like in winter.

Sage and rue will make your drinks safe. If you add the flower of the rose, it will strongly diminish your lust.

Seasickness will not trouble a man who has taken seawater mixed with wine before the trip.

From sage, salt with wine, pepper, garlic, and parsley make a sauce, mixing it together in a sprightly manner.

If you want to be healthy, wash your hands often. Washing after a meal gives you two benefits: It cleans your hands and makes your eyes keen.

Bread should be neither warm nor stale. It should be leavened, raised, well-baked, moderately salted, and chosen from the best grains. Do not eat the crust, since it causes burning choler. Bread that is salted, leavened, well-baked, pure, and healthy should be of great benefit to you.

If you eat pork without wine, it is worse than mutton. If you add wine to pork, then it is food and medicine. The intestines of pigs are good; those of other animals are bad.

Must interferes with urination and acts as a laxative. It causes stoppage of the liver and spleen, and engenders kidney stones.

Drinking and eating at the same time may be harmful, since water cools the stomach, and the food is liable to remain undigested.

FOLK MEDICINE

Veal is very nourishing.

Chicken, duck, turtledove, starling, pigeon, quail, blackbird, pheasant, thrush, partridge, chaffinch, orex, wagtail, and water fowl are nourishing.

If fish are soft, they should be eaten when they are large in size; if fish are hard, they are more nutritive when small in size.

Pike, perch, sole, whiting, tench, shrimp, plaice, carp, gurnard, and trout are all edible fish.

Eating eels is bad for the voice as those who know anything about medicine will attest, and cheese and eel are harmful when eaten together in great quantity, unless you drink wine often.

During the meal take small drinks often. If you eat an egg, make it soft and fresh.

We decided both to praise and to reproach the pea: Without the pod, peas are rather good; with the pod, they cause gas and are harmful.

Goat's milk is healthy for consumptives, and next after that camel's milk, but most nutritious of all is ass's milk; cow's milk is also nutritious and likewise sheep's milk. If your head is feverish or aches, milk is not very healthy.

Butter softens; it is moist and acts as a laxative when there is no fever.

Whey cuts through and washes, penetrates and purifies.

Cheese, is cold, constipating, crude, and hard, cheese and bread are good food for a man who is healthy; if a man is not healthy, then cheese without bread is good.

"Ignorant doctors say that I am harmful, nevertheless they do not know why I should do harm."

Cheese brings help to a weak stomach. Taken after your other food, it properly ends the meal. Those who are not ignorant of medicine will attest to these things.

During the meal take small drinks often, so that you do not become ill, do not wait to drink in between courses.

After each egg drink another cup of wine; after fish have nuts, after meat serve cheese. One kind of nut is good, a second is harmful, a third kind brings death.

Add a drink of wine to your pear, and the nut is medicine against poison. A pear tree produces our pears. Without wine its pears are poison; if pears are poison, then damned be the pear tree!

If you cook them, pears are an antidote, but uncooked they are a poison. Raw they aggravate the stomach; cooked, pears relieve the aggravation. After the pear, drink wine; after the apple empty your bowels.

From eating the cherry, you will derive great benefits: It purges the stomach, its pit removes your kidney stone, and from its pulp will come good blood.

Plums are quite beneficial to you: they are cooling and cathartic.

You should take peaches with must, just as it is customary to eat grapes with nuts. Raisins are bad for the spleen, but good for a cough or for the kidneys.

Fig in a poultice removes scrofula, tumor, and glandulas; add poppy and it mends together broken bones.

The fig generates lice and lust, but it resists anything.

Medlars cause excessive urine and constipation. Medlars are good hard, but better soft.

Must causes urine, is laxative and brings on gas.

Beer nourishes thick humors, gives strength, fattens the flesh, produces blood, provokes urine, has a laxative effect, causes gas, and has a cooling effect. Vinegar has more of a drying effect: It cools, makes a man thin, induces melancholy, decreases the number of sperm, harms those of dry humor, and dries up the nerve of the fats.

The turnip helps the stomach, produces gas, causes urine, and may do harm to the teeth. If it is served under-cooked, it may give you a stomach cramp.

The heart of all animals is slow to digest and hard to excrete. Similarly the stomach is harder to digest and excrete than its extremities.

Tongue gives good medicinal nourishment. The lung is easily digested and is quickly expelled. The brain of chickens is better than any other animals.

The fennel seed loosens gas.

Anise improves vision and comforts the stomach. And sweet anise works better.

The ashes of certain vegetable matters stop hemorrhage.

The salt dish should be placed on the table at mealtime.

Salt wards off poison, and adds taste to a man's food, for food which is served without salt does not taste good. Very salty foods hurt the eyes, decrease sperm, and engenders scabies, pruritus, or vigor.

These three flavors have a warming effect: the salty, the bitter, and the sharp. The sour, like the styptic, and the acidulous have a cooling effect. The unctuous, the tasteless, and the sweet yield a balanced effect.

Wine soup has a quadruple effect: it cleans the teeth; it gives sharp vision; what is lacking it supplies; what is overabundant it reduces.

I prescribe a regular diet for all people: I recommend keeping that diet unless it is necessary to change it. Hippocrates attests that disease may result otherwise. A proper diet is one of the foremost goals of medicine; attend to your diet, or you foolishly direct your other efforts and take care of yourself badly.

What kind? what? when? how much? how often? where to be given? These things a doctor should quickly take note of while prescribing a diet.

Cabbage broth has a laxative effect; its substance is astringent; when taken together they act as a laxative.

The Ancients called mallow "malva" because it softens the belly. The roots of the mallow act as a laxative; they bring movement to the womb and cause menstrual flow to occur often.

Mint would not be mint if it were slow to expel dangerous intestinal worms of the belly and stomach.

Why should a man die in whose garden grows sage?

Against the power of death there is not medicine in our gardens, but sage calms the nerves, takes away hand tremors, and helps cure fever. Sage, castor bean, lavender, primrose, nasturtium, and athanasia cure paralytic parts of the body. Oh sage the savior, of nature the conciliator!

Noble is rue since it gives you keen eyesight. With its help, certainly as a man, you will see sharply. Rue decreases coitus in man and increases it in women. Rue makes man chaste, intelligent and cunning. When cooked, rue makes the house safe from fleas.

The doctors do not seem to agree on onions. Galen says that they are not good for those of choleric humor, but he teaches that they are quite salubrious for phlegmatics, and especially good for the stomach and the complexion. By frequently rubbing your bald spots with ground onions, you may restore your head of hair.

The mustard seed is small, dry, and hot. It causes tears, relieves the head, and expels a poison.

Drunkenness and headache are relieved by the violet. They say that it also cures epileptics.

The nettle gives sleep to the sick, stops vomiting, relieves chronic cough, and is a remedy against colic. It takes away your chest cold as well as abdominal tumors, and it helps in all diseases of the joints.

The hyssop is an herb that purges your chest of phlegm. When it is cooked with honey it is good for the lungs. It is said to restore a healthy coloring to your face.

Chervil ground and mixed with honey is a remedy for the canker. When it is taken with wine it cuts off pain; it often stops vomiting and loose bowls.

Fleabane taken with wine expels black bile; they say it also cures chronic gout.

The mother swallow uses celandine in restoring sight to her blinded young whose eyes have been plucked out, according to Pliny.

The willow's juice kills worms when poured into their ears; its bark cooked in vinegar cures warts; the juice of the fruits and the flower are harmful to human reproduction.

The saffron, being cheery, is said to comfort; it aids weak parts of the body and helps the liver.

Phlegm makes man weak, stout, short, and fat, while the blood humor makes men of medium build. Men of phlegmatic humor tend toward leisure rather than work, and dullness of senses, slow movement, laziness, and sleep are typical. Those sleepy and sluggish men, who spit often, are dull of senses and white in coloring.

If eaten often, leeks make girls fertile. You may also stop nosebleed with them.

Because pepper is black, it is not slow to dissolve. It will purge phlegm and help digestion. White pepper is good for your stomach and useful for the pain of cough. It will ward off the attack of fever and its rigor.

Both sleep and too much movement soon after eating, as well as drunkenness, are usually bad for the hearing.

Fear, long fasting, vomiting, a blow, a fall, drunkenness, and cold cause a ringing in your ear.

Baths, wines, Venus, wind, pepper, garlic, smoke, leeks, onions, lentil, weeping, beans, mustard, the sun, coitus, fire, work, a blow, spicy foods, dust: These things hurt the eyes, but staying up late hurts them more so.

Fennel, verbena, the rose, celandine, rue: From these mix juices to sharpen your eyesight.

Likewise take care of your teeth: gather the seeds of the leeks, burn them with the juice of the henbane, and direct the smoke toward your teeth through a funnel. Nuts, olive oil, head cold, eels, drinking, and raw apples make a man hoarse.

Fast, stay awake, eat hot food, work hard, breathe warm air, drink little, hold your breath: Do these things well if you want to get rid of a cold.

If the cold goes down to the chest it is called catarrh. When it goes to the fauces, hoarseness; to the nose, coryza.

Mix sulfur with orpiment. And add quick lime, then combine them with soap. Mix these four together, and when they are mixed your fistula will be cured, when these four steps are completed.

Man has two hundred and nineteen bones. He has thirty-two teeth, and three hundred and sixty-five veins.

Elecampane is good for the diaphragm. If its juice is mixed with that of rue, there is nothing more healthful for those with hernia.

Nasturtium juice spread over the head is said to stop hair from falling out; it also cures toothache; and the juice mixed with honey cures scales.

Four humors make up the human body: Blood, choler, phlegm and melancholy. Earth corresponds to melancholy, water to phlegm, air to blood, fire to choler.

Fat and jolly of nature are those of sanguine humor. They always want to hear rumors, Venus and Bacchus delight them, as well as good food and laughter. They are joyful and desirous of speaking kind words.

These people are skillful for all subjects and quite apt. For whatever cause, anger cannot lightly rouse them. They are generous, loving, joyful, merry, of ruddy complexion. Singing, solidly lean, rather daring, and friendly.

Next is the choleric humor, which is known to be impulsive: This kind of man desires to surpass all others. On the one hand he learns easily, he eats much and grows quickly. On the other hand, he is magnanimous, generous, a great enthusiast. He is hairy, deceitful, irritable, lavish, bold, astute, slender, of dry nature, and of yellowish complexion.

There remains the sad substance of the black melancholic temperament, which makes men wicked, gloomy, and taciturn. These men are given to studies, and little sleep. They work persistently toward a goal; they are insecure. They are envious, sad, avaricious, tight-fisted, capable of deceit, timid, and of muddy complexion.

These are the humors which give to each his skin coloring:

From phlegm comes a fair, white complexion.

From blood a ruby color, and a rather tawny complexion from red choler.

If blood is overabundant, the face turns red, the eyes protrudes, the cheeks swell up, the body is too weighed down, the pulse is frequent, full, and soft; great pain occurs, especially in the forehead; the bowels are constipated. A dry tongue and thirst result, and dreams are completely red in color. The saliva is sweet, even when tasting bitter things.

Phlebotomy is scarcely needed before a person is seventeen. The more productive spirit will escape with your blood during phlebotomy, but these spirits will soon be replaced by drinking wine, and any harm done by the humors will be gradually repaired by food.

Phlebotomy clears your eyes, freshens your mind and brain, makes your marrow warm, purges your bowels and restrains your stomach and belly from vomiting or menstruation; it purifies the senses, brings on sleep, takes away weariness; it cultivates and improves hearing, speech, and strength.

These are the good months for phlebotomy - May, September, April, which are lunar months just as are the Hydra days.

Neither on the first day of May nor the last day of September or April should blood be drawn or goose be eaten. In the old man or in the young man whose veins are full of blood, phlebotomy may be practiced in every month. These are the three months: May, September, April, in which you should draw blood in order to live a long time.

Cool constitution, a cold region, great pain, bathing, sexual intercourse, youth and old age, long illness, heavy drinking, and eating; if you are in one of these situations or if you are nauseous, then phlebotomy is not good for you.

What should you do when you want to be phlebotomized? Or when you are bloodletting or when you will have blood let? Ointment, drink, washing, bandages, and movement should be kept well in mind.

Phlebotomy cheers the sad, calms the angry and helps

cure madmen.

Make the wound rather large, so that quickly the vapors may escape, and blood come out more abundantly and more freely.

When blood has been taken out, stay awake six hours, so that the vapors of sleep will not harm your sensitive body. To avoid damaging a nerve, do not let your wound cut deep. After being cleansed by blood, you should not eat immediately.

You should avoid all milk products, and refrain from drinking after phlebotomy. Keep away from cold things, since cold is bad for you.

While in this condition, avoid walking outside during cloudy weather, but raise your spirits by walking outside in good weather. Rest is appropriate for all, and movement could prove harmful.

Practice phlebotomy at the beginning of acute and very acute illnesses. Take a lot of blood from those of middle age; from children and older persons take only a little. Take twice as much blood in spring, but only the normal amount in other seasons.

In summer and spring take blood from the right veins; in autumn and winter from the left.

These four parts of the body- the head, the heart, the feet, the liver- should be relieved of blood.

The heart in spring, the liver in summer, the following in the order of the seasons- the head in winter, the feet in autumn.

Opening the salvatella vein gives you many small

benefits: It purges the liver, the spleen, the chest, the diaphragm, and the voice; it also takes away any unnatural pain from the heart.

If your headache is from alcohol, drink water, for from too much alcohol an acute fever may occur.

If the top of your head or forehead has a burning pain, rub your temples and forehead moderately at the same time, and wash them with warm morel that has been cooked.

Fasting in summertime dries out the body. Vomiting is profitable in every month, for it purges harmful humors, and it washes the circuits of all the stomach. Spring, summer, autumn, and winter are the seasons of the year.

In springtime the air is warm and humid, and no time is better for phlebotomy. In spring lovemaking is beneficial to man in moderation, as are exercises, laxatives, sweating, and baths. In that season the body should be purged with medicines.

Summer is usually hot, and is known as a dry season. The summer encourages the occurrences of red choler. In summer food of cold and humid qualities should be served, and lovemaking should be avoided;

Baths are not good then, and phlebotomy should be rare. Rest is useful, and drink is good in moderation.

THE END

VARIOUS FOLK REMEDIES

This present section will derive from a number of works and includes all folk remedies for ailments which are not alchemical in nature. Some of them are rather funny, and others a bit more serious. The following list includes works alluded to:

I. John George Hohmans' *Pow Wows*. An early 19th century grimoire of sorts.

II. Albertus Magnus' *Egyptian Secrets*. Another 19th century work, translated into English be DeLaurence at the dawn of the 20th. Some of its lore overlaps with *Pow Wows*.

III. The *Petit Albert*. This mid 18th century grimoire contains a great deal of folk medicine along with workings with alchemy, talismans, and various spells both malevolent and benevolent.

IV. *Frays Golden Recipes*, which is an 1897 work containing a series of basic herbal and other remedies in alphabetical order.

V. *Valuable Herbal Prescriptions* from the Bradford Medical Institute, of 1895. This work contains various preparations, herbal in nature.

VI: *The Useful Family Herbal* by John Williams. This 1829 work is fairly short and contains a laundry list of folk cures.

VII: *The Family Companion and Physician* published by Dr. J Wilson in 1862. I have selected only the section on diseases and remedies out of this intermediate-length work.

FROM "POW WOWS"

Remedy for hysterics and for colds

This must be attended to every evening, that is, whenever you pull off your shoes and stockings, run your finger in between all the toes and smell it. This will certainly effect a cure.

To banish the whooping cough

Cut three small bunches of hair from the crown of the head of a child that has never seen its father; sew this hair up in an unbleached rag and hang it around the neck of the child having the whooping cough. The thread with which the rag is sewed must also be unbleached.

To banish convulsive fevers

Write the following letters on a piece of white paper, sew it on a piece of linen or muslin, and hang it around the neck until the fever leaves you:

A b a x a C a t a b a x
A b a x a C a t a b a x
A b a x a C a t a b a
A b a x a C a t a b
A b a x a C a t a
A b a x a C a t
A b a x a C a
A b a x a C
A b a x a
A b a x
A b a
A b

A very good remedy for the colic

Take half a gill of good rye whiskey, and a pipe full of tobacco; put the whiskey in a bottle, then smoke the tobacco and blow the smoke into the bottle, shake it well and drink it. This has cured the author of this book and many others. Or, take a white clay pipe which has turned blackish from smoking, pound it to a fine powder, and take it. This will have the same effect.

To make a good eye water

Take four cents' worth of white vitriol, for cents' worth of prepared spicewort (calamus root), four cents' worth of cloves, a gill of good whiskey and a gill of water. Make the calamus fine and mix all together; then use it after it has stood a few hours.

A very good remedy for the white swelling

Take a quart of lime which has not been slaked, and pour two parts of water on it; stir it well and let it stand over night. The scum that collects on the lime-water must be taken off, and a pint of flax-seed oil poured in, after which it must be stirred until it becomes somewhat consistent: then put it in a pot or pan, and add a little lard and wax; melt it well, and make a plaster, and apply it to the parts affected. The plaster should be renewed every day, or at least every other day, until the swelling is gone.

A good cure for wounds

Take the bones of a calf, and burn them until they turn to powder, and then strew it into the wound. The powder prevents the flesh from putrefying, and is therefore of great importance in healing the wound.

To make an oil out of paper which is good for sore eyes

A man from Germany informed me that to burn two sheets of white paper would produce about three drops of oil or water, which would heal all sores in or about the eye if rubbed with it. Any affection of the eyes can be cured in this way, as long as the apple of the eye is sound.

To destroy crab lice

Take capuchin powder, mix it with hog's lard, and smear yourself with it. Or boil cammock, and wash the place where the lice keep themselves.

For deafness, roaring, or buzzing in the ear and for toothache

A few drops of refined camphor-oil put upon cotton, and thus applied to the aching tooth, relives very much. When put in the ear it strengthens the hearing and removes the roaring and whizzing in the same.

For vomiting and diarrhea

Take pulverized cloves and eat them together with bread soaked in red wine, and you will soon find relief. The cloves may be put upon the bread.

To heal burns

Pound or press the juice of male fern, and put it on the burnt spots and they will heal very fast. Better yet, however, if you smear the above juice upon a rag, and put it on like a plaster.

Very good cure for weakening of the limbs, for the purification of blood, for the invigorating of the head and heart, and to remove giddiness

Take two drops of oil of cloves in a tablespoonful of white wine early in the morning, and before eating anything else. This is also good for the mother-pains and the colic. The oil of cloves which you buy in the drug stores will answer the purpose. These remedies are also applicable to cure the cold when it settles in the bowels, and to stop vomiting. A few drops of this oil poured upon cotton and applied to the aching teeth, relieves the pain.

A well tried plaster to remove mortification

Take six hen's eggs and boil them in hot ashes until they are right hard; then take the yellow of the eggs and fry them in a gill of lard until they are quite black; then put a handful of rue with it, and afterward filter it through a cloth. When this is done add a gill of sweet oil to it. It will take most effect where the plaster for a female is prepared by a male, and the plaster for a male prepared by a female.

Cure for dropsy

Dropsy is a disease derived from a cold humidity, which passes through the different limbs to such a degree that it either swells the whole or a portion of them. The usual symptoms and precursors of every case of dropsy are the swelling of the feet and thighs, and then of the face; besides this the change of the natural color of the flesh into a dull white, with great thirst, loss of appetite, costiveness, sweating, throwing up of slimy substances, but little water, laziness and aversion to exercise.

Physicians know three different kinds of dropsy, which they name:

1. Anasarca, when the water penetrates between the skin and the flesh over the whole body, and all the limbs, and even about the face and swells them.

2. Ascites, when the belly and thighs swell, while the upper extremities dry up.

3. Tympanites, caused rather by wind than water. The belly swells up very hard, the navel is forced out very far, and the other members fall away. The belly becomes so much inflated that knocking against it causes a sound like that of a large drum, and from this circumstance its name is derived.

The chief thing in curing dropsy rests upon three points, namely:

1. To reduce the hardness of the swelling which may be in the bowels or other parts.

2. To endeavor to scatter the humors.

3. To endeavor to pass them off either through the stool or through the water.

The best cure therefore must chiefly consist in this: To avoid as much as possible all drinking, and use only dry victuals; to take moderate exercise, and to sweat and purge the body considerably.

If anyone feels symptoms of dropsy, or while it is yet in its first stages, let him make free use of the sugar of the herb called *Fumitory,* as this purifies the blood, and the *Euphrasy* sugar to open the bowels.

FROM "EGYPTIAN SECRETS"

A very good Recipe for the Colic

Take a spoonful of olive or sweet oil, pounded crab eyes, and four carefully dried and pulverized peels of oranges, dissolved in good, warm wine. It relieves the pain immediately.

An Easy and Efficacious Remedy for the Dysentery

The patient need only take a piece of the red mortar from a bake oven, as large as an egg, prepared as follows: Pound it in a mortar, and boil in river water, but take it cold. The ailment will cease almost instantly.

An especially approved Powder for the Gravel

Burn the blood of a hare and the entire skin in a new earthen pot to ashes, and give it to the patient dissolved in warm water. Let him take a spoonful before breakfast. It is astonishing what a powerful effect this powder exercises.

Secret Remedy of the great Theophrastus Paracelsus for Healing the Cancer

This celebrated recipe is composed as follows: When a human being takes hold with his right hand of a live mole, and keeps the mole so long with a tight grip until it dies, such a hand obtains by dint of this miraculous proceeding, such marvelous power, that cancer boils, repeatedly rubbed, by moving up and down with this hand will break open, cease to form again, and entirely vanish.

An excellent Ointment for Old Sores on the Feet

The following articles are necessary to make this

ointment: one ounce of deer's tallow, two ounces of bees' wax, a like portion of white rosin, half ounce of white lead, three ounces of white bolus, six ounces of sweet oil, two ounces incense and mastic. The rosin and oil are left to boil together, and melt the wax therein, until it becomes stiff. After it has cooled off mix all the other articles to it; after they have been pounded, stir them well, and save up for use. Before applying this ointment to old sores, wash them first with warm sweet wine, then apply the ointment, and all wilt be well done to effect a result.

For Arthritis or Pains in the Limbs

Take two handfuls of fresh juniper berries, bruise them, boil them in a pint of old wine, add a glassful of brandy and put the whole in a cloth that is folded four times, and this apply to the place where the pain is located. It is an approved remedy.

Hysterics accompanied by Fainting

Take the warts commonly growing on the shanks of steers cut them fine, dry them in an iron pan over a glowing flame until they become yellowish, bruise them gently and give of this powder as much as the point of a table-knife will hold, in wine or other liquor, to the patient, who must keep herself warm.

A Remedy hitherto Secret against Sloth and Slough, commonly called Sweeny

Dig three burdock roots on a Friday before the sun rises cut off every one of these roots, three round slices, sew them in a cloth, bind them over the sweeny limb or member, and let it remain there from two to four days, repeat as before until the part affected stops to ooze matter. The roots may be green or dry, it is all the same, if you only take care to dig them on a Friday before sunrise. Has been sufficiently tried on man and beast.

Against Violent Headaches

Iron herb hung around the neck, or the essence thereof sprinkled upon the brow and temples, will cure the most violent headaches.

For Costive People

Take half of a scruple or veronica or speedwell. Probatum est!

Ointment for the Scurvy

Take a glass of wine, a glass of brandy, unwashed butter, smear soap, white beeswax, salt, pepper, cloves and a little of sulfur flower.

A Secret Art to banish Chicken Lice

Strew malaxis herbs upon the floor of the hen-house, let it remain eight days therein, then wash it all clean again and the lice will have vanished.

For Bad Hearing

Take the oil with which the bells of churches are greased, and smear it behind the afflicted ears, and relief will not fail to come at once.

How to drive away Bed Bugs

Fern leaves gathered between the last two days of the month of June, and put under the bed, will drive away the bed bugs sure.

How to Kill Bed Bugs

Take of wormwood and rue a handful of each, mix them with common oil, also enough water, so that both water and oil will cover the herbs; after this boil the mass so long until all the water evaporates, whereupon squeeze the herbs in a press to obtain all the oil possible, and add a like quantity of mutton tallow; with this saturate the bedsteads, and the bugs will die.

For Stitching Pains in Woman or Child

Take goats' milk and a warm roll, and boll together, and apply the poultice as warm as possible upon the ailing spot and tie a towel around it It will be cured.

To Drive away Swellings

Take aniseed oil, turpentine oil, of each one-half an ounce, stir well and apply upon the swelling. It will soon improve.

A Remedy to cure the Cough

When cherries are in season, dry the stems of black cherries between two sheets, of paper to prevent them from becoming dusty, save them in a paper box. Draw tea therefrom, for every drawing take about four saucers full of water, and as many cherry stems as may be held between three fingers. Boil like any other tea, and continue to take this tea till the coughing ceases. The most violent cough may be cured by this remedy.

For Colic

Take a few bay leaves and soak them in brandy in a warm room. As soon as the colic is felt, take from one to four spoonfuls of this remedy.

To cure Frosted Feet

Take a white woolen cloth which has never been used before, burn it to ashes, strew these ashes upon the afflicted feet and they will heal.

To strengthen the Procreative Organs

Take twelve ounces of imperial spices, two pounds of white sugar, twenty-four grains of opium, one ounce of borax, four ounces prepared steel filings, twenty drops of cinnamon oil, twenty drops of oil of cloves; of these articles prepare a powder. Take a pinch, or as much as covers the point of a table knife, every hour throughout the day. Bathe the body often in warm water, and the organs in cold water. After this cure you will be stronger than ever before.

For a Plaster

Take olive or sweet oil, camphor, red lead, five cents' worth of each, and prepare into an ointment.

A good Plaster for Open Sores

Take five cents' worth of bees-wax, the same quantity of ropemakers' resin, some few ounces of beef suet, a few teaspoonfuls of sweet oil, that is, the same quantity in weight of each of the ingredients, boil over a quick fire to the substance of a salve, and use like a plaster.

To Ascertain whether a Sick Person will become well again

Cut a piece of bread, rub the patient's teeth therewith, and throw it before a dog. If he eats it, the patient will recover. Otherwise, the disease is dangerous.

To Drive away Lice and Nits from the Head

To drink powder of hartshorn dissolved in wine, prevents the growing of these vermin on the head. If such powder is strewn upon the head, all lice and nits will surely die.

For Gravel, a Simple and Effective Art

This herb boiled in beer, and drank mornings and evenings, is a miraculous remedy.

How to draw the Poison from a Body

Drink four ounces of rosemary water, it will neutralize the poison and strengthen heart and brain.

A Good Salve for Itchy Hands

Take meadow rue, boil in olive oil, mix a little beeswax therewith, so that it becomes a salve. Grease the hands with It, and soon they will be all well.

To Restore Manhood

Buy a pike as they are sold in the fish-market, carry it noiselessly to a running water, there let whale oil run into the snout of the fish, throw the fish into the running water, and then walk stream upward, and you will recover your strength and former powers.

Another Remedy for the Above

Take a new fresh laid egg, if possible, one that is yet warm. Pour Whale oil over it, and boil the egg in it; the oil then should be poured into a running water, stream downward, never then open the egg a little, carry it to an ant's hill, of the large red specie, as are found in fir-trees forest, and there bury the egg. As soon as the ants have devoured the egg, the weak and troubled person will be restored to former strength and vigor.

Remedy for the Hydrophobia

The "Swabian Mercury," a German work, printed at Stuttgart, Germany, contains in No. 181, Mommy, September 10, 1810 the following article, with regard to hydrophobia, which deserves to be reproduced and embodied into this book:

"The county physician, Dr. Schaller, in Baireuth, has recently performed a very successful cure, at the country-seat of the Master of the Royal Forest, Baron de Hardenberg in Karo-linenreuth. The doctor has successfully restored to her wonted health a four-year-old girl, who was bitten by a mad dog, despite all the symptoms of hydrophobia, having already been developed, by the application of belladonna and water of distilled laurel-berries. Thus it was proven that there is verily a remedy for this terrible malady, even after it has taken hold of the unfortunate victim. A similar power is ascribed to aniseed oil, If several drops thereof, poured into the wounds, made by the biting of the rabid animal, or of any other poisonous animal or bird. The oil put on a cloth, and laid upon the wound, will draw the poison therefrom, and leave no injurious effects.

An Excellent Recipe for Pestilence

Take garlic and rue. Boil in good wine vinegar. Drink this mornings and evenings. It is a sure cure.

How the Oil of Earth Worms are Made, and what Good Use is made thereof

It serves in cases of arthritis or neuralgia as well as for the withering of limbs and warts on hands and feet, corns on feet, heels, ruptures, and other injuries of all kinds. Put the earthworms into a pot and wrap the same up in a loaf of bread, bake it in a bake oven as long as is necessary for bread to bake, then put it in a glass vessel, and distill in the sun.

The Usefulness of Black Snails

They cure withered limbs and warts on hands and feet, corns on feet, heels, ruptures and other hurts. Put the snails into a pot. add a good deal of salt and keep it nine days in the ground. After this distill in a glass in the sun.

To make an Ointment for the Cure of the Itch

Take green corn or broom seed, press the sap therefrom, trail it in the same manner that a mush is cooked, add five cents' worth of sulfur and quarter pound of lard. Rub the body with it every night.

For Hysterics

Take dried chicken manure, grind it to powder, and give a pinch of it to the patient in a prune. It is a quick remedy.

For a Felon on the Finger

Take fresh ox gall, boil it, and apply as warm as one can bear it, by dipping the finger therein, and keep it there until it becomes cold. Thus the felon or worm dies soon.

When a Person has a Cancer on Breast or Check

One ounce of sassafras boiled in beer, the pot well sealed, so that the fumes do not evaporate. Drink thereof. If the sore is open, pulverize bones of a corpse, and strew into the wounds. This, also, heals constant discharge from the bladder, etc.

For the Fever

Take the water of the patient and mix it with some flour and make a dough thereof, of which seventy-seven small cakes are made, each one as large as a lintel; proceed before sunrise to an ant-hill and throw the cakes therein. As soon as the insects have devoured the cakes, the fever vanishes. Probatum.

For Falling of the Womb and Cough

Take orange peels, aloes one drachm, and five cents worth of carrots. Put in a bottle, shake well, and take evenings and mornings a good draught of it till the cure is effected.

To stop the Bleeding of a Wound

Paint the wound with nitric spirit.

To make a Blister

Take cantharides (Spanish fly powder), 4 ounces; turpentine, 8 ounces; yellow bees' wax, 4 ounces; linseed oil, 6 ounces. Mix these ingredients to a plaster.

For the Erysipelas

Take a quart of fresh milk, dog's waste stirred therein and strained through a cloth. This is a good internal medicine.

Or make for External Use:

Tormantil wort: 1 drachm
Dragon blood: 2ounces
Red chalk stone: 1 drachm
Mix together and put in milk.

An Approved Oil for Lame Limbs

Take wool, herb flowers, put them into a glass, and after this in an ant hill one knee deep, and tie a bladder around the glass. Let the glass remain there for ten days and the contents will turn to water, wherewith anoint the limbs whenever they pain.

To make an Herb Wine

1. Horse Radish.
2. Rockmoss Flowers.
3. Stone Flowerets.
4. Coxcomb.
5. Veronica.
6. Rue.
7. Sage.
8. Grape Hyacinth.
9. Lung Wort.

Of each a handful; five cents' worth of rose blood, one half pound of barley, one quart of water and one quart of wine, wherein the herbs have to be boiled until one pint evaporate. Drink morning and evening one glassful thereof.

An excellent Eyewater for Man and Beast

When blind, and the eyes are covered with a skin, or the eyes are darkened and dim, take the eggs of red ants and put them into a small glass. Draw a water therefrom. This glass containing the eggs must be kept well corked, so that nothing may ooze out, then put the phial into dough of rye flour and bake in the oven with other bread, and when taken from the oven let cool off with the other loaves, then carefully remove the bread from the glass, so as not to break the same and the ant eggs will prove to have turned into water. This water apply four or five times, as may be necessary, to the afflicted eye, every time one drop only. This has been tried on man and beast.

A Plaster for a Sore Breast

1 quart of rosin, 1 quart of wax,
1 quart of lard, 1 quart of linseed oil.
Unwatered butter, Saffron for five cents.

All these articles boil together, and strain through a white cloth, and let it grow cold.

When a Man has Trod on a Thorn or Briar, Glass, Etc

Buy red lead or minium, paint the sore spot, and draw it out.

For the Flux

Take camphor gum, Venetian soap, green juniper berries, and cognac brandy; put all in a little bag and apply.

For Open Sores

Take hogs' lard, of the size of a bean. Heat it, get the yolk of an egg and some saffron therein. Stir it well together, it helps.

For Swellings

Aniseed five cents; oil of turpentine five cents; oil of juniper five cents. Mix and stir well. Grease the swelling therewith.

A Good Ointment for Wounds

Take one-half quart of vinegar, one-half pint of honey,

one ounce of verdigris, one ounce of dragon's blood, one ounce of bolus minium, two ounces mastic, one ounce incense, and three ounces oil of turpentine. All mixed well together.

How to Prevent Feeling Cold in Winter

Take nettlewort, garlic, pour lard to it, and boil together. When hands and face are greased with this ointment, one will not feel cold.

An Excellent Remedy for Apoplexy

Take a considerable portion of linden-tree blossoms and May flowers, six ounces of fresh bay leaves, bruise in a mortar to a mush. Then take a pint of blue violet sap, in this dissolve white rock candy sugar as much as will dissolve therein; pour this over the mush and mix well in the mortar Then strain all the juice out through a cloth; wormwood salt dissolved in a half pint is added thereto and all is to be rectified in a retort, also through an alembic distill so that no phlegm remains in the mixture. Thus an excellent spirit will be obtained, which must be kept in a glass vessel hermetically closed.

Whoever is attacked with apoplexy may take one-half teaspoonful of this spirit dissolved in linden blossom water, or other distilled water in good wine, etc. It will certainly prove a good remedy, and secure good health for future.

To make a good Green Salve

Butter, five cents; Grease, five cents; Balm Oil, five cents; Verdigris, five cents; mix together; or take ashes, lard, and anguish honey, of a like quantity, and make an ointment thereof by mixing.

When a Person has Sprained Himself

Take juniper berries and hay flowers, bruise them and boil in good old wine. Apply as a poultice.

For the Breaking of Felons

Take Venetian glass, half an ounce of pepper, honey, beef gall. Mix all these articles and pound them. Spread them upon a hairy cloth, and tie around the felon of the horse. Let it remain from three to four days.

For the Felons

Give the first three scraps from the hoof of a horse which is being shod for the first time.

For Dysentery

Boil an egg and eat it as hot as you can, without bread or salt.

An Ointment for various kinds of Pimples and Boils, also for Small-Pox, etc

Take some unwatered butter, raw bees' wax, pitch, saffron, for five cents, some sulfur; the sulfur must be melted in a pan, afterward add the wax, pitch, saffron, and last the butter, let it boil well together, as long as a soft egg, or till it foams over. Put it upon a rag and tie as warm as it can be borne upon the pimples and kept tight by means of another band. This is an excellent thing for poisonous eruptions of all kinds. Probatum.

For Putrid Mouths or the Scurvy

Brunnelle water, Norway maple leaves and strawberry

water. With these waters rinse the mouth clean, and with a horn-scraper well scraped, roast mush meal upon a new lid, put it in rose honey and paint the mouth therewith.

A Gargle for a Putrid Mouth

Take turnips, autumn roses, juniper berries, lancet herbs, white iron herbs, blackberry roots, of each a handful, boil in a clean pot, and with this water gargle.

For Mole and Liver Spots

White camphor, Venetian borax, of each one ounce, bean meal, four points of a knife full, white precipitate of mercury, two ounces lemon, rose water, sugar, parsnip water, white lily water, of each one ounce, prepared saltwater lozenges and a few grains of linseed. Distill for three days in the heat, afterward press through a cloth and put in a cool place. This will be an excellent water for liver spots. Before washing with it, add a little alum and the white of an egg, and a little of red snails, and grease therewith. It is a great medicament.

How to Beautify the Face

In the first place take twelve or twenty-four fresh eggs, put them in a glazed pot, pour boiled vinegar over the eggs, cover this well and keep it for eighteen days in a cellar; then pour the vinegar off, soak two loaves of wheaten bread in a quart of goat's milk, then take white wort, cut fine and mix together, put all in an alembic and distill to a water.

A good Black Plaster

Take one-half pound of olive oil, a quarter of a pound of silver litherage, a quart of good vinegar; rose vinegar would be the best for the purpose. Stir all these articles together in a pan placed upon the fire till the mass becomes black. Then pour it into pure water, and grind it upon a stone or board together. It is a good remedy for all sorts of injuries.

For Bloodshot or Red Eyes

Take white autumn roses, soak them three hours in aqua rosarum (rose water), then tie them over the eye, but do not expose yourself to the open air for the day.

A good Herb Wine for a Laxative

Take white waywort roots, three ounces of alantis roots, one and one-half drachm white nettle blossoms, one and one-half ounce benedictus roots, a stem of wormwood herbs, all together a good handful, one-half ounce of lemon peels; also of rhubarb, one-half ounce, one and one-half ounce of senna, half an ounce of prepared coriander, a few white andrones, a little aniseed, one-half ounce violet roots, sweet angelica, one ounce of good sloe blossoms. Take for dinner and supper, in soup, a spoonful of this mixture, or take every day twice the cardo-benedictus powder.

How to distill a Water to cause a Perspiration

Take a good handful of cardo-benedict herbs, same quantity of wormwood centifolium, cut fine and put into a dish, sprinkle these well with some good old wine. Let it stand and soak for four days; then take a drachm of cinnamon, a whole lemon put into a glass, pour again good old wine over it, and let it stand again for four days, cut it into fine pieces and distill in the alembic. The result will be an excellent water for sweating the patient.

FROM "THE PETIT ALBERT"

To Prevent Rabies

As the bite of a rabid dog is infinitely dangerous, it is thus good to have quick remedies to defend against the fatal consequences of this malignant bite. So crush laserwort seed sprouts with good vinegar and make a plaster that you apply to the bite wound, and anoint it as well with balsam oil. Fresh wild rose root, being crushed and applied, is, as the words of Pliny suggest, also a speedy remedy against the bite of the rabid dog. Good naturalists assure that taking the beast and burning it to ashes, and drinking good wine in the same setting, provides healing as well. Reduce river crabs to ashes with fire during the summer, in the transit of the moon as a crescent, when the Sun enters the sign of Leo, and powder the burned crabs. Give half a drachm in broth of the same to the patient, evening and morning for fifteen days, and he will heal. Galen ensures that this remedy has never failed him in need. But I suggest that we do not rely so much on any single remedy, for we can do all those little remedies in the way.

To Prevent Drunkenness

As man has nothing more valuable than his reason, and it becomes absent when too much wine is drunk, it is proper to give him a method to protect against it. When you are invited to a meal where you fear to succumb to the sweet violence of Bacchus, drink before you sit two table spoons of figwort and a dollop of good olive oil, and you can drink wine safely. You shall observe the glass or cup in which you will be served a drink, do not sate yourself with sweet foods or potato because both of these foods contribute much to drunkenness. If one becomes intoxicated he must, for the man, wrap his genitals in a cloth that is soaked in strong vinegar, and the woman who has succumbed to the intoxication should put a similar cloth on her nipples, and they will come back to their senses.

To Defend Against Illness

Foul smells are naturally contrary to the human health and the stench is sometimes fatal, as Fioraventus wrote, who says that if you take the filth of human blood and phlegmatic fluids well dried up, if it is mixed with styrax and these are burned in a room, the stench will be fatal. To be protected against these deadly infections, I will propose a sovereign antidote which will triumph over all kinds of venoms and poisons.

You will take in the growing season the leaves of hypericum, before it casts its flower as much as you are able to hold in your hands. Put them in the sun with four pounds of olive oil for ten days and then expose them on the stove in a water bath, in hot water, and then press the juice out of the leaves, and put it in a vessel or bottle or strong glass jar and when the wort is flowered and seed, you will put a handful of that seed and the flowers in the jar as well and will boil it all on the fire in a water bath for one hour. Then you will add thirty scorpions, a serpent, and a green frog, you shall cut off their heads and feet, and after a bit, boil it also. You will put two ounces of each herb following in thereafter; crushed gentian root, white dictamnum, the root of the tormentil, rhubarb, the Armenian bole, thus prepared. The ointment ought to be green in color. All this must be exposed to the sun during the scorching days of midsummer, after having well sealed the jar, and finally you must deposit the jar for three months in composting manure. And after that time you will remove the jar from the manure, and keep the treasure in a vase of tin or strong glass to use it. The usage is to rub around the heart, the temples, the nostrils, the sides and along the spine, and you will know that this is an antidote against all kinds of poisons. It is also good to cure the bites of venomous beasts.

Balm to Prevent Plague

This recipe can destroy any plague, it was a gift of a King of Spain to his daughter, Queen of France, designed by his own physician. It is simple enough so that anyone may concoct it. You must obtain twelve black salsify roots, and cook them in three quarts of white wine, and make sure that the pot where they cook is well covered for fear of too much evaporation of the alcohol; then being cooked you place them in a cloth and press the roots to extract the juices soaked into them. Add to this liquor juice twelve lemons, a half ounce of ginger, half an ounce of cloves, a half ounce of cardamom, half an ounce of aloe wood, all well crushed.

To this mixture you must join one ounce or so of the following; elderberry, brambles, and frank sage. You will boil it all together and quite slowly until decreasing the liquid to one quart, and then very quickly the material must be cooled. Then put it in a glass jar strong and sealed tightly. Drink the potion on an empty stomach every morning for nine days and by this means you will be the test of the miasmas, when even you are among plague victims. For those who are already infected, add to the drink the juice of a bugloss root and dried scabiosa, and this will be an antidote to the contagion within them. For plague wounds, mix pileront leaves, brambles, elderberries, mustard seed, and coal dust, and make this into a poultice to apply to the wounds. By God's help they will heal.

To Cure Gunshots or Other Wounds

You will make a decoction as listed thus: Taking two crown's weight of dutchman's pipe, some laurel seed, and crayfish dried in a smith's oven and harvested on a full moon, also powdered musk, of one shield's weight, and four crown's weight of comfrey or brunelle grass. It is necessary this final herb is harvested with its flowers, and dried in the shade between two cloths. You will reduce all these to fine powder, and after having mixed well, you will put them in a sachel of new cloth, which is closed with a wire; then you will have an earthen pot, glazed, in which you put your bag, with twenty small branches of periwinkle and three pints of the best white wine you can find, and after having plugged your pot with three or four sheets of paper, such that steam can be released only from a small area, you will put it into a charcoal fire, and it will boil and be reduced to a third of its original volume. When you remove it from the fire, and having allowed it to cool, you must place this decoction in a double fine linen, and lay it in a strong glass jar to serve you in need; beware above all that the jar is closed such that air does not enter it.

Here is how it is used for healing wounds. You will have a small syringe made of copper, which is always kept clean, so that it may be used on wounds that are hollow as follows. You gently clean the wound with a small white cloth, soaked in the decoction as listed, and then you use the syringe to inject the decoction into the wound three or four times, and you will cover the wound with the cloth and with the leaf of a red cabbage to seal it and put more of the decoction into the leaves forming a compress. Wrap the wound lightly, and it will heal shortly. Beware to keep it clean as the wound closes, as to not let the wolf into the sheep's pen, so to speak.

A Healing Powder

All those who have used this wonderful secret, until now, have endeavored by great physical arguments to prove the reality of the same. As it is difficult to speak clearly about something that is in itself extremely obscure and hidden, it is no wonder that these physicists have not converted many unbelievers nor convinced academics by reasoning; Digby Knight attempts to explain the powers he speaks of but yet the masses neither believe nor understand these works, for he presumes these secrets to be real, while we all seek the reason behind the secret and evidence for the same. He also presumes the principles behind the same secrets.

You have to have good Roman vitriol that is calcined, or rather which is purified of its superfluous humidity, exposing it for three or four days in the hot sun, being enclosed in a glass vial well corked. The Vitriol must be diluted in a small bowl of rainwater, filtered into the fire, about one ounce to a pint of water. If this is to be done in summer, one does not bring the water close to the fire, because it is necessary that it is neither cold nor hot, but in a just temperament between the cold and the hot; then this concoction has a linen dipped into it and some of the patient's blood is dipped into the same with the linen.

If the patient is away from the place that the operation is taking place, it could not be more convenient for evidence of the healing and supernatural power we speak of; it suffices to dip the same linen at noon into the vitriolic water, and to hold this bowl in a cool place. Every time the linen is mixed with the blood, the patient will feel their pain relieved to the degree of the work of a skillful surgeon. The patient will be cured in a very short time, by the invaluable virtue of vitriol, which we shall have occasion to speak of also elsewhere.

Making A Wash To Cure Facial Blemishes

Take saltpeter and wrap it in a thin cloth; soaking the same with pure water. Touch your blemishes with this cloth soaked as said. There is also a water that is a good use to beautify the face, and I advise this method more readily than what I just said regarding saltpeter. You will take two quarts of water in which you cooked Fajolles beans, until they are reduced almost to a paste; this water is then put into a still. You shall join two bundles of chickweed, two of silverweed, one pound of ground veal, with six fresh eggs, and to all this a pint of white vinegar. You distill this mixing in a water bath, and you'll have made an excellent water to dispel blemishes, washing with the same in the evening and the morning. I know there are countless people who fear that these distillations will not restore youth; but here is one that has such an effect, smoothing the skin: You mix bread with three pounds of wheat flour, bean flour, a pound of goat's milk, with mild sourdough; when you have baked the same mix, you shall dissolve any crumbs by adding new milk cheese and six egg whites with a sponge. Add one ounce of calcined shell egg and mix this all together in a still. You will make a distillation of this with fire, and you will have an excellent rejuvenating water, rubbing your face every day with the same, it will make the skin polished like a mirror. It will also whiten the skin as well, using the true water of Venice, which is done in the following manner. You will take two pints of milk, the blood of a black cow taken in May, a pint of water from a grape vine bleeding its sap, four lemons with four oranges, slicing the same, with two ounces of candy sugar, half an ounce of well pulverized borax, four onions pounded thoroughly, and narcissus bulb, and you put all this together to distill and cook in a water bath, and you will keep this water in a bottle well corked.

A Powder To Exfoliate The Face

You will take thirty sheep hooves and six hooves from calves. You must strip away all the flesh, which may take some time. You grind the bony hooves the best you can, and take good care to remove the marrow that you will find, cooking them all in a pot, skimming the foam gently to remove the debris and fats. When they are boiled for the space of three hours, you should cool them and chill the same; then with a silver spoon, fat will rise to the surface. Skim off and take this fat, and for every half pound of skimmed fats you'll add a dram of calcined borax and as much rock alum, with two ounces of grapeseed oil, and boil it all together in a pint of white wine, which is very clear, and let it cool down. Take this fatty solid and wash it several times in rosewater until it becomes very white and powdery, and lay it in small pots for you to use as desired.

A Soap For Faces and Hands Alike

Take a pound of iris from Florence, four ounces of storax, two ounces of sallow sandalwood, half an ounce of cloves, half an ounce of fine cinnamon, and the same of nutmeg, with a grain of ambergris. All this is to be reduced to a powder and sieved with the ambergris powdered separately. Then take two pounds of good white soap, grate it into three pints of water spirits to soak for four or five days; then knead this with water in which oranges were boiled and you will make a paste with starch finely sieved into it. Now you can mix your ambergris dissolved with a little tragacanth liquefied in water. This paste you will form into bars of soap you then lay in the shade, and all of this should be stored in boxes with cotton for preservation.

Preventing Foul Breath

Take a bit of myrrh before going to bed and hold it in your mouth, such that it dissolves.

Curing A Bad Fever

Take blessed thistle, absinthe wormwood, and saffron. Steep it in boiling water and drink it in the same way as tea, every day, or a bit more as a fever begins, and you will be healed.

A Secret To Maintain Good Health

At noon each day, take four rue stems, nine grains of juniper, a nut, a dry fig, and a little salt; mash it all together and eat it on an empty stomach.

Curing Bladder Stones

This disease is caused by the Moon; thus observe that it is the hour of Mars or Mercury. Take scorpions, put them in a new earthen pot that has a narrow mouth, and put it in an oven that is not too hot. In six hours, crush the baked scorpions and eat them.

Curing Colic

This disease is caused by the Moon; thus observe that it is the hour of Mars or Mercury. Take the laurel fruit, and make it into a powder, and add two drachmas of weight of the same to aromatic wine; it will take away the pain.

Curing Urination Problems

This disease is caused by the Moon; thus observe that it is the hour of Mars or Mercury. Take the seeds of abrotanus, and boil them in water. Add a decoction of cantharide beetles without head, feet and wings. Let the powder settle and drink a spoonful to urinate.

Curing Oedemas

This disease is caused by Saturn; thus observe that it is the hour of Mars or Venus. Take a pheasant, kill it and drain the blood. Drink two glasses of the same and the disease will be healed.

Curing Stomach Pains

This disease is caused by the Sun; thus observe that it is the hour of Mars, Mercury or the Moon. Take a chicken and kill it, and remove the stones from its belly and powder them. Drink this with wine for a cure.

FROM "FRAYS GOLDEN RECIPES"

Abscess: A flour and treacle poultice is a quick cure for either an abscess or a boil.

Appetite: Half-an-ounce of Peruvian bark to half-a-pint of boiling water, and, when cold, mixed with half a pint of port wine, is good to restore the appetite. Take a wine-glassful in the forenoon.

Asparagus for the Lungs: The frequent use of asparagus is strongly recommended in affection of the lungs and chest; it is a very wholesome and agreeable vegetable.

Asthma: For difficulty in breathing, or asthma, live chiefly on boiled carrots or leeks for a month; or, drink a pint of new milk morning and evening. This has cured an inveterate asthma.

Backache: The plant, Golden Rod, used in the manner of tea, 1 ounce to a pint of water, is a simple remedy for back pains.

Baldness: Rub the head night and morning with a decoction of boxwood. One ounce to a pint of water, boil for a quarter of an hour in a covered vessel, cool and strain, add an ounce and a half of Eau de Cologne or lavender water to make it keep.

Bilious Complaint: Hot water drunk before breakfast is a good remedy for bilious complaint; or, bilious attacks are prevented by taking one tea-spoonful of black currant preserves before breakfast.

Bleeding of the Nose: May generally be stopped by putting a plug of lint into the nostrils, or dip the lint in Friar's

Balsam; in obstinate cases, the sudden shock of a cold key, or cold water cloths placed in the nape of the neck will often stop the bleeding instantly. An effectual means of stopping bleeding of the nose is to move the jaws up and down as if going through the process of mastication. If the patient is a child put some paper in his mouth and tell him to chew it thoroughly. This method is ridiculously simple, yet it has never been known to fail in the most aggravated cases.

Blood Purifier: A recipe invaluable: The simplest and best blood purifier known is a sliced lemon, two table-spoonfuls of black currant preserves, and ten red sage leaves, to a quart of boiling water, sweetened to taste, which makes a most agreeable drink.

Bowels, Pain in: To relieve an attack of this complaint take a tea-spoonful of spirit of nutmeg, and a like quantity of syrup of ginger in water, and apply hot fomentations sprinkled with turpentine.

Bronchitis: Bronchitis is greatly relieved by drinking very hot water,sweetened with brown sugar candy, and not to sleep in the same underclothing worn during the day; or, a piece of wash-leather is good to wear constantly on the chest for bronchitis.

Breath: Bad breath is cured either by mint tea or the free use of strawberries; or, when caused by bad teeth, chew a piece of orris root. But cleanliness is the best remedy. Try rinsing the mouth with weak Condy's fluid and water.

Bright's Disease: Take a teaspoonful of sweet spirits of niter, and the same quantity of digitalis each night, and 20 drops of tincture of steel after breakfast. Eat meat sparingly.

Broom Tops: There is no remedy so healthful to those who suffer from heaviness of the limbs and tendency to dropsy as a decoction of fresh broom tops. Half an ounce of the tops should be boiled in a pint of water down to a gill. A wine-glassful every three hours.

Bruise: To prevent a bruise turning black, apply a treacle and brown paper plaster.

Bunions (to Cure): Paint them night and morning with tincture of iodine.

Burns: Flour and cold water will cure a burn instantaneously, whether large or small. Renew the same again and again.

Cancers: A recipe worth a fortune- In ten cases of cancer this simple remedy has failed in none. Bed clover tops are to be used in the manner of tea. This unpretentious plant cannot be urged on the public too strongly for its wonderful power and direct action over a cancer or for any cutaneous affection. The writer of this prescription says: "Fifteen cases of cancer that my brother physicians have abandoned as incurable I have cured with the wonderful remedy red clover tops." All that is required is to make tea of it. 1 ounce to a pint of boiling water, and drink freely during the day; wet a cloth with the tea and apply to the cancerous sore.

Change of Life: On change of life take a little electuary of senna occasionally. Try it.

Chilblains: Put the hands and feet once a week in hot water in which two or three handfuls of common salt has been dissolved, if the skin is broken apply marshmallow ointment.

Cholera: Should the cholera show itself in the district, to prevent its attack take a tea-spoonful of cinnamon in hot water frequently; or, this simple remedy for cholera has never been known to fail- first, give the patient hot water to cause vomiting, which cleanses the stomach; next, toast an oatcake, and put it in a pint of boiling water and drink freely.

Composition Essence, if used by out-door workers, or factory or foundry bands before going to work, would prevent thousands from having colds or sickness through exposure to cold morning air. Mix one tea-spoonful to a glass of hot water and milk, this drink before setting out. Travelers using it before or on their journeys will find it invaluable as a stimulant. Children half quantity.

Complaints of any sort: Vinegar, mixed with honey, with a pinch of mustard in it, and taken freely, stops any complaint from advancing. For any complaint a mixture of bread crumbs, mustard and vinegar is good to use inwardly.

Corns: For a troublesome corn, rub it now and again with spirits of turpentine and it will soon depart company; or, corns are speedily cured by first paring, then bind a slice of lemon over them. Tried with good effects.

Coughs or Colds: Most useful to refer to- Half a drachm of carminate of ammonia, one ounce of syrup of tolu, a quarter of an ounce of spirits of niter, half a drachm of laudanum, and six ounces of water; take one table-spoonful three times a day. This cures any sort of cold. Or, severe colds are cured with the herb yarrow, which bears a white and pink flower- the pink should be chosen; use it in the manner of tea, sweetened with treacle, and drink it freely on going to bed. Tickling coughs are quickly cured with one ounce of honey and one tea-spoonful of paregoric, mixed with the juice of a lemon, and taken going to bed.

Croup, to which children are very subject is dangerous. The best remedy is a tea-spoonful of ipecacuanha wine every five minutes until sickness is produced; or, a tea-spoonful of goose grease three times a day.

Dandruff is a disease of the scalp, for which a solution of borax is a very good remedy- used as a wash.

Deafness: Deafness, if to be cured at all, is by equal parts of the oil of cloves, the juice from the foxglove flower, and rum, dropped on a little cotton, and placed in the ears; or, syringe with hot water, and a little carbonate of soda is also a good remedy.

Despondency: The best comforter for a depressed or desponding mind is equal parts of agrimony and rosemary, made and used in the manner of tea.

Diabetes: Avoid sugar, and all food containing sugar, also much drink of any kind, and prepare the following; Peruvian bark, Colomba root, sumac berries, and the plant known as queen of the meadows, one ounce of each; boil in three pints of water, down to one quart, and take a wine-glassful four times a day.

Dim Sight: Strong tea dims the sight. The true sign of good health is in a sparkling eye.

Dock Ointment: A favorite country remedy of great value in the treatment of skin diseases. Clean and bruise half-a-pound of common yellow dock root, simmer for two hours in three gills of water, strain and evaporate to half a tea-cupful. Add gradually six ounces of prepared lard and an ounce of yellow wax, which have been previously melted together. Stir the whole till cold, and apply freely.

Drink: The use of cloves stay the craving for drink. Those using the least drink of any description are the most nourished. One of the latest treatments for obesity or stoutness is to abstain as much as possible from liquids of all kinds.

Dyspepsia: Dyspepsia may be cured by the free use of

oysters.

Ear-Ache: The ear should be bathed with a strong decoction of chamomile flowers and poppy-heads, as warm as it can can be borne.

Eczema: Is one of the most difficult skin diseases to cure, but by applying and persevering with the following it will be found to have a wonderful effect over this most obstinate complaint. Wash with plain soap and paint with glycerin of carbolic acid, wash often from five to fifteen minutes and apply Vaseline.

Epilepsy: Take 1 ounce each of mistletoe, valerian root, pellitory, and black horehound, boil in 3 pints of water, clear off, and when cold, add 1 ounce of tincture of skullcap. Dose: A wine-glassful four times a day. Used with good effect.

Erysipelas: Erysipelas is a well-known dangerous complaint, which may be cured by two sprigs of wormwood, a quarter of an ounce of senna, and a quarter of an ounce of chamomile flowers to a pint of boiling water, and drink freely. Tried with speedy relief. Erysipelas is very infectious. Even the Apple, as an article of diet, cannot be praised too much for its phosphorous qualities, it so soon acts on the brain, as well as the spinal cord and a sluggish liver.

Excitement: The common meadow plant, Ladies' Slipper, used as tea, is good for spasms, hysteria, cramps, nervous headache, fits, neuralgia, hypochondria, fevers, colic, debility, etc, and, wherever it is required to quiet the nervous system, is safer than opium and will act where opium fails. One ounce to a pint of boiling water.

Eyes, Inflamed: For inflammation in the eyes bathe them in boiled milk, with a white poppy in it.

Eye (Sty): Poultices and hot fomentations multiply stys and boils. Take a table-spoonful of brewers' barm three times a day, and apply to the eyelid an ointment of 3 oz. of lard and 1 oz. of white wax, melt together, then add ½ oz. of nitric oxide of mercury in very fine powder, stirring all the time. It is an excellent remedy.

Eyes, Watery: For watery eyes, dissolve ten grains of sulfate of zinc in five ounces of water, and bathe the eyes with it night and morning.

Eyes Weak: For weak eyes bathe them in cold water with a few drops of vinegar in it.

Feet, to Wash: The neglect of washing the feet is often visited by a quarrelsome temper, and other bodily complaints.

Female Complaints: Steel, quinine, and pennyroyal pills answer for irregularities, hysteria, headache, costiveness, loss of appetite, pains, lassitude, etc.

Gall Stones may be treated successfully with olive oil A tea-spoonful after every meal.

Goiter: Goiter or swelling of the neck has been cured by taking daily 15 bruised nettle seeds.

Hair Falling Out: Anxiety will cause the hair to fall off. When the hair falls off, damp it frequently with sage tea; or 1 oz. each of rosemary, boxwood and marshmallows to a quart of boiling water, and when cold used as a bath, prevents the hair from falling off, and good to cure baldness.

Hair, to Destroy: Mix in the following proportion sulfide of barium (not sulfate) 3 oz., white starch 2 ½ oz., oxide of zinc 2 ½ oz. Make into a thin paste with water and apply to the growth of hair with an ivory or other suitable pencil. Allow to remain on about ten minutes, then wash off with water, and apply cold cream.

Head Ache: Head ache and stomach complaints- often complained of- mix one drachm of sweet niter, one drachm of sal volatile, and two drachms of carbonate soda, in a tea-cupful of cold water; two table-spoonfuls to be taken three times a day.

Hoarseness: Take a fresh egg, beat it, and thicken it with pulverized sugar. Take freely.

Hysteric Fits: The smell of spirits of hartshorn is good for those subject to hysteric fits or a drowsy feeling.

Impure Blood: For all impurities of the blood, the hop used as tea cannot be too highly recommended.

Indigestion: Indigestion is a breeder of disease, but may be cured by mixing one drachm of powdered colomba root, one drachm of ground ginger, and half a drachm of carbonate of soda; this divide into twelve powders, and take one in a little milk three times a day; or, one ounce of colomba root to a pint of boiling water is a most excellent and cheap remedy for indigestion. Take a wine-glassful three times a day. Tried with every satisfaction.

Jaundice: For jaundice, a quarter-pound of Venice soap, made into moderate sized pills with eighteen drops of the oil of aniseed; three of these pills to be taken night and morning.

Kidney Disorder: Take red meats very sparingly, live principally upon fish and fresh green vegetables, drink equal parts of lime water and pearl barley water, take a tea-cupful three times a day; or, lemon water mixed with salts is good for diseased kidneys. Take a wineglass full in a morning.

Liver, Enlarged: Enlargement of the liver is dangerous.

If the disease is severe the diet should be of the simplest; drink nothing very hot, and make free use of stewed prunes for a fortnight.

Lungs, Diseased: Important- Iceland moss or seaweed, made into a jelly with boiling water, and sweetened with sugar candy, is good for diseased lungs; or, the free use of sugar is good for diseased lungs.

Mad Dog Bites: To be bitten by a mad dog, the danger is four times greater if bitten in any other part than the leg. For the bite of a mad dog apply wet salt and soda immediately.

Mouth Sore: For a sore-mouth apply the white of an egg, beaten in vinegar and lump sugar.

Mumps: There is seldom much to apprehend from this disease, though it is generally infectious. Keep the head and face warm, and guard against taking cold. Should the tumor in the neck suddenly disappear, its return must be promoted by warm fomentations. To abate the fever take of nitrate of potass 1 drachm, tartarised antimony 1 ½ grains. Mix together, divide into six powders, one to be taken every four hours.

Nervous Debility: Nervous debility and palpitation is greatly relieved by mixing 2 drachms of chloric ether, 2 drachms of tincture of gentian, 2 drachms of sal volatile, 2 grains of iodide of potassium, add half-pint of cold water (first boiled), take a table-spoonful three times a day. As a stimulant it has no equal.

Nervousness: Nervous people will find that sage and thyme, used as tea, will give them relief.

Nightmare: The best remedy for the fearful complaint, nightmare, is the herb thyme, used in the manner of tea.

Pains: By applying a bag of hot moist bran gives relief, and soothing relief.

Palpitation: When very troublesome, take 8 drops of oil of caraway on a little lump sugar, and use the stairs or steps as little as possible.

Piles: Pile ointment should be made from 2 oz. of lard, 1 pennyworth of opium, 1 oz. of gall; these mix and apply night and morning for a cure.

Pleurisy: Pleurisy is cured by the use of elder flowers in the manner of tea; or, take seven drops of laudanum in a little cold water on going to bed. If the pain is violent apply a hot fomentation of cayenne tea for half an hour at a time, and then a cloth wrung out of the liquor, and a dry one bound on the top.

Psoriasis: Is an affection of the skin and nails, dependent upon blood disease. Bathe with good carbolic soap and take an infusion of buchu leaves. Pour 3 gills of boiling water on 1 oz. of leaves, when cold take a wine-glassful three times a day.

Quinsy: Quinsy is cured by figs boiled in milk and hot water, with a little sal ammonia in it; this to be used as a gargle, and some of it drunk, which acts on the glands with wonderful effect.

Rheumatic Gout: Hot water drunk frequently is a good cure for rheumatic gout.

St. Vitus's Dance: Mistletoe and skullcap, of each 1 oz., boil in a quart of water. Dose; a wineglass full four times a day. Quinine wine, beaten up eggs and fresh milk, with complete brain rest, has also been successful in this complaint.

Salve for Cuts and Burns: Take three carrots, grate

them, place in a vessel and cover with fresh lard, simmer half-an-hour, strain, and add sufficient bees-wax to make a paste; this is a valuable ointment for cuts, burns, or wounds of any kind.

Scorbutic: Scorbutic or roughness of the skin is cured by 1 oz. of olive oil to 1 oz. of white wax melted in it. Mix, when near cold, with one penny-worth of white precipitate, and use as an ointment; or, scorbutic persons will find the free use of celery invaluable.

Scurvy: Take fresh vegetables of every kind especially lemons. Sulfur and cream of tartar clear the blood. An ounce of the decoction of oak bark twice daily gives tone to the system.

Sea-Sickness: Before going on board take a substantial meal, and on the voyage 1 tea-spoonful of the fluid extract of cocoa in a little water every one or two hours.

Sleeplessness: Sleepless nights are prevented by eating a few grapes before going to bed; or, by taking a tea-spoonful of magnesia in a wine-glass of water on going to bed.

Sore Mouth: Take a tea-spoonful of the tincture of gum myrrh diluted with water and rinse the mouth three times a day.

Sprained Ankle: Immerse at once in a pail of hot water and keep it there for fifteen or twenty minutes. Bandage with cloths wrung from hot water and salt.

Stoutness: Diet is the main treatment, avoid pork, carrots, potatoes, turnips, beetroot and parsnips. Dry toast is best at breakfast and tea, little sugar should be taken and only skimmed milk. Strong black coffee is an excellent anti-fat; take three cups in the day with a tea-spoonful of fresh infusion of digitalis in each.

Swellings: Nothing is so good to take down swellings as a soft poultice of stewed white beans put on in a thin muslin bag, and renewed every hour or two.

Sting of a Bee: May be relieved by applying a thick slice of raw onion. This should be renewed about every ten minutes until the pain is removed. The acid of the onion draws out the poison and prevents the injured parts from swelling.

Tapeworms: Tapeworms are killed in a grown-up person by first taking a little opening medicine, next fast for a day, or even two, then take a thimbleful of the oil of male fern in a table-spoonful of water before breakfast, and this repeat.

Teeth White: To have teeth very white, clean them with charcoal mixed with honey.

Throat, sore: One of the best old remedies for sore throat is to roast a potato, then crack it, place it in a piece of flannel, and apply it very hot, when the steam from it will be found to have made a cure in one night; or, an obstinate sore throat is cured with a little alum dissolved in sage tea, sweetened with honey. Tried.

Tooth Powder: A good tooth powder is made from the following- Powdered Peruvian bark 1 oz., powdered myrrh 1 oz., camphor 1 drachm, prepared chalk 1 oz.

Typhus Fever: for typhus fever, mix together 3 drachms of liquid acetate of ammonia, 2 drachms of syrup of ginger, 1 oz. of cinnamon water, and 30 drops of laudanum. This draught to be given early in the evening, when the most beneficial effects will result to the patient, who can procure sleep by no other means.

Ulcers: For ulcers, piles, or smallpox use the root of the plant tormentil. Take I oz. of the root, bruised or in powder, to 1 pint of boiling water. Take a tea-cupful as warm as convenient three or four times a day. It also makes a good wash for the sores.

Warts: The juice from the stem of the elder will soon cure a wart, or rub occasionally with castor oil.

FROM "VALUABLE HERBAL PRESCRIPTIONS"

RHEUMATISM

The joints and muscles are the parts affected, the movement of the same causing pain, in severe cases the joints swell and become very much inflamed. When in the joints it is described simply as Rheumatism or Rheumatics, when in the muscles it is described as Muscular Rheumatism.

Causes: Taking alcoholic drinks to excess, getting the clothes wet through, sleeping in damp beds, lying on damp grass, getting one cold on top of another, etc.

Treatment: Have a vapor or Turkish bath every week if possible, and guard against chill. Prepare the following:

Agrimony ½ oz
Bogbean ½ oz
Raspberry Leaves ½ oz
Arcticum Lappa ½ oz
Achilloe Millefolium, the herb ½ oz

Boil in a quart of water slowly for 5 minutes, strain, and when cold take a wineglass full three times a day; and at bedtime take a pill of the following:

Lobelia Herb 2 drachms.
Gum Arabic 2 drachms.
Capsicum 1 drachm.

Mix with Gum Mucilage, and make into 4 grain pills. Dose: One pill at bedtime.

SCIATICA

Causes: Taking cold, general debility, impaired vitality, etc.

Symptoms: Acute pain in the hip, and sometimes extending from the hip to the knee, in advanced cases extending to the foot. It is sometimes tedious of cure.

Treatment:

Populus Tremuloids, the bark 1 oz
Juniper Berries 1 oz
Myrica Cerifera ½ oz
Ginger ½ oz

Boil in a quart of water (slowly) for 5 minutes, strain, and when cold take a wineglass full 3 or 4 times a day. The medicine must be kept in a cold place.

Lotion:

Spirits of Hartshorn 1 oz
Sweet Oil 1 oz
Tincture of Myrrh 1 oz

Shake well the Bottle and gently but perseveringly rub into the affected parts twice a day.

KIDNEY AND BLADDER TROUBLE

Symptoms: Heaviness, drowsiness, pains at the bottom of the back, sometimes a shooting pain, at other times a dull pain, dizziness in the head, variable action of the heart, scanty urine with frequent desire to pass same, etc. When dropsical swellings take place the disease is advanced, and is then styled

Bright's Disease. Eat sparingly; let your diet be plain but substantial; avoid that mentioned later in this work.

Treatment:

Dog's Grass ½ oz
Pellitory of the Wall ½ oz
Clivers ½ oz
Juniperus Communis, the berry ½ oz
Alchemilla Arvensis ½ oz

Boil slowly in a quart of water 5 minutes, strain, and when cold take a wineglass full 3 or 4 times a day, indulge as much in open air as possible. The medicine must be kept in a cold place.

One pill at bedtime. The same pill as for Nervous Debility, shall be given.

SORE EYES

Keep the eyelids clean, and night and morning foment the same a minute or so with equal parts milk and water, warm; and afterwards rub in gently a little of the following ointment:

Ointment:

White Wax 1 oz
Olive Oil 2 drachms
Mutton Suet 2 drachms
Oil of Roses 1 drachm

Melt the mutton suet and wax, add the oil and roses, and stir until cold.

If vitiated blood be the cause take also the following medicine:

Rubus Strigosus, the leaves 1 oz
Galium Aperine ½ oz
Ground Ivy ½ oz
Child's Powder ½ oz

Boil in a quart of water slowly for 3 minutes, strain, and when cold take a wineglass full 3 times a day. The medicine must be kept in a cold place. It may be sweetened with sugar if desired; dose for children must be reduced accordingly. Open air exercise should be indulged in as much as possible. Inherited sore eyes can seldom be cured, but even in these cases this treatment should prove very beneficial.

ULCERATED THROAT

Causes: Working or living in an impure atmosphere, unwholesome food, neglected cleanliness, etc.

Treatment:

Agrimony ½ oz
Raspberry leaves ½ oz
Galium Aperine ½ oz
Gentian root ½ oz
Cassia ½ oz

Boil in a quart of water slowly for 3 minutes, strain, and when cold take a wine glass full three times a day. The medicine must be kept in a cold place.

Gargle: 1 part tincture of myrrh to 7 parts water, and add 15 drops tincture of cayenne; with this gargle the throat 3 or 4 times a day, and keep the bowels nice and regular if not already so.

ULCERATED STOMACH

Causes: Long continued stomach derangement, unwholesome food, debility, excess in alcohol drinking, etc.

Symptoms: Dull heavy sensation at the pit of the stomach, occasional swelling of the same with occasional cramp feeling, sickly feeling with sometimes a tendency to vomit, restlessness and variable pulse, depressed in spirit, temporary absence of strength, if the disease be advanced the tongue also becomes somewhat ulcerated.

Treatment:

Clivers ½ oz
Arctium Lappa, the root ½ oz
Raspberry Leaves ½ oz

Boil in a quart of water (slowly) for 5 minutes, strain, fill up to a quart and when cold take a wineglass full 3 or 4 times a day. The medicine must be kept in a cold place. And at bedtime 2 pills composed as follows:

Solid Extract Cascara 2 drachms
Capsicum 1 drachm
Extract of Chamomilla 2 drachms

Mix with Gum Mucilage. Make into 4 grain pills.

HEADACHE

Causes: The causes are too numerous to mention: constipation, obstructed blood circulation in the head, overeating, brain worry, disordered stomach, etc; in females obstruction of the menses is a common cause.

Treatment:

Scullcap ½ oz
Rosemary ½ oz
Taraxacum, the herb ½ oz
Menthe Viride ½ oz
Verbena Herb 1 oz

Boil slowly in a quart of water 3 minutes, strain, and when cold take a wineglass full three times a day. The medicine must be kept in a cold place.

Keep the bowels nicely regular with the following pills:

Solid Extract Cascara 2 drachms
Lobelia Herb 2 drachms
Turkey Rhubarb 2 drachms
Extract of Dock 2 drachms

Form into pill mass, make into 4 grain pills.

Dose: One or two pills at bedtime three nights a week. Indulge in open air as much as possible, and also follow instructions in bedroom ventilating (if possible.)

NERVOUS DEBILITY (Constitutional)

Nervous debility is so well known that it scarcely needs describing, and shows itself in a dozen different ways. Fears (groundless), tremors, dread of coming evil, lack of courage, startled at the least unexpected sound, buzzing noises in the head, ringing in the head, restlessness, shy of company, lacking confidence in one's everyday work; in advanced cases trembling (or shakiness) of the hands, etc; at the commencement of the ailment one or two of the symptoms only may be present, followed by the rest as the debility advances.

Treatment:

skullcap ½ oz
Mistletoe ½ oz
Menyanthes ½ oz
Gentian ½ oz

Boil in a quart of water slowly for 5 minutes, strain, and when cold take a wine glass full 3 times a day. The medicine must be kept in a cold place.

Pills as follows:

Lobelia herb 2 drachms
Gum arabic 2 drachms
Capsicum 1 drachm

Mix with gum mucilage and make into 4 grain pills. Dose; 1 pill at bedtime.

BLOOD DISEASES (Constitutional)

Causes: Living in thickly populated districts, closely confined rooms, working in vitiated atmosphere, free use of malt alcohol, eating tainted food; it is sometimes left in the train of scarlet fever, measles, etc., and is often inherited.

Symptoms: The symptoms are too well known and too numerous to need describing.

Treatment:

Sassafras Bark ½ oz
Achilloe ½ oz
Sarsaparilla ½ oz
Arctium Lappa ½ oz

Galium Aperine ½ oz
Guiacum Raspings ½ oz
Astragalus (the root) 6 drachms

Boil the lot in a quart of water slowly for 15 minutes, then strain, boil the same a second time in a pint of water 5 minutes, strain, add to the other, and when cold add the juice of a large lemon, and take a large wineglass full (or a half-tumblerful) three times a day. Keep this medicine in a cold place. Sponge the body with equal parts vinegar and cold water, rub briskly until thoroughly dry with a coarse bath towel, this may be done every other day if possible, it is not absolutely necessary but highly beneficial. A vegetable diet is good, also lean beef, lean mutton, or fish; avoid fat, coffee, cheese, pork, stew, sausage, all highly seasoned dishes, jams, and pickles. When procurable an occasional Turkish bath is highly beneficial. Spend plenty of lime in the cooling room and guard against chill on leaving the baths.

PILES

Piles come under two classes, bleeding and blind. There are numerous causes; wine drinking, excessive purging with pills containing aloes, pills containing mercury, highly seasoned food, thoughtlessly sitting on cold or damp stone, etc. In others the disease is inherited, in inherited cases there is no certainty of a permanent cure, when cured it is liable to return at any time.

Treatment:

Pile Powder 1 oz
Honey 4 oz

Mix into a soft paste and take a teaspoonful 4 or 5 times a day.

Boil 1 oz. Marshmallow Root in a quart of Milk slowly

for two minutes (carefully watch it or it will instantly boil over and you will lose the lot), drink freely of this as often as you please; if too cloggy composed of all milk, use equal parts milk and water; this must be kept in a cold place. Night and morning wash the seat (anus) and sponge a few minutes with cold water, dry with a cloth, and gently but perseveringly rub in a little Pile Ointment composed of Gall.

Keep the bowels easy with turkey rhubarb advised for constipation.

LIVER AFFECTIONS

This disease shows itself in many different forms, with some people the symptoms are very prominent, whilst in others very obscure; there are numerous causes. Symptoms: Sallow complexion, languidness, variable appetite, depression of spirits, sometimes constipated, at others a kind of prickly purge; when the white of the eye is a yellow tint the ailment is advanced.

Treatment: Eat sparingly, do not overload your stomach, let your diet be plain and simple, avoid all kinds of highly seasoned dishes, stews, cheese, pork, jam, pastry, pickles, and all kinds of sweets. Indulge in open air as much as possible, and if in the habit of taking intoxicants let them rest for 6 or 8 weeks.

Taraxacum Root ½ oz
Myrica Cerifera ½ oz
Agrimony ½ oz
Hydrastis Canadensis ½ oz
Stomach Bitters (powder) a half teaspoonful.

Boil in a quart of water slowly for 5 minutes, strain, and when cold take a wineglass full 3 times a day. This medicine must be kept in a cold place. The following Pills are very valuable in helping the cure:

Gentiana Lutea 2 drachms
Lobelia Herb 2 drachms
Taraxacum 2 drachms
Golden Seal 4 drachms

Mix into pill mass with Gum Mucilage, make into 3 grain pills. Dose: One pill twice a day immediately after meals.

LUMBAGO

Symptoms: In some instances kidney trouble could easily be mistaken for lumbago, as also rheumatism, but the most pointed symptoms of lumbago are, when rising from a sitting position, there is much difficulty in straightening one's self, with sometimes a dull pain in trying to do so, pains at the bottom of the back in the region of the kidneys.

Cause: It mostly arises from chill, or repeated chills (colds) in the back.

Treatment:

Juniper berries ½ oz
Tanacetum Vulgare ½ oz
Uva ursi ½ oz
Bog bean ½ oz
Caulophyllum 1 drachm

Boil very slowly for 5 minutes in a quart of water, strain, and when cold take a wineglass full 3 times a day. This medicine must be kept in a cold place.

The following pill may be taken at bedtime:

Lobelia herb 2 drachms

Gum arabic 2 drachms
Capsicum 1 drachm

Mix with gum mucilage and form into 4 grain pills.

GRAVEL AND STONE

Causes: Excess in alcohol, especially fermented wines, rich diet, inactivity, drinking well water, etc.

Symptoms: Sickness, sometimes a desire to vomit, disturbed urine, sometimes tinged with blood, red deposit sticking to bottom of chamber utensil after urine, sometimes gritty, occasional pain extending to the bladder, sometimes swelling of the leg or thigh, difficulty in passing urine, etc.

Stone: Urinary obstruction, sometimes passing very small pebbles, dribbling urine, occasional pains at the bladder neck, at times thick, milky looking urine with very strong smell.

Treatment:

Pellitory of the Wall ½ oz
Gravel Root ½ oz
Parsley Peirt ½ oz
Achilloe ½ oz
Wintergreen ½ oz
Althoea ½ oz

Boil in a quart of water slowly for 5 minutes, strain, and add to the hot liquid 2 oz. of honey, mix well. Dose when cold: A wineglass full 3 times a day. This medicine must be kept in a cold place.

If the bowels are not nicely regular a 3 grain pill at bedtime composed as follows may be taken:

Extract of Taraxacum 1 drachm
Turkey Rhubarb 2 drachms
Oil of Menthe Viride 10 drops

Form into pill mass and divide into 3 grain pills.

Dose: One pill at bedtime 2 or 3 nights a week.

BLACKHEADS

Blackheads, commonly called grubs, should be gently squeezed out as they appear; always wash in water with the chill taken off (never really cold water) and use a coarse flannel to wash with sulfate of zinc ointment is as good as anything that can be used.

PIMPLES

There are many varieties of pimples, but all that need concern the patient are the two kinds which may be described as the soft and the hard, the soft ripen and fill with a cream tinted matter which can be pricked with a needle and the matter gently squeezed out, it then dries up and disappears; thc other kind do not contain matter and might justly be described as skin eruptions; both kinds are constitutional, that is to say not a disease; the same may be said of blackheads and acne. There are few cases which can be permanently cured, they are liable to return at any time. Zinc lotion or zinc ointment will do all for them that can be done.

ACNE

Acne spots might justly be described as choked up perspiration, and need precisely the same treatment as for Blackheads.

A small bottle of zinc lotion can be procured at any chemist's for a few coppers. Zinc ointment in penny, two penny or three penny tins. Those really desirous of trying an internal treatment cannot adopt anything better than the medicine for Blood disease, see prior, but as previously stated there is no certainty as to the cure being permanent.

GASTRIC TROUBLE

Symptoms: Food turning to acid bile, or acid gas, heaviness and sluggishness until it passes away; sometimes gas fumes rise into the throat or mouth.

Cause: Indigestion.

Treatment:

Hydrastin 32 grains
Xanthoxylin 32 grains
Avenin 32 grains
Sodi Bicarb 160 grains
Water to 4 ounces

Dose: A teaspoonful in a wineglass of water three times a day, soon after each meal. Also follow bedroom ventilation (if possible) and diet.

ACIDITYOF THE STOMACH - BILIOUSNESS

Much akin to the above named, same treatment. Open air as much as possible, and walking exercise considerably helps the cure of the above; also see diet particulars.

WATERBRASH

Symptoms: Clear liquid (waterlike) and of an acid taste rising into the mouth after eating a little cheese, an unripe apple, or anything of a nondigestive nature; it is mostly found in young people.

The following simple things will usually counteract the acid; crush a piece of school chalk under the blade of a knife, crush it into a fine powder, put as much as would cover a shilling on the tongue and wash it down with a little milk and water. Another simple counteraction is a pinch of salt in a quarter of a glass of milk, fill up the glass with hot water and slowly drink it.

FITS

Loss of the senses, followed by inward convulsions, but the symptoms are so well known both by the afflicted and the non-afflicted that it is useless to dwell on them.

Cause: The causes are numerous, the most frequent being injury to the back of the head by falling or otherwise; run down constitution, nerve troubles, or anything which diminishes vitality.

Treatment:

Tanacetum (the herb) ½ oz
Pellitory of the Wall ½ oz

Leonurus Cardiaca ½ oz
Mistletoe ½ oz
Rue ½ oz

Boil in a quart of water slowly for five minutes, strain, and when cold take a wineglass full three times a day This medicine must be kept in a cold place. And the following pills at bedtime:

Lobelia Extract 2 drachms
Asafoetida Extract 2 drachms

Form into 4 grain pills and take two every night.

Sponging the body three times a week with equal parts vinegar and cold water, afterwards rubbing briskly until thoroughly dry with a coarse bath towel would be very helpful.

Also follow instructions as to ventilated bedroom.

INDIGESTION

I have always maintained that indigestion is incurable, and have not yet had cause to alter my opinion. When people tell me that I or anyone else have cured them of indigestion, I know that they never really had it, and by close questioning usually find that they had cured themselves of excessive eating; that by reducing the quantity of food they were in the habit of consuming they had assisted the stomach in performing its proper functions.

These cases cannot be described as indigestion in the true sense of the term, they might justly be described as overtaxed stomachs; there is a vast difference between an overtaxed stomach and indigestion, the former will perform its functions if not overtaxed, without medicine, but the latter would also need medicinal aid; or to describe it more accurately we might call the former an abused stomach, not a non-digestive stomach. The nondigestive stomach is the real source of trouble, a stomach not up to much when at its best, whether studying diet or not, and herein lies the true definition of the word Indigestion. Another remarkable thing connected with indigestion is there is no rule as to diet. The writer of this book having all his life had to study his diet must be allowed to know a little on this subject, few people having tried more remedies, and although he never met with that infallible cure one reads of in the newspapers, he is still living, with little to complain of, and long life is what we seek to attain.

There never was nor ever will be an infallible cure for indigestion. The food which would digest with one person would fail to digest with another, and the best means to adopt is to take particular notice of the kind of food which best agrees with you and keep to it, allowing your stomach to be the judge. The same may almost be said of medicines, but I recommend the two prescriptions here appended, because of their general effectiveness during a long and varied experience.

Causes: Impaired vitality, overloading the stomach, worry, excess of brain work, closely confined rooms, sedentary occupation, spitting whilst tobacco smoking, excessive drinking of ardent spirits, in fact excess in any kind of alcohol; whilst a large number inherit this dcfcct.

Symptoms: The symptoms are numerous, the following being only a few. A sense of heaviness in the stomach, sometimes attended with a dull pain, a feeling of sluggishness soon after meals, occasional sensations of dizziness in the head, heart palpitation; certain kinds of food will turn to acid, belching of wind, flatulence. If allowed to continue unassisted the person becomes a confirmed dyspeptic, hypochondriac, etc. in progressive cases only one or two symptoms may be observed, whilst in advanced cases many, and in old standing cases the lot. Proceed as follows:

Eat slowly of the food which you know from experience best agrees with you; if you have not taken notice of this, take notice. Always cease eating when you could eat a little more; you do not benefit from the large quantity eaten, the true benefit is derived from the reasonable quantity digested. You may with advantage avoid the following; cheese, pork, stews, hash, sausage, all kinds of highly seasoned dishes, pickles, and jams.

Treatment:

Agrimony ½ oz
Raspberry Leaves ½ oz
Galium Aperine ½ oz
Centarium ½ oz
Stomach Bitters (powder) ½ teaspoonfull.

Boil slowly in a quart of water 3 minutes, strain, and when cold take a wineglass full 3 times a day. This medicine must be kept in a cold place. Also take the following digestive pills:

Lobelia Herb 2 drachms
Capsicum ½ oz
Turkey Rhubarb ½ oz
Caryuphyllus ½ oz

Form into pill mass with Extract of Gentian, make into 4 grain pills, and take one pill 3 times a day with each meal, immediately after meals. These pills (apart from the herb medicine) answer for many people, consequently a shilling box could be sent without the herbs. Also follow the open air particulars on, and the bedroom ventilation instructions.

CONSUMPTION, BRONCHITIS AND ASTHMA CURE

Prescription:

Marshmallow Root 2 drachms
Licorice Root 2 drachms
English Linseed ½ oz
Iceland Moss ½ oz
Hydrastis Canadensis 2 drachms
Life Root 2 drachms
Pleurisy Root 2 drachms

Directions: Place the whole of the ingredients into two pints of cold water and simmer or boil slowly for 5 minutes, occasionally stirring; whilst hot strain through a piece of muslin or fine sieve, then add and dissolve 2 oz. of sugar, or 10 pieces of lump sugar of ordinary size. If for a cough absolute, add double quantity of sugar and 2 tablespoonfuls of best vinegar. The sugar must not be added until the liquid is strained from the herbs. When cold fill up to a quart. The mixture must not be taken until cold; and must be kept in a cold place; and if bottled the bottle must be thoroughly cleaned after each making (for simple cough it may be taken warm).

Dose: A wineglass full three or four times a day, between meals if possible. This medicine must be kept in a cold place.

FALLING HAIR

As an outward application to arrest falling of the hair and to promote its growth, have the following made up at any first-class herbalists:

Cantharides 1 oz
Bay Rum ½ oz

Musk 2 drachms
Rosemary 2 drachms
Water 4 oz

Shake well the bottle and rub a little into the roots of the hair once a day. This prescription is both harmless and effective.

CHILD'S CORDIAL

For disturbed sleep and gripes in children.

Lobelia Syrup 3 oz
Tincture of Valerian 2 drachms
Essence of Aniseed 1 drachm

Dose: A teaspoonful every two or three hours.

SOOTHING SYRUP

For green stools, looseness of the bowels and gripes in infants.

Rhubarb 2 oz.
Aniseed 1 oz
Marshmallow Root 1 oz

Boil in a quart of water for 5 minutes, strain clear, place the liquid again into the pan and add i lb. of lump sugar, boil slowly a minute or two, stirring the while, lift off the scum floating on the surface, allow it to stand until cold, then bottle.

Dose: A teaspoonful five or six times a day.

WHOOPING COUGH

Best Treacle ½ lb
Tincture of Lobelia 1 oz

Aniseed Water 1 oz

Make the treacle hot, and whilst hot add the lobelia and aniseed water, and stir until cold.

Dose: A teaspoonful occasionally.

TROUBLESOME PERIODS

Treatment:

Matricaria (the herb) ½ oz
Rue ½ oz
Leonurus Cardiaca ½ oz
Wintergreen ½ oz

Boil in a quart of water (slowly) 5 minutes, strain, and when cold take a wineglass full 3 or 4 times a day. The medicine must be kept in a cold place. Take two pills at bedtime composed as follows :

Hiera Picra 2 drachms
Mentha Pulegium (Extract) 2 drachms

Make into 4 grain pills.

Ladies subject to troublesome periods can greatly alleviate their suffering by proceeding with the above treatment about three days before the time, and continuing the medicine until the close, one packet will serve the time.

CONSTIPATION

For constipation take as much of the best powdered Turkey Rhubarb as would cover a sixpence, dissolved in a little milk and water at bedtime every night; and the following morning on awakening drink a half-pint of hot water. To move the bowels by natural means is the object; pill purging, or any kind of purging, is injurious, and sure to make you more constipated afterwards. Turkey Rhubarb also cleanses the stomach, and with most people answers splendidly. A good way of ensuring the quality of the rhubarb would be to buy it in the root (in the piece) and powder it yourself, the simple nutmeg grater will answer the purpose. The dose may be increased or decreased as occasion demands (some people being much easier moved than others) but avoid purging.

GOUT (Rich Man's)

The rich man's gout in nine cases out of ten arises from excess of too rich food, wines, etc; the remedy would be to live on a plain diet for a few weeks, avoiding all kinds of wines, beer, and stout; an occasional drop of whiskey may be indulged in if desired, much open air, and walking exercise as soon as able.

An eminent Welsh doctor, regarding the rich man's gout, said; Live on sixpence a day and earn it, and you need not fear its return.

GOUT (Poor Man's)

The poor man's gout arises from too little, or too poor food, causing an impoverished state of the system; the remedy (were such possible) would be to exchange tables with the rich man, this (perhaps) not being possible the substitute is: Live well on good substantial food, the very best you can afford, with, if you can afford it, an occasional glass of good port wine, or Guinness's (harp label) stout.

DYSPEPSIA

The same treatment as for indigestion, dyspepsia being indigestion in an advanced stage.

NERVOUS BREAKDOWN

The same treatment as for nervous debility, the trouble in this instance being either more advanced, or taking place more suddenly, it is then described as nerve collapse.

LACK OF THOUGHT CONCENTRATION

The same as for nervous debility, the only difference being that this inability often takes place without any of the other symptoms named in nervous debility being present.

ANEMIA (Bloodlessness)

Anemia will be better known to the reader as poor blood, or bloodlessness, which through some unaccountable reason is more frequently found in females than in males, and may arise from various causes which have a tendency to debilitate the system; among which may be named closely confined workrooms, or closely-confined rooms of any kind, poor diet, the breathing of impure air, insufficient attention to keeping the pores of the skin open, and various other causes too numerous to mention.

This is why we see so many pale, weary, and debilitated parents, and in numerous cases, weak, puny offspring. One would hardly expect to find a strong healthy child born of weak, debilitated parents. Such is scarcely in accordance with the laws of nature. Healthy plants are not produced from inferior seed and poor soil, and it is impossible for strength to be born of weakness. When the blood in its richness is not up to its proper gravity, taking into consideration that the liver, kidneys, heart, lungs and brain must be fed with it, it sounds to sense that such organs must fail to perform their proper function; and when these organs do fail or are feeble in their action, the local symptoms following are too numerous to mention, and the patient invariably begins to treat the local symptoms. The cause of course (in the majority of cases) is entirely overlooked-consequently, if the cause be not attacked the field of advertised specifics have full play, and the afflicted look in the paper for the (so-called) specific for their particular class of symptom or symptoms, as the case may be, and no doubt the majority of these proprietary medicines are very good, and will stimulate the organs for which they are adapted, but fail to produce any permanent beneficial effect in cases where the remedy is not adapted to the cause; whereas had the organs he was treating been at fault, the medicine in question would justly be termed a specific, because its influence on these particular organs would perform a cure.

Therefore where the symptoms mentioned arise from poorness of blood, whilst the patient is battling with first one specific and then another the debility is gradually gaining ground, and eventually the nervous system begins to relax, and constitutional nervous debility eventually makes its appearance.

When the patient reaches this stage he or she of course begins to be low-spirited, moodiness and despondency are prominent, everything- even their daily routine of business-seems a trouble, and yet rest makes little difference. Eventually all the local symptoms attending a deranged system are prevalent, and one begins to think there is no one on earth so badly dealt with, whereas there are thousands just thinking similarly of themselves; and if this state of affairs is allowed to continue it is not so very long before the stomach becomes weakened, and incapacity for digesting the food takes place; and if allowed to continue, dyspepsia (swelling after meals), but swelling after meals only takes place when the debility of the digestive organs is of long standing. General debility implies much, and would cover a whole category of symptoms. It is styled general debility because the person may appear to be suffering with all the ailments that flesh is heir to, and yet an examination does not show a deficiency of any particular organ, hence it is termed general. There can be no general debility in a healthy person, and there are few unhealthy persons where the blood is rich, pure, and up to the proper standard. The blood is the life, and upon it depends the proper working of the principal functions of the body. The Germ Syrup enriches and forms new blood, and slowly but surely builds up the system; to prove this you only need to weigh the patient before and after treatment on the same scales.

FROM "THE USEFUL FAMILY HERBAL"

For the King's Evil

The king's evil may be cured by a plant called king's evil weed. It grows in wild shady land, under almost all kinds of timber, and in the form of a plantain, but the leaves are smaller, and are spotted, green and white- a very beautiful plant. When it goes to seed, there comes up one stalk in the middle of the plant, six or eight feet high, and bears the seed on top of the stalk in a small round bud.

Take this, root and branch, pound it soft, apply it to the tumor for a poultice or salve, and let the patient drink a tea made of the same for constant drink. If the tumor is broken, simmer the root and leaf in sweet oil and mutton tallow; strain it off and add it to bees wax and rosin until hard enough for salve. Wash the sore with liquor made of the herb boiled, and apply the salve and it will not fail for a cure.

The Best Remedy for Rattles in Children

Take bloodroot, powder it, give the patient a small teaspoon full at a dose; if the first dose does not break the bladder in half an hour, repeat again three times. This has not been known to fail for curing.

Valuable Remedy for the Bilious Colic

Take of west india rum, one gill, of west india molasses, an ounce, of hog's lard, one gill, and the urine of a beast, one gill; simmer them together. This composition will seldom fail of performing an effectual cure for life.

For a Felon

Blue flag root and wild turnip root, a handful of each, stewed in half a pint of hog's lard- strain it off- add to it four spoonfuls of tar, and simmer them together. Apply this ointment to the felon til it breaks. Add bees wax and rosin to the ointment for a salve to dress it with after it is broken. This is an infallible cure without losing a joint.

For the Salt Rheum

Take swamp sassafras bark, boil it in water very strong. Take some of the water and wash the part affected; to the remainder of the water add hog's lard, and simmer it over a moderate fire til the water is gone. Anoint the part affected after washing; continued four days it never fails for a cure.

Salve for a Burn

Take wild lavender, the green of elder bark, chamomile, and parsley. Stew them in fresh butter; strain it off, and add it to bees wax, rosin, and white diacalon, equal parts- if a burn is of long time standing and discharges very much take mutton suet before it is tried, pound it up with chalk to the consistency of salve. This cures the most inveterate sores of the kind.

The Best Salve for Women's Sore Breasts ever Found

Take one pound of tobacco, one pound spikenard, half a pound comfrey, and boil them in three quarts chamber lye til almost dried; squeeze out the juice, add it to pitch and bees wax, and simmer it over a moderate heat to the consistency of salve. Apply it to the part affected.

An Ointment to Relax Stiff Joints and Shrunken Sinew

Take a pound of hog's lard, put into it a small handful of melolat green, stew it well together, strain it off, add it to one ounce rattlesnake grease, an ounce of olive oil, and ten drops of oil lavender. Mix them well together. Anoint three times a day and rub it in well with the hand.

Valuable Cure for Inveterate Old Sore Legs

Take the bark of cavron wood or shrub maple, boil it very strong, take part of the liquor and boil it down to a salve, and wash the part affected every time it is dressed. Apply new salve twice a day. Make a tea of the same, and drink it three times a day.

To Cure the Bite of a Rattlesnake

Take green horehound tops, pound them fine, press out the juice, let the patient drink a tablespoon full of the juice morning, noon, and night, or three times in twenty four hours. Apply the pounded herbs to the bite and change them twice a day. The patient may drink a spoonful of sweet olive oil. This seldom fails curing.

Cure for the Itch

Take half a pound of hogs' lard, four ounces spirits turpentine, two ounces flour sulfur, and mix them together cold; apply it to the ankles, knees, wrists, and elbows, and rub it on the palms of the hands, if there be any raw spots; apply a little three nights when going to bed.

The Red Salve for Swellings in Formation

Take linseed oil, one pound, sweet oil or fresh butter,

half a pound, red lead, one pound, boil them all together, stir it boiling, then slack the heat and add to it two pounds of bees wax, one pound of rosin, and stir them together til cold.

Foote's Ointment

Take one pound of hog's lard, one pound of mutton tallow, half a pound oil spike, and heat them over a moderate fire until united; then add as much bees wax and rosin as will make it to a salve- the renowned Foote's Ointment. This cures all common sore where there is no inflammation.

A Certain Cure for Corns on the Feet or Toes

Take white turpentine, spread a plaster, apply it to the corn, and let it stay on til it comes off itself. Repeat this three times- it never fails curing.

A Cure for Warts on Any Part of the Body

Make a strong solution with corrosive sublimate, and wet the wart with it three or four times a day- it never fails curing.

An Excellent Family Bilious Pill

This pill, made frequent use of, prevents all kinds of fevers. Take one pound sweet rind aloes, four ounces jalap, four ounces pulverized blood root, two ounces cloves, and two ounces saffron, and beat them all to a fine powder. Pill them with molasses- mix them well in a mortar. The common way of using them is to take every night one, of the size of a pea, if you have a bilious habit. But if you wish them to act as a physic, take four or five on going to bed. They give no pain in the operation.

For the Toothache, if the Teeth Be Hollow

Take gum opium, gum camphor, and spirits of turpentine, equal parts, rub them in the mortar to a paste, dip lint in the paste and put it in the hollow of the tooth every time after eating. Make use of this three or four days, and it will generally cure the tooth from ever aching.

For the Bilious Colic

Take the above mentioned bilious pill, add it to half its weight in calomel, give four or five pills, and repeat the dose, and it is a certain cure for the bilious colic. Or take mandrake root, dried and pulverized; a large teaspoon full is a dose. This must be repeated several times.

A Sure Cure for Canker in the Mouth

Take one pound of fresh butter, put it into an earthen vessel well glazed, set it on the fire and let it boil; while boiling add to it four common green frogs- put them in alive, let them stew until the frogs are dry, then take them out and add to it a little chamomile and parsley; when cold stir in a little burned alum, pulverized, and if the fever is high, give a little rattlesnake gall, dried in chalk. This will cure the most inveterate canker in the mouth, throat, or stomach.

A Medicine to Cure Inward Ulcers

Take sassafras root bark, two ounces, coltsfoot root, two ounces, bloodroot one ounce, gum myrrh one ounce, winter bark one ounce, socotrine aloe one ounce, steep them all in two quarts of spirits and drink a small glass every morning, fasting.

For Cramp in the Stomach or Any Inward Part

Take ten drops of the oil of lavender on sugar or in wine. Repeat the dose once an hour if required.

A Cure for the Flying Rheumatism

Take princess pine tops, horseradish roots, elecampane roots, prickly ash bark, bitter-sweet bark off the root, wild cherry bark, and mustard seed- a small handful of each- one gill of tar water into one pint of brandy, or the same proportion. Drink a small glass before eating, three times a day.

Valuable Remedy for Wind Colic in Women and Children

Take equal parts of ginseng and white root, half as much calamus or angelica seeds, dry them, pound them very fine, and mix them together; a teaspoon full is a dose for a grown person- for children according to their age. Repeat this dose once in half an hour, if required, It rarely ever fails.

For a Hectic Cough

Take three yolks of hens' eggs, three spoonfuls of honey, and one of tar. Beat them well together, and add to them one gill of wine. Take a teaspoon full three times a day, before eating. Or a syrup made of barley, turnips, and elecampane; boil them in fair water, three quarts to one pint of barley, one pound of turnips, four ounces of elecampane; boil it down to one pint, and add to it one pound of honey or loaf sugar, and half a pint of brandy. A tablespoon full is a dose, three times a day. Or wild licorice, half a pound, brook liverwort half a pound, elecampane two ounces, solomon's seal four ounces, spikenard half a pound, gumfire four ounces, boiled in four quarts of water to one; add it to two pounds of honey in one pint of old spirits. Half a glass is a dose before eating.

For the Erysipelas, or Saint Anthony's Fire

Make egg wine rich and good for drinking; drink a part of it and wash the part affected with the other part. This is a valuable remedy.

For the Rheumatism in the Loins

The oil of sassafras, used internally and externally; ten drops on loaf sugar is a dose. Anoint the part affected with the same. Repeat it as often as needed. Or sit over hemlock boughs and drink poke berries in brandy for three weeks every day. Only seat three times. Or shower with cold water and drink brandy all the time. Or drink brandy and bathe the part affected with salt and rum, hot as can be borne, by a fire. Repeat it six days.

For the Quinsy

Bleed under the tongue, in the first stage of it, and sweat the throat and neck with carduus, a thorny herb, growing in gardens. Boil it in milk and water, and sweat powerfully three or four times. This has not failed in one instance to cure.

Remarkable Plaster to Ease the Pain of Felons or Frog Felons, or Any Such Tumor, on the Hands or Feet or Elsewhere

Get a pitch pine knot from an old log, the side next to or in the ground. Split the knot fine, boil out half a pound of pitch; take four ounces of strong tobacco, boil it in water, strain out the tobacco, boil the resin until it is thick, then add the pitch to the resin, simmer it over a moderate heat, and stir all the time til it forms a salve altogether. If the swelling be on the hand or finger, lay the plaster on the wrist. If on the foot or toe, lay the plaster on the ankle. Or wherever it may be, lay it above the next joint-this will take out all the pain in a short time. Dress the sore with any other salve that is best. This cure is infallible.

For the Phthisic

Take four ounces of hens' fat, and a seed bowl of skunk cabbage, that grows in the bottom of the leaves close to the ground. Cut it fine, stew it in the fat til it is dry, then strain it off. A teaspoon full is a dose to take three times a day. Make a syrup of white swamp honeysuckle blossoms and queen of the meadow roots, sweetened with honey; add to it a quart of syrup, and half a pint of brandy.

To Cure a Wen

Take clean linen rags and burn them on a pewter dish, gather the oil on the pewter with lint, and cover the wen with it twice a day. Continue it for some time, and the wen will drop out without any further trouble.

An Excellent Remedy for Asthma

Take spikenard root, two ounces, sweet flag root two ounces, elecampane root two ounces, common chalk two ounces; beat very fine in a mortar, add to it a pound of honey, and beat it well together. A teaspoon full is a dose three times a day.

Excellent Pill for Hysteria

Take a quantity of white root, otherwise called Canada root- boil it in fair water- when it is boiled very soft, strain out the roots, and boil the liquor to the consistency of a thick paste, so that it may be pilled. Let the patient take two or three pills at a dose when the disorder is coming on.

Cure for Bleeding at the Stomach

Take a pound of yellow dock root, dry it thoroughly, pound it fine. Boil it in a quart of sweet milk, strain it off, and drink a gill three times a day. Take also a pill of white pine turpentine every day to heal the vessels that leak.

For the Dropsy

Take half a pound of blue flag root, half a pound of elecampane root, boiled in two gallons of fair water to one quart, sweetened with one pint of molasses. Let the patient take half a gill three times a day before eating.

For the Canker Rash

White birch root, pulverized very fine, given in small doses three or four times a day. Make a tea of the same, for constant drink. For the fever, give rattlesnake gall, three grains at a time.

For any Hemorrhage of the Blood

Take a handful of bloodweed- it grows in old fields and is called by some, horsetail, or white top; is about waist or shoulder high, one stalk from the bottom and has a very bushy top- when it is green. Pound it, press out the juice, and give the patient a tablespoon full at a time, once an hour until it stops. If it be dry, boil it strong, and give tea very strong three or four spoonfuls at a time.

Cure for the Gravel in the Bladder or Kidneys

Make a strong tea of the herb called hearts' case, and drink it plentifully. Or take the root of Jacob's Ladder, make a very strong tea, and drink freely; it is a most certain remedy.

Jacob's Ladder is a vine that often grows in rich interval soil, near a wood or bush that stands near grass lands. It comes up with one stalk about breast high, then springs off into a number of branches covered with green leaves, and the fruit is a large bunch of black berries. When ripe, the bunch hangs down under the leaves by a small stem. This is proved to be the best cure that has been found.

Valuable Remedy for the Piles

If the piles are outward, make an ointment of chamomile, sage, parsley, and burdock, the leaves of each- simmer them in fresh butter or hog's lard, and sweet oil. Anoint the parts with it, and drink tar water half a gill three times a day. But if they are inward, or blind piles, drink tar water twice a day and essence of fir every night going to bed, half a small glass. This effects a cure in about two months.

For the Toothache if the Tooth be Hollow

Put into the hollow a piece of blue vitriol, as much as the hollow will contain. Repeat it for several days and it will kill the marrow.

For the Common Canker in Children or Adults

Take canker root, or cold water root- so called because it is used with cold water- wash the root, pound it; steep it in cold water and wash the tumor with it, and drink of it. This root grows in rich soil, in meadows, by fences, stumps, or log heaps. It comes up with a stalk from the ground, a yard or two high, and then branches out very large. Its leaf is like clover. The top of the root is yellow as gold, in a bunch, then branches out into many fibers, some like plantain.

For the Whooping Cough

A Syrup made of elecampane root and honey, four ounces of the root to half a pint of honey. Bake it in a well glazed earthen pot, in an oven half hot. If the root be green, it needs no water. If dry, add half a pint of water. A teaspoon full of the syrup for a small child (add a little if older) three times a day.

For Rickets in Children (In the Bowels)

One ounce of rhubarb, powdered in one ounce of enceviniris, put into one quart of wine or brandy. If a child is a year old, it may take a tablespoon full at a time; if older take more, to half a gill for an adult. If any part of the body is affected with the disorder, bathe the part with brandy, and drink turkey root, steeped in wine, three or four times a day.

Sure Remedy for Women's Sore Nipples

When the infant stops sucking apply a plaster of balsam fir. It will cure in three or four days.

Cure for Itching Heels or Feet, or Ribbed Heels

Take any kind of tallow and tallow the part affected with it and rub it in by a hot fire, at night, on going to bed. Repeat it three or four times.

Preservative Against All Sorts of Bilious Fevers

The fullness of bile is the cause of all sorts of fevers, and jaundice, bilious colic, and cholera. Physic often with blood root and mandrake root mixed together, once a quarter, and make small beer with elder roots, spruce boughs, burdock roots, hops, white ash bark, sarsaparilla roots, and spikenard. Make a bitter with unicorn roots, and bark, white wild roots, and the yellow dust of hops. If a family will continue this method they will never be troubled with fevers.

For Convulsion Fits

Take convulsion roots, make a tea of them, and drink, or powder them and take the powder in small doses. Convulsion root grows in timber land, and comes up in July, with a bunch of white stalks about six or eight inches high, with a little knob on the top. It has no leaves. The top and root are for use. The root is a bunch of small fibers very numerous, and full of little knobs about the size of mustard seed. They grow just under the leaves.

For the Consumption (Tuberculosis)

Take half a bushel of barley malt, put it into a large tub, take six pails of water, make it boil, pour it on the malt, let it stand six hours, take half a bushel of white pine bark, one pound spikenard roots, one pound Syria grass, boil them in the water that the malt is soaked in, half away, then put it into a keg, add yeast or emptyings to it. Let it ferment, then bottle it up and drink a pint a day.

For the Quinsy in the Throat

Sweat the throat with spotted carduus boiled in milk and water by holding a pot of it under the throat as hot as can be borne. Hold some of it in the mouth, and when the swelling has gone down, wear a piece of black silk about the neck constantly and it will prevent the quinsy from ever coming again.

For Swellings that Come of Themselves

An ointment of alder tags and sugar of lead simmered in hogs' lard, and melilot and saffron, simmered all together. Strain off and anoint the part affected; it will scatter the swelling if taken in time. Give the patient something to guard the stomach before anointing.

Excellent Poultice for Old Inveterate Sores

Scrape yellow carrots, wilt them on a pan or fire shovel, very soft. It takes out the inflammation and the swelling; and is an excellent poultice for a schirrous breast.

Excellent Medicine for Inward Pains or Ulcers

Take elecampane, comfrey, spikenard, masterwort, angelica, and ginseng roots, of each a pound, boughs of fir two pounds, chamomile one pound; put them into a still with a gallon of rum and two gallons of water; draw off six quarts, drink a small glass night and morning.

Another Excellent Essence, Good for All Sorts of Inward Weakness, Inward Fevers, Coughs, or Pain in the Side, Stomach, or Breast

Take twenty pounds of fir boughs, one pound of spikenard, four pounds of red clover; put them into a still with ten gallons of cider; draw off three gallons and drink half a gill night and morning.

For Diabetes

Take a wether sheep's bladder, put it into a glass bottle that will hold about a quart, fill it up with good Madeira wine, and let it stand forty eight hours, then drink three or four times a day, about half a gill at a time. A deers' bladder is preferable.

For Stoppage of Urine

Take a spoonful of honey bees, as much buds of currant bushes, steep them in hot water very strong, and drink two spoonfuls at a time every half hour.

For Sore Eyes

White vitriol, one teaspoon full; sugar of lead one ounce; gunpowder two ounces to one quart of fair water, mixed and shaken well together six or eight times. Wash the eyes three times a day- an infallible cure.

For Dropsy

Sassafras bark of the root, one pound; prickly ash bark, one pound; spice wood bush half a pound; three ounces of garlic, four ounces of parsley root, four ounces of horseradish roots, four ounces of black birch bark- boil all in three gallons of malt beer. Drink a gill three times a day.

To Stop a Fever Sore from Coming to a Head, and Carry it Away

Sweat it with flannel cloth dipped in hot brine. The cloth must be changed as often as it becomes cold for three hours; then, washed in brandy and wrapped in flannel, repeat it three or four times.

To Stop Puking

Take gum camphor, pound it, pour on boiling water, and let the patient drink a spoonful every ten minutes. It must be sweetened with loaf sugar. Or take a handful of green wheat or green grass, pound it, pour a little water on it, press out the juice, and let the patient drink a spoonful once in ten minutes.

For the Lockjaw

When any person is taken with the lockjaw, give him five grains of Dovers' powder, then set him in a rub of water as hot as he can bear it; bathe his head with camphorated spirits; let him sit or stand in the water as long as he can bear it without fainting, and bleed him if possible. Repeat this three or four times; then out of the water put him in a warm bed wrapped in flannel.

For the Numb Palsy

When a person is taken with the numb palsy, let blood freely if possible; give a tablespoon of flour of sulfur once an hour; bathe the part affected with spirits of hartshorn, take one pound of roll brimstone, boil it in four quarts of water to one quart- let the patient drink a tablespoon full once an hour. If applied early it will finally cure.

To Cure Vegetable Poison, Poison Ivy, Poison Elder, or Any Other

Take rosemary leaves or blossoms; make a tea of them to drink morning and night, like bohea tea or any other. Or take wild turnips, if green, pound them and press out the juice; if dry, boil them in fair water; wash the part affected with the clear liquor. Take part of the liquor, add to it a little saffron and camphor and drink to cleanse the fluids and guard the stomach.

For the Spina Ventosa that Comes on the Breast

Take spikenard root, comfrey root, yellow oak bark, and tobacco; boil them in water strongly; take out some of the liquor to wash the tumor; add to the rest hog's lard or mutton tallow, beeswax and rosin; simmer it over a slow fire, stir it constantly, until it is salve. Apply it to the sore and physic with mandrake roots three or four times; bleed once.

To Cure Inward Ulcers

Sassafras root bark, two ounces; coltsfoot root two

ounces, bloodroot two ounces, gum myrrh one ounce; steeped in two quarts of spirits. Drink a small glass every morning. Live on a simple diet as much as possible- for constant drink make a beer of barley malt, one peek, spikenard root two pounds, comfrey root one pound, burdock root two pounds, black spruce boughs five pounds, angelica root one pound, fennel seed four ounces- for ten gallons of beer. Drink one quart a day. Let your exercise be light.

For the Catarrh in the Head

Take yellow dock root, split it and dry it in an over; bloodroot and scoke root four ounces of each; cinnamon one ounce, cloves half an ounce- pound them all very fine and let the patient use it as a snuff eight or ten times a day. Every night smoke a pipe full of cinnamon mixed with a little tobacco, and sweat the head with hemlock, brandy, and camphor. Pour a little camphorated spirits and brandy into the hot liquor to sweat.

For an Inflammation of the Head

Take red beets, pound them very fine, press out some of the juice, let the patient snuff some up into the head, and make a poultice of the beets, and lay it on the mould of the head. For the fever, use rattlesnake gall, cream tartar, and head bitney. Bleed as often as once a day. Physic with deerweed root, or wild mandrake root, with a little bloodroot. Keep strong drafts to the feet.

To Take a Film from a Person's Eye

Take sugar of lead, make it very fine; take an oat straw, and cut it short, so as to be hollow through- dip the end of the straw in the powder, and blow a little of it into the film morning and night. After the film is almost consumed apply it to a drop of hens' fat once a day until it is well.

To Cure a Breach or Burst on the Body

Take four or five snails, that crawl about on old rotting wood; you may often find them under loose bark that is moist, or on old logs or stumps. Collect a parcel of them enough to cover the breach; lay them on a linen cloth, bind them on, and repeat as often as the snails are dry. Let the patient drink turkey root, cinnamon, cloves, and maize, made into a tea, or steeped in wine, three or four times a day. This, well attended to, will perform a cure.

To Cure a Schirrous Jaw, or Swelled Face, or the Scurvy in the Mouth or Teeth

Take princess pine and scurvy grass, boil them in water, add it to rum and honey, hold it in the mouth as hot as it can be borne, and boil a large quantity of the herbs, and sweat the head over it.

Receipt to Make the Best Tarlington's Balsam

This balsam of life is a most excellent medicine in consumptive complaints, and also for weak females in all stages of life. For a feverish stomach, let the patient take thirteen or fourteen drops in a small glass of wine in the morning, fasting. It strengthens the stomach and kills the fever. It is good for pain in the stomach or side, nourishes weak lungs, and helps a small whooping cough. It is made this: Gum benzoin four ounces, gum storax callimtee three ounces, balsam tolu one ounce, gum aloe socotrine one and a half ounces, gum albanum one and a half ounces, gum myrrh one and a half ounces, angelica root two ounces, St. John's wort tops two ounces. Pound all these together, put them into three pints of rectified spirits four weeks in a moderate heat, and shake them once a day- then strain it off and it is fit for use. If the gums are not all dissolved, add a little more spirits to the same; shake it and let it stand as before.

For a Relaxation of the Gut or Fundament in Children

Break two or three hens' eggs, part the white from the yolk, take the yolks and put them into a frying pan washed clean from grease, set them over a slow fire, let them stand a while, then turn them over and squeeze them until the oil comes out. Be careful not to burn them. Collect the oil, anoint the gut when it is down, then boil an egg very hard, let it be whole, and whilst it is warm, wrap it up in a linen cloth and bind it on the fundament after you have put up the gut.

For the Common Phthisic in Children

Take four ounces of seneca snake root, four ounces of spikenard, four ounces of parsley root, and two ounces of licorice stick. Boil them all together in four quarts of water; strain it off, sweeten with loaf sugar or honey, and let the patient drink a small glass night and morning.

For Shrunk Sinew or a Stiff Joint

Half an ounce of yellow basilicon, half an ounce of green melilot, half an ounce of oil amber, and a piece of blue vitriol as big as a chestnut: Simmer them together to a salve or ointment, and apply it to the part affected, and the joint above. Repeat it often and it will perform a cure.

For Rheumatism

Take a handful of princess pine, a handful of horseradish roots, elecampane roots, prickly ash bark, bittersweet root bark, wild cherry bark, mustard seed, and a pint of tar water. Put it all into two quarts of brandy. Drink a small glass every morning, noon, and night, before eating. Bathe the part affected with salt and rum by a warm fire.

Remedy for Weakness in the Urinary Vessels, for Children who Cannot Hold their Water

For those so troubled take two ounces of good red bark, and steep it in one quart of wine for twenty four hours; let the patient (if two or three years old) drink a tablespoon full. If older, a little more at a time. Or red beech bark taken off a green tree; dry it well, pulverize it fine, and use it the same way.

For a Nosebleed

Take common nettle roots, dry them, carry them in the pocket and chew them every day. Continue this three weeks.

To Cure a Consumptive Cough or Pain in the Breast

Take a spoonful of common tar, three spoonfuls of honey, three yolks of hens' eggs, and a half pint of wine- beat the tar, eggs, and honey well together in a dish, with a knife or spoon. Bottle it up for use. A teaspoon full is a dose, morning, noon, and night, before eating. Use barley tea for constant drink.

For Weak Obstructions in the Female Sex

Heart's Case herb, spikenard roots with the pith removed, a small part of bloodroot, turkey root, wild licorice, a few roots of white pond lilies, and a good parcel of female flowers, so called (it often grows by the sides of ponds and has a leaf and blossoms some like cowslips but it grows single, one root or stalk by itself, and some smaller than the cowslip; the leaves are green and the blossoms yellow. This is one of the finest roots for female use in the world.) Use double the quantity of this, and equal parts of the others- make a syrup of them; boil them in fair water until the substance is out; then strain it off, and sweeten it with honey, and add as much rum to it as will keep it from souring. Drink half a gill on going to bed every night. This will strengthen the system and throw off all obstructions. It is best for persons so complaining to wear a thick piece of flannel on the small of the back.

For Children Troubled with Worms

There are many things helpful to children troubled with worms. Take the bark of witch hazel or spotted alder, steep it in a pewter vessel, let it boil on a moderate heat very strong; a child of a year old can take a tablespoon full- if older more, according to age. Let them take it four or five times a day for several days. It is sure and safe. Or take sage, powder it fine, and mix it with honey- a teaspoon full is a dose. Sweetened milk, with a little alum added to it, is very good to turn the worms.

Flour sulfur mixed with honey, is very good for worms. Take a piece of steel, heat it very hot in a smith's fire, then lay it on a roll of brimstone, melt the steel, let it fall into water, and it will be in round lumps; pound them very fine, and mix the dust with molasses- let the child take half a teaspoon full night and morning, fasting. Or get mandrake roots, dried and powdered, mixed with honey- give a child of a year old as much of the powder as will lie on a sixpence; take it in the morning, fasting, three or four times successively. If a child is taken with fits, by reason of worms, give as much paregoric as the child can bear; it will turn the worms and ease the child. To prevent children from having worms, let them eat onions raw or cooked- raw is best. Salt and water is good to turn worms; and giving a dose or two of flour sulfur, mixed with molasses or honey, afterward, brings off the worms without anything else.

A Cure for the Polypus

Two ounces of dried bloodroot, pounded fine; a quarter of an ounce of calix cinnamon, two ounces of scoke root- snuff it up the nose, it will kill the polypus. Then pull it out with a pair of forceps and use the snuff until it is cured. If the nose is so stopped that it cannot be snuffed, boil the same and gargle it in the throat, and sweat the head with the hot liquor til it withers so as to use the snuff.

For a Frog Under the Tongue

When the frog is first perceived take weak lye and hold it in the mouth as hot as can be borne; and if it is grown tough, touch it in three or four places with caustic until it is sore, then apply the lye.

For Childbed Fevers

In childbed fevers, take rattlesnake gall, five grains malitel, sweat balm tea, once an hour til the fever abates, and every time the fever rises continue the same. Keep the body loose.

Cure for Phthisic

Roast three egg shells brown- pulverize them rather coarsely, mix with half a pint of molasses, and take a spoonful morning, noon, and night. The cure is certain, unless the disease is hereditary.

For Dysentery

Half an ounce of pomegranate bark, pulverized and steeped in a pint of wine, or good cider, and taken a gill at a time, before eating.

Valuable Remedy for Dysentery and Bloody Flux

Take of white pine bark after the ross is off, three pints, or water three pints, let it simmer down to one quart- strain it all off, add half a pint of west india rum, and half a pint of west india molasses. The whole composition for a grown person- half for a child. This remedy is simple but may be depended on as effectual; it will seldom if ever fail.

To Destroy Worms in a Safe and Sure Way

Take a large teaspoon full of the rust of tin; mix it with a tablespoon full of molasses. This is a valuable remedy. It may be given in sickness or health.

FROM "THE FAMILY COMPANION AND PHYSICIAN"

Ague and Fever, or Intermittent Fever

Symptoms: This disease may be divided into three classes, namely:

1. The cold stage, the hot stage, and the sweating stage. The cold stage generally begins with pain in the head and loins, weariness of the limbs, coldness of the extremities, stretching, yawning, and sometimes vomiting, shivering and violent shaking.

2. A burning heat, red skin, sensitive to the touch, pain in the head, and flying pains are felt in the different parts of the body, and often flighty; the pulse is quick and strong, the tongue white, the thirst great, and the urine is highly colored.

3. Perspiration is seen first about the neck and breast, and thus continuing until profuse sweat breaks out at every part of the body; the heart diminishes to its usual standard, and the pulsations to their usual number, and all the functions are restored to their natural order- when after a certain, interval the paroxysm returns, and produces the same distressing sensations, generally Once in twenty-four hours.

To Cure: First to put as speedy a stop as possible to the fits when they have occurred, give the patient an emetic, ie: Take equal parts pulv. Lobelia, Ipecac, and Bloodroot, pulv. cayenne pepper one half a tea-spoonful, and repeat every twenty minutes, together with Boneset or Chamomile tea, until the patient vomits freely. This is to be given before the cold stage, and often it breaks up the disease without further medicines. It sometimes happens that the Cayenne cannot be taken; in that case give leas doses, sufficient to vomit a little. Should any peculiar temperament, debility, or state of the system render an emetic injudicious, you will give a cathartic, ie: Mandrake or May apple, and Cream-tartar, in equal parts, one tea-spoonful; add one gill of boiling water; sweeten to taste, and drink. This will cleanse both the stomach and bowels.

But should the cold stage come on, then you will give the patient warm Catnip or Virginia Snakeroot, Boneset, or Peppermint teas, and apply warm bricks to his feet, cover warm, and use every means to promote perforation. These remedies will greatly lessen the other stages.

Hot stage: As soon as the cold stage terminates, you will remove the extra covering, and all warm applications, as well as warm drinks, and give the patient cold drinks. You may also give lemonade freely. This course will allay the febrile excitement.

Sweating stage: At this stage both cold and hot drinks must be discontinued, and those that are tepid given. During the intermission drink ague wine bitters. This will cure in a short time where everything else fails. Drink from a half to one wine-glassful every two or three hours, made as follows: One oz. Peruvian bark, half oz. Wild Cherry bark, half oz. Cinnamon, half oz. Cloves, half oz. Nutmeg, half Oz. Cayenne pepper, one tea-spoonful Sulfur, and one quart Wine. Pulverize all.

Cathartic: Extract the substance from bark of butternut root, and take one pill the size of a pea each night. These remedies will not fail to cure in a short time.

Remittent Fever

This disease is characterized by frequent paroxysms, one succeeding another so rapid, that the former scarcely leaves until they have another symptom much like the former, it being very difficult to discriminate between the two, only as the former attacks with the paroxysm but once in about twenty four hours.

Remedies: First, give an emetic at once, combined with the vapor bath, and repeat if necessary the following day. Second, cleanse the bowels with the Mandrake compound. Third, give the Quieting powder every two or three hours, and bathe frequently the entire body with warm weak lye or warm saleratus water, until you promote perspiration.

You may also give the patient freely warm Lemon tea. Give the patient Slippery Elm, Comfrey root, Mint, or Catnip tea. Often the patient has severe headache. In that case make cold applications to the head and warm to the feet. After the fever is removed, the patient will be weak. In that case you will give him the Wine bitters, a half to one wine-glassful three times a day.

Inflammatory Fever

This disease may be known by great heat, frequent, strong, and hard pulse, redness of the face, and may be distinguished from the former by the increased amount of inflammation, dizziness of the head, etc.

Remedies: This fever should in every way be treated as the remittent fever, omitting the emetics. First give the Mandrake compound once in four hours, until you promote a healthy action of the bowels, and then follow up the remedies as directed under
that head.

Regimen: Nutritious liquids should be given, such as corn meal gruel, toasted bread and water, ripe fruits, roasted fruit, and water, etc.

All kinds of fever may be broken in a short time by the use of the emetic or mandrake compound and vapor bath, if taken in time.

Continued Fever

This fever is characterized by debility, inactivity, heaviness, yawning, stretching, coldness in the back, which continues to spread until it sweeps over the whole system, accompanied with chills, etc; stomach nauseated, and frequently confusion of intellect. Finally the coldness passes off, and then the skin becomes dry, face red, dull pain in the head, the pulse quick and full, great tendency of blood to the head, costiveness, urine highly colored and scanty.

Remedies: Follow the directions as laid down under the head of Remittent and Inflammatory Fevers. At the beginning give the Emetic, and in eight or ten hours after give the Mandrake compound, and repeat every four hours until you obtain a lively action of the bowels. Give the Sweating powder every night, and plenty of Motherwort tea to drink, and bathe the whole body frequently with weak lye; give the patient from three to five grains of Ipecac three or four times a day. If he has much pain of the bowels, you will simmer Catnip, Smartweed, Wormwood, Hops, etc, in vinegar, and apply to the parts; warm and change frequently.

In the latter stages, when the patient is much reduced, and the fever abates, you will stimulate- give wine, or wine and water. Should the stomach assume a putrid state, you may give him two or three table-spoonfuls of yeast, three or four times a day.

Regimen: Avoid all stimulating drink and food at the commencement of this fever, but when weak and reduced, give more nourishing food, and Wine and raw Eggs. Oysters, etc.

Scarlet Fever

Symptoms: Commences with a chill, like other fevers, nausea and sometimes vomiting, thirst, headache, eyes red and frequently swollen, pulse high, breathing quick; subsequently the flesh begins to swell, and a pricking sensation is felt; red blotches usually appear about the neck and breast, then sweep over the entire body; usually in two or three days perspiration takes place, and the eruption disappears, and the scale or cuticle peels off.

Remedies: Very little medicine is required in this disease. Only cleanse the secretions of the body, with a cool diet, and prevent the patient from taking cold. But a second form sometimes appears, in which the throat and mouth are much inflamed, and soon succeeded by grayish sloughs, and give the parts a speckled appearance, and render the breath fetid. This is a gangrenous form, for the patient often dies in a few days, or if he recovers it will be very slowly, accompanied, by many unfavorable symptoms, such as Dropsy, Ulcers of the throat, nose, etc.

Remedies: In this as other fevers, cleanse the stomach and bowels, give the Sweating Powder once in four hours, with the free use of warm Lemon, or Catnip teas, until he sweats; bathe the body in warm Saleratus water freely and frequently, and give Saffron tea frequently. You may also give three or four Ipecac powders during the day. This will not only relax the bowels, but promote perspiration, and is also an expectorant.

Bathe the throat if swollen and painful, with the Sassafras Liniment; gargle with Shoemake bolls or berries, 1 oz. to 1 pint of water, steeped strongly; also with Yeast and water; weak Lye is also good. Apply Mustard poultices to the feet. Should the patient be very restless, give the Sweating; Powder at night, or two Pills as large as a pea, of Motherwort Extract.

Should there be symptoms of inflammation of the brain, apply warm wet cloths, or cold applications such as Brandy or Rain Water and Vinegar; Camphor is also good.

Regimen: Give glutinous drinks such as Slippery Elm, Flaxseed, Comfrey, or Marshmallow Root teas. Food mild and cooling; room neither cold nor hot; keep the air pure. You may also give Snakeroot tea occasionally.

Infantile Fever

Symptoms: The child is peevish, lips dry, hands hot, breath short and quick, head aches, pulse quick, often from 100 to 140 in a minute, lays stupid, sleep disturbed, food rejected, sometimes bowels are relaxed, and sometimes costive, evacuations slimy, often delirious and sometimes speechless, generally drowsy; sometimes seems quite well, but peevish. This fever is mild at the beginnings slow in its progress, and uncertain in its results.

Remedies: As in many other fevers, give an Emetic; then cleanse the bowels with Senna and Manna two or three times a week. Promote perspiration, bathe the entire body with warm water, apply cloths wet in vinegar and water, to the head, and a mild mustard poultice to the feet; give Elder Blow tea freely, also the Ipecac and Sweating powders. When the fever abates and the child is weak, give a Tonic, such as Chamomile Flowers, Gentian, or Colombo teas. Diet as in all fevers.

Inflammatory Diseases

These diseases are characterized by redness, heat, pain and swelling of a part, or the whole body, either acute or chronic, and may attack any or either organ or member of the body:

Inflammation of the Brain

The patient is attacked with favor symptoms, such as redness of the face and eyes, retires from light and noise, headache, delirium, pressure of the head, throbbing of the temples, feet cold and head hot, etc.

Remedies: Bring the heat from the head to the feet as soon as possible, by cold applications to the head and warm bathing of the feet, draughts, etc. Give a Cathartic once in four hours, until an action is procured, and then repeat two or three times a week the Mandrake compound, and promote perspiration as in fevers. But should the symptoms not abate, you will apply a Mustard Poultice between the shoulders, and foment the head by applying Hops simmered in vinegar, warm, and change frequently, and if restless give 1 to 3 Motherwort pills at night.

Regimen: Food cool and mild. Drink mucilaginous teas.

Inflammation of the Ear

Symptoms: The pain is very acute, ear inflamed; more or less fever, and sometimes delirium, attended with throbbing. Suppuration takes place, and often continues for years.

Remedies: If the pain is very acute, simmer bitter leaves in vinegar and water, and foment the parts; repeat until the pain abates. If this fails, take 1/2 oz. of Sassafras Oil, 1 oz. Olive Oil, and 1 drachm Camphor; mix all, and drop it on wet on a little cotton, and put into the ear. Onion Juice, Laudanum, etc, is also good; the Vapor Bath is also good, applied to the head, Hickory wood Sap is also good, as well as for deafness. If the ear suppurates, inject with an ear syringe Olive Oil, Castile Soap Suds, decoction White Oak, etc.

Mumps

The glands of the neck upon one or both sides, become enlarged, hard and painful; difficulty often of both breathing and swallowing; the swelling often extends to the testicle, and becomes very dangerous as well as painful, increasing for three or four days. It is frequently attended with fever.

Remedies: Promote perspiration; give Cathartic (gentle). If very painful, immerse raw cotton in the following: Castile Soap, scraped, 1 drachm, Sassafras Oil, 1/2 oz., Olive Oil, 1 oz., Camphor, 3 drachms, apply to the parts, and give the patient warm tea freely. If the testicle is swollen, take equal parts of good old Jamaica Rum, Tinct. Camphor, and Laudanum; mix and warm a little, and bathe frequently; or wet cotton and apply. You may also give an Emetic, and Sweating Powder, etc.

Quinsy

This disease is characterized by redness of the tonsils, difficulty in swallowing and breathing, hoarseness and dryness of the throat, fullness of the tongue, difficulty in expectoration; it is attended with fever, pulse full and hard, often from 100 to 150. This disease occasioned the death of Washington.

Remedies: Give an Emetic, Purgatives; steam the head with bitter Herbs and Vinegar, inhaling the same freely, and repeat frequently until the symptoms abate. Bathe the affected parts freely with the Rum Liniment. The Sassafras Liniment is also good. To the latter add a little Hartshorn. Gargle the throat frequently with Shoemake liquor, namely, 1 oz. of the berry and pint of water; you may add a little Sage, Alum, Borax. etc. A little yeast is also good with the above. Saltpeter is also good. Weak Lye is also valuable. If the throat is badly swollen, make a Poultice of Flour, Slippery Elm, and Buttermilk; apply warm, and change frequently. Henbane simmered in spirits, and applied, is also very valuable.

Regiment: Avoid all cold or stimulating drinks; food mild, as in all other inflammatory symptoms.

Croup

Symptoms: A whistling noise, frequently hoarseness, when coughing, like the barking of a hoarse dog, great thirst and restlessness, difficult expectoration.

Remedies: Carry off the mucus as quick as possible by means of an Emetic, and cleanse the bowels as soon as practicable; bathe the feet in warm water, or apply Mustard Poultices to the same, repeat the Emetic every day, or oftener if necessary, also keep the bowels open, bathe the throat and stomach with the Sassafras Liniment, you may also steam the parts, and inhale Horehound, Catnip, and Hops, simmered in Vinegar, and bind them about the neck warm, and repeat. You may also give a tea-spoonful of the following: Onion Juice sweetened with honey, 1/2 to 1 tea-spoonful every hour. Diet the same as Quinsy.

Whooping Cough

Symptoms: A tightness of breathing, thirst, quick pulse, and some symptoms of fever, hoarseness, cough, expectoration difficult. It assumes this character ten to twelve days, and then is attended with a peculiar kind of hooping at intervals, and is quite violent, and in its advanced stages the patient frequently chokes, and then vomits either from the stomach or lungs, or both, and often bleeds from the nose or ears. It sometimes continues for months and even for years.

This disease is not curable; the symptoms can only be mitigated by proper remedies. To lessen the unfavorable symptoms you will give emetics frequently, sufficient to vomit lightly, so as to keep the phlegm as clear from the stomach as possible. Give the patient Poppy tea freely and frequently. Pennyroyal, Hyssop, Spearmint, Comfrey, Slippery Elm, and Flaxseed teas are all good. Give Castor Oil frequently, to keep the bowels open. Olive Oil is also good. Immerse the feet in warm weak Lye every night. You may also apply mild solutions to the feet and breast frequently. You may also apply a plaster between the shoulders, made as follows: 3 parts Hemlock Gum to 1 part White Pine Gum.

Regimen: The food should be light and easy of digestion, and drinks warm.

Colds and Coughs

Symptoms: It is not necessary to describe the symptoms of this complaint; they are too well known to be mistaken. I would only admonish you, and say that this is the forerunner of many of the ills of life. And as the Apostle admonishes us to flee from the appearance of evil, so I would say flee from these attacks as soon as possible. No time should be lost, lest a viper more terrible fastens upon you.

Remedies: First take the Steam Bath; an Emetic next, cleanse the bowels, and drink bitter Herb teas, such as Smartweed, Boneset, Hoarhound or Penneroyal, Spearmint, Chamomile, etc. You may also make a Syrup of Onion Juice and Honey, or Poppies. Should your cold continue you may take the Cough Drops.

Regimen: Avoid everything of a heating and stimulating character both in food and drink. Corn Meal Gruel or Bean Porridge is the best food. Keep warm, dry, and free from cold atmosphere. Drink warm teas freely, and immerse the feet in warm weak Lye each night on going to bed.

Inflammation of the Lungs

Symptoms: The patient is attacked with violent pain in the side or chest; difficulty of breathing, cough, dryness of the skin, heat, anxiety, and thirst, pulse hard, strong, and frequent.

Remedies: Employ a counter-irritant at once- the best one is a mild Mustard Poultice; leave it on until the skin is reddened, but not blistered. Give the Ipecac Tincture to loosen the mucus; this will promote perspiration, expectoration, and action of the bowels. You may also give the Cayenne Powder, this will both lessen cough and inflammation, and give quiet and ease.

Drink Comfrey, Flaxseed, Slippery Elm, or Marshmallow tea freely. Buttermilk Soup is also valuable. Immerse the feet every night in warm weak Lye, from twenty to thirty minutes.

Regimen: The best food the patient can eat, is Buttermilk or Indian Meal Gruel- these are both food, drink, and medicine. Avoid everything of a stimulating nature both in food and drink.

Pleurisy

Symptoms: The patient is attacked with chills, fever, thirst, restlessness, and then a sudden violent pricking pain in the side, extending to the shoulder blade and back and sometimes over part of the breast, with frequent cough, expectoration, etc. The mucus thrown off at first is small in quantity, and then often having streaks of blood, and as it progresses it becomes more gross and more impregnated with blood. Pulse very strong and tight, like the string of the violin.

Remedies: Give to an adult 2 teaspoons full of Sudorific Drops in Catnip tea, and if not relieved in half an hour, repeat. Bathe the feet in tepid Water or Ley. Apply Mustard Poultices to the side and Draughts to the feet. Camphor, Whiskey, and warm Water, applied by wetting cloths, are all good; or you may take 1 pint Alcohol or brandy, and 1 oz. of Cayenne Pepper- simmer a little, wet flannel and apply, and change as often as cool; or, you may boil bitter Herbs in Vinegar, and apply warm, and change frequently. Give Pleurisy Root Tea freely through the day, say 1/2 oz. of the root to 1 pint of boiling water; you must first bruise the root. Should the inflammation not abate, you may give 15 to 20 drops of Tincture of Foxglove, in Pleurisy Root Tea, and give the Sweating Powder each night.

Regimen: Food cool, slender, and diluted. Avoid all stimulants, whether solids or liquids.

Inflammation of the Stomach

Symptoms: Burning heat, pain, and swelling, frequently hiccough, vomiting, cold extremities; hard, quick, and tense pulse, pain increased by pressure, thirst and pain increased by drink; restlessness and weakness.

Treatment: To case the pain, give 20 drops of the Cholera Compound, once in fifteen to thirty minutes, until the pain is relieved. Drink Slippery Elm Tea freely, Flaxseed, Comfrey, and Marshmallow Root Teas arc all good. Foment the stomach with bitter Herbs, or if very urgent, apply a Mustard plaster. Give a dose of Castor or Olive Oil frequently, sufficient to keep the bowels rather relaxed. Should the patient continue to vomit, give Spearmint Tea and bind the herb upon the stomach. Do not give an Emetic in this case; if you do, you may endanger life. Carefully avoid eating or drinking anything of a heating, acrimonious, or irritating nature. Avoid all Spirits, Wine, or Malt Liquors. Food, Corn Meal Gruel, Buttermilk Pap, simple Toast prepared in water, mild Mutton or Chicken Broth. Drink, neither cold nor hot; it should be chiefly Slippery Elm Tea.

Inflammation o f the Womb

This disease often occurs from injury, such as Childbirth, Difficult Labor, Puncturing, Pollution, or Cold, and Obstructed Menstruation, etc.

Symptoms: Heat of the bowels, burning pain, urine high colored and scanty, sensitive or painful to the touch, and sometimes bloating; the pulse is hard and frequent, countenance dejected, depression of strength, heat of the whole body, thirst, and sometimes a nausea.

Remedies: fomentation's should at once be employed, such as Camphor Compound, Drops simmered in vinegar and applied in a bag warm, and changed frequently. Catnip Tea should be drank freely. The Sweating Powder should be given from two to three times a day. Cathartic, give a small dose of Compound Mandrake three or four times a week, and give the Compound Tincture frequently and freely.

Inflammation of the Bladder

Symptoms: Acute burning and pain at the lower part of the abdomen; a frequent desire to urinate; a partial and sometimes entire obstruction of the urine, frequent desire to evacuate, a frequent and hard pulse, sometimes vomiting etc., and frequently blood and matter passes with the urine.

Remedies: Employ counter irritants; a Mustard Poultice, bitter Herbs simmered in water or vinegar, or the Camphor Compound, warm, and change frequently; inject warm wafer with a small syringe, give from a 1/2 to 1 tea-spoonful of the White Drops three times a day. Also give the Compound Tincture of Burdock. Wild Carrot. Wild Parsley Seed, and Rush teas are all good. Diet, chiefly Gruel, Buttermilk. etc. Drink, cooling and mucilaginous, such as Slippery Elm, Flaxseed, and Pumpkin Seed teas, which are all good.

Small Pox

Symptoms: This disease is divided into two distinct classes. It is known as Distinct and Confluent. In the Distinct Small Pox the disease begins with an inflammatory fever. Cold stage, great languor and drowsiness. A hot stage soon comes on, and then is characterized by great drowsiness, and frequently a numb sensation, and often when the patient closes his eyes, it appears to him as if the entire members of his body were enlarged. From three to five days after the attack, the eruption appears and spreads over the entire body. At this stage the fever entirely subsides. At first, numerous red spots appear, and then gradually rise into pimples, which first appear upon the face, and at the sixth day arc filled like a bladder. The fluid, and afterwards a pit, form at the center. Between the eruptions the skin assumes a scarlet hue, the eyes red, face swollen, until the eyes are often closed.

At the eleventh day the swelling abates, the pustules are quite full; on the top of each a dark spot appears and then breaks, and a portion of the matter oozes out, and forms a crust or scab over the surface, and some days after, the scab falls from the skin, leaving a darkish spot.

Confluent form: In this species the foregoing symptoms arc much aggravated. The pulse is increased, more fever, increased drowsiness, and frequently delirium, and sometimes vomiting, and with the young frequently epileptic fits, and often proves fatal before the eruption appears, and when they do appear, they are in clusters like the measles, and often run together, mid the entire face and other parts assume a black or crusty appearance. The eruption does not properly fill, but assumes a watery hue. and evidently indicates putrefaction. It is always attended with fever, and the more fever the greater the danger.

Remedies: If vomiting, give the patient Spearmint tea warm and freely, and if violent and difficult to check, bind the herb warm upon the breast; or you may give him Saleratus water to drink- when this is accomplished, give the Mandrake Compound, and repeat once in four hours until the bowels are thoroughly cleansed. Then promote perspiration; give warm tea of Catnip and Saffron, equal parts; frequently immerse the feet in warm weak Lye, and bathe the surface of the entire body once or twice a day. If fever increases at any time, see that the bowels and stomach are kept well cleansed, and give the Sweating Powder every night. Should there be much pain in the head, apply Mustard Poultices to the soles of the feet, and bathe the head with equal parts of Rain Water, Vinegar and Spirits.

Should the throat be sore, gargle it with equal parts of Hyssop and Sago, sweetened with Honey, and three or four times a day give a wine-glassful of yeast. Should the patient manifest restlessness, give him Virginia Snakeroot weak tea to drink at night. Should he be languid and weak, give him Buttermilk to drink, not too sour, or made in Pap: A little wine whey, etc.

Should the eruptions not till, you will give him Ale and Molasses well warmed, to drink freely. Should this fail, give him warm milk punch freely. Or after the eruptions fill, should they strike in, you will pursue the same treatment.

Secondary fever: This is the most dangerous of all other stages. This generally occurs when the eruptions begin to turn dark. Many are carried off at this stage. To correct this at once, give a Cathartic, even though the bowels may be relaxed. By this method you will carry off the impurities of the body. The above treatment to be pursued in either of the forms of the disease.

Regimen: If the pox is well filled, there is no occasion for alarm. Give him Corn Meal Gruel, Buttermilk, Roasted Apples, Mush, or Hasty Pudding. Let his diet be cooling and yet nourishing. Avoid all stimulants except in such cases as you are directed to use them. Keep the room well cleansed, with fresh air, but of moderate temperature. If there should be much irritation of the eruptions. Poultice with Buttermilk and Flower of Slippery Elm.

Measles

Symptoms: This disease is characterized by uneasiness, chills, shivering, headache sore throat, heaviness, and sometimes vomiting, etc, but more commonly with heaviness of the eyes, redness, tears, and inflammation, resistance of light, and frequent sneezing; the heat increasing rapidly, a dry cough, violent pain in the groins, and frequently looseness, tongue coated, thirst great, etc, the eruption appears from the third to the fifth day, and the spots dry up; the skin peels off and a new one comes on; from the ninth to the eleventh day, no redness is seen upon the surface, but unless the secretions and excretions have been well cleansed, the cough will continue and fever increase, and bring on great distress and danger.

Remedies: I know of no better remedies or course of treatment for Measles, than that I have laid down under the head of Small Pox. Except that of Pulmonary symptoms, where the mucus has accumulated, you will give the patient a mild Emetic, and repeat if necessary.

Regimen: Diet the same as for Small Pox. While recovering, eat light food, and in small quantities, for some time.

Delirium Tremens

Symptoms: Vomiting, belching of wind, etc. This disease is gradual in its progress, and is a number of days before it arrives at its worst stage. It causes restlessness, wakefulness, and a constant disposition to walk to and fro; delirium, spirits agitated, sudden frights, and often visions of ghosts, snakes, devils, etc. It is attended with fever and costiveness, and often terminates in fits of epilepsy, but with proper treatment the patient may recover.

Remedies: You should give the patient brandy or gin. which frequently affords immediate relief. Should the blood rush to the head, which may be known by the redness of the eyes, palpitation of the heart, etc, immerse the feet and limbs at once in warm, weak Lye, and give Motherwort tea freely. You may also apply Mustard Poultices to the feet and back of the neck. Also give Cathartics and Emetics, and 2 to 3 Motherwort Pills the size of a pea, on going to bed.

Regimen: Care should be taken that during the fit he does not do violence to himself. His food should be chiefly Corn Meal Gruel, and he should be kept quiet and easy.

Cholera Morbus

Symptoms: The attack is sudden and violent, causing nausea, vomiting, pain in the stomach, accompanied by griping and pain in the bowels and purging. The stools are at first thin and watery, and often accompanied with green bile. As the disease advances, these symptoms arc more violent, and cause a spasmodic affection of the muscles of the bowels and extremities. The patient is drawn nearly into cramps by every paroxysm, and often screams at the top of his voice from the most excruciating pain.

Thirst great, but when gratified, causes voiding. The pulse becomes feeble, small, and intermitting; extremities cold, countenance pale, and a cold sweat breaks out over the entire surface. It is a violent and dangerous disease, and often proves fatal in a few hours.

Remedies: When first attacked, give from 20 to 30 drops of the Cholera Compound, and Motherwort tea freely; repeat every thirty minutes. Should these remedies fail to check, which is seldom the case, you may give the Neutralizing Powder, namely, to 1 large tea-spoonful add half a pint of boiling water, and loaf sugar to sweeten, and when nearly cold, add 2 table-spoons full of brandy, and give two tablespoons full every half hour. In violent cases you may add to each dose a few drops of laudanum, and continue until the symptoms abate. Attention must also be given to the bowels, to which you may apply a small bag of Oats, simmered in water, warm, or Hops simmered in vinegar, or bitter Herbs, steeped, and changed, and applied warm to the parts. If costive and full of flatulence, take one pint of sweet Milk, and a quarter of a pound of hog's lard; warm and inject every few minutes until ho gets an action of the bowels. Immerse his feet in warm Ley or Water, and apply warm bricks or bottles to his extremities, and promote perspiration. Give him to drink all the Oat Meal or Indian Meal Gruel he can conveniently drink, a little warmed. After the patient recovers, in about twelve hours give him a mild Cathartic.

Asiatic Cholera

Symptoms: They are much the same, only in a more violent form, and consequently should be treated much the same as Cholera Morbus, only as the symptoms are much more argent, of course the doses should be larger. The Cholera Compound was used during the prevalence of Cholera in Cincinnati, with almost perfect success, and my opinion is, that no remedy can be found in either of the above diseases, more efficient.

Cholera in Children

This disease is known as Cholera Infantum, and resembles somewhat Cholera in adults. Although there are many variations, it is more commonly known as Summer or Bowel Complaint. It frequently attacks children during the summer, and is often occasioned by eating green corn and fruits, and by teething. Etc.

Symptoms: It commences with a mild fever; diarrhea, nausea, and subsequently vomiting, stools very offensive, of a slimy, whitish, frothy, or colorless, watery fluid. In its progress the child begins to sink, becomes very weak and pale; extremities cold, skin dry and shriveled, and heat of the head and bowels, eyes sunk and dull, pulse weak and irregular, patient dull and sleepy, and when asleep, eyes partly open.

This disease may assume a chronic form, and the child become a mere skeleton and linger a number of months; or it may die in a few days, unless the most efficient remedies are employed.

Remedies: If the patient is vomiting, give the neutralizing powder. Dose according to age and urgency of the case; this, however, will be required in an advanced stage. If when first attacked you will give the Cholera Drops in proportion to age and strength, you will invariably check the disease in one hour; but you should always give a Cathartic after the disease is checked. If the skin is dry, bathe the entire surface with warm weak Lye or Saleratus Water, once or twice a day, and give the Sweating Powders every eight, together with Catnip tea, and drink freely Slippery Elm, Comfrey, or Flaxseed teas.

Remedies: Keep the atmosphere pure, and clothes clean.

The best diet is boiled milk, thickened with wheat flour; it may be spiced with a little nutmeg, cinnamon, or cloves.

Vomiting

Symptoms: Extreme loathing of food, nausea, vomiting, general debility, lassitude, frequent straining and cramping of the stomach, returning about once every hour- great distress and burning of the stomach, and frequently hiccough and belching of wind; tongue slightly furred, breath offensive, etc.

In a more advanced stage the patient becomes stupid, and sometimes the eyes set in the head, and occasionally vomiting of black matter, and often destroys the patient in a few hours. He is dizzy, trembles, staggers, etc.

Remedies: To allay the irritability of the stomach, give Spearmint tea, and add a little Saleratus, say 1 tea-spoonful of Saleratus to 1 pint of the tea, and give a table-spoonful every hour until relieved; when the stomach is relieved, give the Neutralizing Powder, until it produces a little action of the bowels. Should this fail, you may give the Mandrake Compound. Smartweed tea is said to be good; or you may give an Emetic in the beginning; or the Cholera Drops, which have cured in a few minutes.

Water Brash

Symptoms: Usually attacks in the morning and forenoon, when the stomach is empty. It comes on with pain in the stomach, similar to cramps, after which a great deal of water is thrown from the stomach, of an acid and sometimes insipid taste, and is sometimes ropy, resembling the white of an egg, and after awhile passes off. This disease seldom proves fatal.

Remedies: Take 8 oz. of Compound Tincture of Senna, 1/2 an oz. of Balsam of Tolu Tincture; mix, and take 1 table-spoonful every morning.

Regimen: Avoid all greasy and acid foods. Pepper, Horseradish, Mustard, etc. may be eaten.

Cramp in the Stomach

You will immediately apply a lively friction to the stomach, and take 20 drops of the Cholera Compound, and repeat in fifteen minutes if necessary. You may also take Catnip, Motherwort, or Smartweed, or Set Teas.

Heartburn

When attacked, take 1 tea-spoonful of Carbonate of Magnesia, morning and evening, in milk. Or you may take a mild Emetic, and avoid eating anything which produces flatulence.

Hiccough

Causes: Inflammation of the stomach; flatulence; drinking ardent spirits, swallowing tobacco juice. If from either of the two latter causes, give half a table-spoonful of Hog's Lard and one tea-cupful of sweet Milk warmed. Or a mild Emetic. Should it be from inflammation, give a little Laudanum, after which give Slippery Elm tea freely.

Bleeding of the Nose

This may generally be stopped in a few minutes by holding a piece of silver between the teeth, or applying cold water to the head and nape of the neck. But sometimes these remedies fail. You will then wet cotton in brandy, and saturate it in pulv. alum, and plug the nose. I was called in one day to see two ladies, who were bleeding at the nose until they had bled nearly to death, and soon succeeded in stopping the blood with the above remedies. Grated dried beef is said to be good; plug the nose with it. It may be important in some cases to immerse the feet in warm lye.

Jaundice

Symptoms: Loss of appetite; dullness, costiveness, soon the skin turns yellowish, first of the eye, then the nails, urine high colored, stools gray, skin dry, with frequent pricking sensations; generally drowsy and sleepy, sometimes over wakeful, as the disease advances, the skin becomes more yellowish.

Remedies: As this is an obstruction of the bile in its passage into the duodenum, you will first give an Emetic rather mild, and then in a day or two give a half tea-spoonful of equal parts of pulv. Mandrake Root, pulv. Cloves, and Cream Tartar, and repeat if necessary. Then take the following, namely: 1 drachm Yellow Dock Root, 2 drachms Bitter Root, 2 drachms White Poplar Bark, 1 drachm Capsicum, 1 drachm Wild Cherry Bark; cover with boiling water, then add 1 pint Holland Gin. Dose; to 1 wineglass full three times a day. At the same time take No. 4 Powder each morning, from 3 to 5 grains, or sufficient to keep the bowels a little relaxed.

After the disease is thoroughly broken up, you may take the following: 2 drachms each of Spikenard, Comfrey, and Sol Seal, and 1 drachm of Cherry Bark, 1 drachm of Babary, one of Columbo, and 1 of Chamomile Blows; add boiling water, and let stand one hour; then add 1 quart of good old Port or domestic Wine, and take from a half to one wineglass full three times a day.

Inflammation or Ague of the Breast

Symptoms: Redness, Swelling, Pain, Obstruction of Milk, etc.

Remedies: Drink Yeast and Water freely until it purges; at the same time apply the Rum Liniment, to which you may add a little pulv. Black Pepper. Wet cloths and apply warm and keep moist. But should you fail to remove the inflammation with this remedy, then there has evidently matter formed, and the treatment must be changed.

You will then poultice as follows: take Slippery Elm and weak Lye, make a poultice, and change frequently. You may apply a little Oil or Butter to the parts first, to prevent from adhering. Should the pain be intolerable, you may take now and then a pill or two of Motherwort Extract as large as a pea, or an Opium pill the same size. You may also give the Sweating Powder at night, and immerse the feet in warm water. Promote perspiration, and if necessary have the breast opened with a lancet. It is better, however, to be patient and let Nature do its own work. After the breast has suppurated and the inflammation has subsided, you may apply any healing salve until well.

Diet, the same as in other inflammatory cases.

Locked-Jaw

Causes: This disease proceeds from violent cold, stabs, punctures, bruises, cuts, etc, which must in every case demand our first attention.

Treatment: Poultice with Slippery Elm and weak Lye, or steam with bitter Herbs the affected parts if much inflamed, and repeat three or four times a day. Or you may immerse the parts in weak Lye. Also take the Vapor Bath, immerse the head as well as the body; set until you sweat freely, say from fifteen to twenty minutes. At the same time give an Emetic. You may add a little Capsicum. Repeat the dose every twenty minutes until he vomits freely. If the bowels are constipated, give an injection of hog's lard and sweet milk, and after the stomach is thoroughly settled, you may give 1 oz. Of Olive or Sweet, or Castor Oil, and repeat if necessary. You may also give the Sweating Powders, two or three a day, and frequently drink warm Catnip, Horehound, Pennyroyal, or Motherwort tea.

Inflammation of the Eye

First remove the cause. It sometimes happens that dust, or sand, or cinder, or an eyelash gets into the eye, and produces inflammation. Should this he the case you will open the lid outward and remove the cause. But from other causes such as scrofula, injuries, heat, bright light, bleak wind, the use of liquors, or from measles, smallpox, or syphilis, then you will poultice the eye at night with the pulverized slippery elm and buttermilk. During the day anoint with the Brown Ointment three times a day, or you may use an eye water made as follows: Take the pith of sassafras root, extract its strength in rainwater, add equal parts of Spirits Camphor and Laudanum.

Wash the eyes frequently. Give an Emetic every week and Cathartic twice a week. The Vapor Bath is also good. You may also give the Sarsaparilla Syrup.

Felon

The first thing to be done is to lessen inflammation and pain, when this has taken place. In its first stage, however, it may frequently be removed by immersing the finger in warm weak Lye, and holding it there a long time. But should it continue obstinate, you will take Tansy, Catnip, Hops, Smartweed and Wormwood; boil fifteen to twenty minutes; add half a teacupful of Soft Soap. Place the hand over it. Cover so as to confine the steam until the hand sweats freely, and repeat three or four times a day, and at intervals you may poultice with Flower of Slippery Elm and weak Lye. Poultice until you discover a small white spot; then take a needle and press gradually until it enters the matter. Should fungus flesh follow the matter, you will apply a little of the Caustic or Potash, and you may introduce a little Caustic daily. It then may be dressed with a little Drawing Salve of any kind. You may now and then take a Cathartic, and let your diet be light and cooling.

Chillblains

These are occasioned by the parts being frosted, and may be corrected at once when it happens, by immersing the parts in snow or cold water, after which, let brisk friction be applied. Then take 2 oz. of olive Oil, 1 drachm of hartshorn, and 1 drachm of Camphor Gum. Mix and shake well. Bathe the parts two or three times a day, and immerse the feet in Lye at night. You should wear linen stockings winter and summer.

Boils

When highly inflamed and painful, you may steam with the hitter Herbs, and make a poultice of Slippery Elm and Flaxseed Oil; first boil the Elm ill rain water or weak lye; after it suppurates and breaks, apply a little healing Salve. To prevent Boils, you limy make a syrup of equal parts Yellow dock and Burdock Roots, and take from a half to one wine-glassful three times a day.

Ague in the Face or Jaw

This complaint frequently comes from colds and other causes. The face becomes swollen and painful, and the pain often becomes intolerable.

Remedies: Bathe the parts with the following preparation, namely: Equal parts of Hartshorn, Sulfuric Ether and Alcohol. Or you may steam with bitter Herbs, and you may immerse a bit of cotton in the Tinct. of Capsicum, and place between the cheek and teeth.

Inverted Toe Nail

Immerse your feet in warm, weak Lye; then poultice with Slippery Elm until the inflammation is reduced, then cut the nail at the side affected a little from the flesh, and carefully skin it from the parts until you can withdraw it by means of a pair of tweezers. Should there be proud flesh, apply a little Caustic and Healing Salve.

Corns and Warts

How to Cure: Take 1/4 lb. of Potash, 1 drachm Extract Belladonna, and 2 drachma Gum Arabic; dissolve in a little water- add wheat flour, and work all into a paste- apply a little to the corn, then work around it with a sharp penknife, and soon it will come out; then apply a little Olive Oil or Vinegar, and be careful not to take cold after it for a few days.

Scalds and Burns

Remedies: Immediately when the accident occurs, you will pulverize charcoal and mix with hog's lard, and spread on a piece of linen and apply to the parts. This will relieve the pain in a few minutes. But should you fail getting this remedy in time, until the parts become inflamed, you will then poultice with Flour of Slippery Elm. First apply a little Lard, fresh Butter, or Olive Oil, so as to prevent the plaster from adhering to the parts, and thus continue until well.

Ringworm

Symptoms: This disease begins with a small red spot, sometimes not larger than a three or five cent piece, and continues to spread until it becomes as large, frequently, as the palm of the hand. When the blood is heated by exercise, the parts itch intolerably, and the sore is greatly aggravated by scratching, so that the patient seldom enjoys rest or comfort.

Remedies: Take Fire Weed Oil or Herb bruised, and mix with hog's Lard; after washing the parts with Castile Soap and water, bathe the parts two or three times a day. Or you may take pulv. Yellow Dock Root, and mix with Lard, and apply in the same form.

Itch

Causes: It is generally taken by coming in contact with some person having it, or Wearing their clothes, or sleeping in the same bed, etc. But it is frequently the result of impure air, improper food, and filthy, dirty clothes, houses, etc.

Symptoms: It first attacks the joints between the fingers, and then continues to spread until it sweeps frequently over the entire body. The pimples arc first small, but frequently increase in size until they become like small boils. It is said that they contain animalculae, which may be seen by means of the microscope.

Remedies: This disease may be cured as follows: Make a syrup of equal parts of Yellow Dock and Burdock Roots, and take from a half to one wine-glassful three times a day, and anoint the parts two or three times a day with the same, as is laid down under the head of Ringworm. The old fashioned way of curing Itch is as follows: Adult- take 1 tea-spoonful Cream Tartar, and 1 tea-spoonful Sulfur, mixed with molasses, three mornings, and at the third night anoint the entire surface of the body, and warm in well. Wrap in an old blanket, and sleep soundly until the next morning. Rise and wash in warm water and Castile Soap Suds. Avoid taking cold for a day or two. I have never known this to fail when properly applied. Although I have known many bad results from the use of these as well as all other minerals, I can only say, if you employ them, be careful that you use them judiciously, and not take cold afterwards.

Sprains

If much swollen and inflamed, you will take Smartweed, Wormwood, Mayweed, and Hops; boil well, place the parts over the vessel, cover well so as to confine the steam until it sweats freely, and repeat as often as painful, and bathe frequently and freely with the Sassafras Liniment. If after tho pain abates you find the joint weak, bathe the parts with the following: Take the inner hark of White Oak, boil a strong liquor, and bathe three or four times a day.

Antidote for Poisons

There is not a family on earth who should not understand the nature and cure of Poisons. They are frequently taken into the stomach accidentally, and their effects are often so sudden and violent, that there is no time to procure a physician, and often when called, he does not know how to cure, or in his practice has not his remedies. It is a consoling thought that no great skill nor foreign remedies are requisite to remove poisonous substances from the stomach.

Nature is the best doctor in the world, if we will only be guided by its dictates. Hence when poison is taken into the stomach, it soon occasions sickness and an inclination to vomit. Thus we are admonished at once what must be done, namely, cleanse the stomach by means of an emetic. There are, however, several classes of Poisons, which I shall notice. They consist of mineral, animal, or vegetable mineral, and are of an acrid or corrosive nature, as Arsenic, Zinc, Iodine, Corrosive Sublimate of Mercury, Antimony, etc.

Remedies: Immediately after you discover the accident, you should resort to one of the following remedies: Drink large quantities of warm Water and hog's Lard, or sweet Milk and Salad Oil; or fresh Butter may be melted and mixed in the milk;

or you may give 1 tea-spoonful of pulv. Tobacco, mixed in molasses, and repeat every ten minutes, and drink large quantities of warm water. Either of the above remedies must be urged and repeated until the patient vomits freely. Or you may give a Lobelia Emetic, or the Emetic Compound. But in every case double the usual quantity must be administered. Pulv. Mustard in water, given warm, will also cause the patient to vomit it from the stomach, and in each ease be sure to give the Oil, Fat, or Butter, with the other preparations.

I mention all these ingredients, in order that you may find some of the above in that moment of peril and fright.

Vegetable Poisons are generally of a narcotic or stupefying nature, as Poppy, Hemlock, Henbane, Berries of Deadly Nightshade, Opium, etc.

Remedies: The same as for minerals are to be employed, and after the poisonous substances, are removed from the stomach, it would lie well to give gentle purgative, such as Olive or Sweet Oil, and should the patient be weak, Tonics or Wine to drink, and let his food be of a mild quality, Flaxseed, Comfrey, or Slippery elm teas freely for two or three days. It would be well, however, to note in addition to the above, that sometimes by taking Opium or Laudanum, the patient becomes stupid and difficult to arouse. In that case it is important to use other means to arouse and keep him awake. In this case he should be shook, tossed, and moved about, you may apply pure Mustard Plasters between his shoulders, legs, or arms, and apply stimulants to his nose; Spirits or Salts of Hartshorn may be held to his nose, or you may let him snuff Cayenne Pepper, etc. You may also give him strong Coffee to drink freely, or you may give him a large tea-spoonful of pulv. black Mustard, mixed with water, and repeat if necessary in ten to fifteen minutes.

Ivy Poison

Both man and beast are liable to get poisoned by a vine very common in this country, known as Poison Ivy, Poison Weed, or Mercury. It produces great heat, itching and burning, swelling and inflammation.

Remedies: Take the Bark of Sweet Elder and simmer in Buttermilk; wash the parts freely and frequently, after which you may apply Sweet Oil. If very irritable, poultice with Slippery Elm. You may also use the Fire Oil Ointment three or four times a day.

Bite of Snake

Remedies: Take the roots and branches of the Red Plantain and Horehouud, equal parts; bruise all in a mortar, then squeeze out the juice and give as soon as possible a large table-spoonful of the juice, and if necessary, repeat in one hour, and apply a tobacco leaf to the wound; change frequently. Or you may apply the caustic to the wound and then the tobacco leaf. Salt is also good. The patient should also have frequent Cathartics.

The following is good: Take a bottle of Spirits of Turpentine, place the mouth over the wound, until the pain is extracted, which will be in a short time.

Bite of a Mad Dog

Remedies: Take ash colored, ground, or pulv. Liverwort, 1/2 an oz., Black Pepper, of an oz. Mix all and divide into four parts. Take one each morning in a half pint of sweet Milk, warm, and after the above medicine is taken, then the patient must be dipped under water head and all, and not remain in over half a minute, for thirty days, and then for two weeks three times a week.

This is old Dr. Mead's remedy. In this I have but little confidence. Dr. Buchan recommends if there be no blood-vessel injured, the parts adjacent to the wound may be cut out. But this must be done soon. But if not practicable, mix Salt and Vinegar, and apply, after which, take Yellow Basilicon mixed with Red Precipitate, and apply twice a day.

Dr. Beach recommends the following, and I have more confidence in him than either or all those noted. First have the wound cupped as soon as possible, after which apply the Caustic Potash until an eschar is formed. Then apply an Yeast Poultice, and keep up a discharge as long as possible. Then make a strong infusion of Skullcap through the day, and Mandrake Compound once a week. But if there be symptoms of Hydrophobia, take a Lobelia emetic every other day and at the same time take the Vapor Bath.

Myself together with two young gentlemen, were bitten by a dog having Hydrophobia, among the Dutch near Schenectady, N. Y. one in the nose, one in the left hand, and the other in the right. A Dutchman prescribed the following strange prescription: Equal parts of the false tongue of a colt, and the jaw bone of a dog, and verdigris, to be taken nine mornings in succession. Also from one quarter to one third of a copper, to he filed, and taken during the day. We all took the above, and neither myself nor they, so far as my knowledge extends of them, have had the disease. I believe, however, they had the wounded parts cut out. but I did not. I am of an opinion that the Red Plantain would cure or prevent the disease, by eating large quantities of the stalk, of the leaf, or squeezing out the juice from the stalk and root, as prescribed for the bite of a rattlesnake, but in that case it would be well to apply Dr. Beach's remedies externally.

Diseases of Children

Infants are frequently afflicted with flatulence and gripes, more frequently from the mother eating improper food than from any other cause. She should therefore be careful about her diet. When the child is thus attacked, you may give it some Catnip, Peppermint, or Pennyroyal tea. But the best remedy, in all cases of griping, teething, nervousness, and disquiet, is to make Syrup of Motherwort, and sweeten, say about the consistency of laudanum, and give the child from ten to fifteen drops, and increase if necessary. This will also cure fits in children. With this remedy I cured one in St. Lawrence County, NY., who had been afflicted with them two years, after all others had decided the case incurable.

Purging or Looseness: This may soon be corrected by giving the child from one to three drops of the Cholera Compound, or by giving both the mother and child the Neutralizing Powder.

Teething: This complaint has cost the life of many a child. It causes heat and pain in the head, restlessness, fever, swollen gums, dysentery, and often fits. Remedies: It may be necessary to cut the gums a little, and administer a little Castor Oil every other day, unless tho bowels are relaxed. You may also give the Motherwort Extract, and Catnip Tea, and promote perspiration. You may give the child a crust of bread, or make a hole through a silver dollar, and hang about the neck.

Sores about the Ears, Groins, Etc: Wash the parts with Castile Soap and Water; wipe dry with linen; then you may sprinkle on the sores a little Flour of Slippery Elm, or apply the Fire Oil Ointment, made as follows: Take 2 drachms Oil and one quarter of a pound of pure hog's Lard. Mix cold.

Sore Mouth: Children arc frequently afflicted with this

complaint. Little small spots appear in the mouth. Give a gentle physic, and wash the mouth frequently with a tea made of Sage and Hyssop, sweetened with honey.

Convulsions from Teething: You will at once immerse the feet in warm, weak Lye, and give the Motherwort Syrup. Onion or garlic may be bruised and applied to the stomach. If there is much heat of the head, you may apply a cloth wet with rain water, spirits and vinegar.

Soreness about the Navel: Apply the same remedies as prescribed for Sores about the Ears, etc.

Rupture: Lay the child upon his back; then press the tumor or protruded parts back, and make a plaster of the Extract of White Oak Bark, and apply; then a compression over it with a bandage, to keep it in its proper place.

Tongue Tied

It so happens that sometimes infants cannot nurse, from the top of the tongue being contracted. In that case, and in that only, should there be a very small incision made with a lancet or a pair of scissors. This cut. however, must, be very small, lest a blood-vessel be severed. Parents are apt to think their child is tongue tied sometimes, when such is not the case.

For Sty of the Eye

Take 1 tea-spoonful of tea in a small bag, turn a few drops of boiling water on the same, and apply at, night, and if necessary repeat the next night. This will certainly cure, unless it be from scrofulous taint.

For Worms

Dry Egg Shell pulverized, and mixed in molasses. Give

the child one tea-spoonful three mornings in succession; then a dose of physic. This remedy will destroy the worms.

To Preserve the Eye, and Restore Partial Blindness

Occasionally press the eye-ball by means of placing the thumb and finger next to the nose and the temple. Take 1 gallon of Water, 2 drachms of Cream Tartar, and 2 oz. Of refined Sugar. Wash the eyes three times a day. This simple remedy has restored the eyesight of those partially blind for many years.

Another Remedy for Felon

Take 1 pint Soft Soap, and add slacked Lime until formed into putty. Fill a leather thimble, made somewhat larger than the finger, and insert the finger.

REMEDIES FROM ALCHEMICAL WORKS

The following sections have been included from works of alchemy specifically dealing with elixirs and medical materials. For those interested in the subject of alchemy in a more broad sense, I published a work this same year on the subject called "Alchemy, a Collection."

These works have been included verbatim from my own prior editions:

I: *A Work of Saturn* by Isaac Hollandus. This short manuscript from 1670 involves creating a sort of medical compound which contains lead, which is dissolved into wine or applied externally to wounds. Under the conception of the four humors of Galen, the sweating and other symptoms of lead ingestion would have been considered medicinal.

II: *Tract on the Tincture and Oil of Antimony*. This work is from the 13th century, translated later. It is purely medicinal and provides instructions for creating a "universal medicine."

A WORK OF SATURN

PREFACE

Courteous reader:

The philosophers have written much of their lead which is prepared out of antimony, as Basil has taught; and I am of the opinion, that this Saturnine work of the most excellent philosopher, Isaac Hollandus, is not to be understood of common lead, (if the matter of the stone be not much more thereby intended) but of the philosophers' lead. But whether the vulgar Saturn be the matter of the philosophers stone, thereof you will receive sufficient satisfaction from the subsequent seventeen considerations or documents. This is published for the benefit of all the lovers of this art, because it expound and declares the Stone of Fire.

A WORK OF SATURN

My student shall know, that the Stone called the philosopher's stone, comes out of Saturn. And therefore when it is perfected, it makes projection as well in mans' body from all diseases, which may assault them either within or without, be they what they will, or called by whatever name, as also in the imperfect metals.

And know, my student, for a truth, that in the whole vegetable work there is no higher nor greater secret than in Saturn; for we do not find that perfection in gold which is in Saturn; for internally it is good gold, herein all philosophers agree, and it wants nothing else, but that first you remove what is superfluous in it, that is, it's impurity, and make it clean, and then that you turn it's inside outwards, which is its redness, then will it be good gold; for gold cannot be made so easily, as you can of Saturn, for Saturn is easily dissolved and congealed, and its Mercury may be easily extracted, and this Mercury which is extracted from Saturn, being purified and sublimed, as Mercury is usually sublimed, I tell you, my student that the same Mercury is as good as the Mercury which is extracted out of gold, in all operations; for if Saturn be gold internally as in truth it is, then must it's Mercury be as good as the Mercury of gold, therefore I tell you that Saturn is better in our work than gold; for if you should extract the Mercury out of gold, it would require a years space to open the body of gold, before you can extract the Mercury out of the gold, and you may extract the Mercury out of Saturn in fourteen days, both being alike good.

Would you make a work of gold alone, you must labor two whole years upon it, if it shall be well done: and you may finish a work of Saturn in thirty or thirty two weeks at the most. And being both well made, they are both alike good; Saturn costs nothing or very little, it requires a short time, and small labor; this I tell you in truth.

My student, lock this up in thy heart and understanding, this Saturn is the stone which the philosophers will not name, whose name is concealed unto this day; for if it's name were known, then many would operate, and the art would be common, because this work is short, and without charge, a small and mean work.

Therefore does the name remain concealed, for the evils sake, which might thence proceed. All the strange parables which the philosophers have spoken mystically, of a stone, a Moon, a furnace, a vessel, all this is Saturn; for you must not put any strange thing unto it, only what comes from it, therefore there is none so poor in this world, which cannot operate and promote this work; for Luna may be easily made of Saturn, in a short time, and in a little longer time Sol may be made out of it. And though a man be poor, yet may he very well attain unto it, and may be employed to make the philosopher's stone.

Wherefore my student, all is concealed in Saturn, which we have need of, for in it is a perfect Mercury, in it are all the colors of the world, which may be discovered in it; in it are the true black, white and red colors, in it is the weight, Saturn is our Latten.

Example: The eye of a man cannot endure anything that is imperfect, how little it may be, though it be the least atom of dust, it would cause much pain, that he can rest nowhere. But if you take the quantity of a bean of Saturn, shave it smooth and round, put it into the eye, it will cause no pain at all; the reason is, because it is internally perfect, even as gold and precious stones. By these and other speeches you may observe, that Saturn is our philosopher's stone, and our Latten, out of which our Mercury and our stone is extracted with small labor, little art and expense, and in a short time.

Wherefore I admonish you my student, and all those who know it's name, that you conceal it from people, by reason of the evil which might thence arise; and you shall call the stone our Latten, and call the vinegar, water, wherein our stone is to be washed; this is the stone and the water whereof the philosophers have wrote so many great volumes. There are many and different works in the mineral stone, and especially in that stone which God has given us for free, whereof so many strange parables are written in the mineral book.

But this is the true stone which the philosophers have sought, because it makes projection upon all the imperfect metals, especially upon quick Mercury, and moreover make projection upon all diseases whatsoever, which may come into mans body, as likewise upon all wounds, cancers, fistulas, open sores, buboes, imposthumes, and all whatsoever can come externally upon mans body, therefore this stone is not under the mineral work, but under the vegetable.

It is the beginning of the vegetable book, and the

principal; this stone is called *Lapis Philosophorum*, the mineral stone is called *Lapis Mineralis*, and the third stone is called *Lapis Animalis*. This stone is the true *Aurum Potable*, the true quintessence which we seek, and no other thing else in this world but this stone. Therefore the philosophers say, whosoever knows our stone, and can prepare it, needs no more, wherefore they sought this thing and no other.

My student shall take ten, twelve, or fifteen pounds of Saturn, wherein is no mixture of any other metal; laminate it thin, have in readiness a great stone jug, half full of vinegar, stopper the jug very close, set it in a lukewarm bath, every three or four days scrape off the calcined Saturn from the plates, and reserve it apart, thus do so long till you have five or six pounds of the calcined Saturn, then grind it very well on a stone with good distilled wine vinegar, so as you may paint therewith, then take two or three great stone pots, therein put the calx of Saturn which you ground, pour good distilled wine vinegar upon it, that two parts of the pot be full, stir it well together, stop the pot close with a polished glass or rounded stone, set the pots in a bath, stir it four or five times a day with a wooden ladle, lay the glass or stone stopper again over it, make the bath no hotter than that you may well endure your hand therein, that is, lukewarm.

So let it stand fourteen days and nights, then decant that which is clear into another stone pot, pour more distilled vinegar upon the calx which is not well dissolved, mix them well together, set it fourteen days in the bath, again decant it, and pour more vinegar upon it as before.

This decantation and pouring on continue so long till all the calx of Saturn be dissolved, then take all the dissolved Saturn, set it in a bath, evaporate the vinegar by a small fire, and the Saturn will become a powder or lump.

Or stir it about until it be dry, you have a mass or powder of a dark yellow, or honey color, then grind the powder again very finely upon a flat stone with distilled vinegar; put it into a stone pot, stir and mix it well together, set it again into a bath, which is but lukewarm, so let it stand five or six days, stir it every day from the top to the bottom with a wooden ladle, cover it again with the glass stopper, then let it cool, pour off that which is dissolved into a great stone pot, pour more vinegar upon it, mix and stir them well together, set it into the bath as before, reiterate this decanting and pouring on so often, till no more will dissolve, which try with your tongue, if it be sweet, it is not enough dissolved, or put some of it into a glass gourd, let it evaporate, if anything remain, it is not yet all dissolved which would be gold, and then what remains in the pot are feces, and sweet upon the tongue; if you find anything in the gourd, it is not yet all dissolved, then may you pour fresh vinegar upon it, till all be dissolved, then coagulate it as before, pour yet more vinegar on it, stir it, set it again into the bath, reiterate this operation of solution and coagulation so long till you find no more feces at the bottom, but all be dissolved into a pure clear water, then is Saturn freed from all its leprosy, melancholy, feces, and blackness, being pure and white as snow, for it is cleansed from all it's uncleanness, because it's coldness stands outwards as Luna does, and its heat is internal, malleable as wax, and sweet as sugar candy.

Why is it white as snow? Because it is purified from all its impurities, and because its coldness stands external as Luna does, and its heat is internal.

Why is it sweet? Because the four elements in it are pure, and separated from all sulfurous stink and blackness, which Saturn received in the mine; it is almost medicinal, and like unto nature: And because it is so pure, it affords some of its internal virtue outwardly as that of sweetness; but the heat is so covered with the cold that it cannot put forth its power externally by reason of the cold which is external (the heat of Saturn lies internal, even as in nitrate salts) as does the taste; the spirit of tasting is the most subtle in all things, as is taught more at large in the book of vegetables, how the air does dilate itself from all herbs and flowers externally; for the spirit of the air lies in the inward part of all things; for God created nothing in this world but it has its peculiar taste or air, the air and the taste are one spirit- the taste goes out of the air, as smoke from the fire.

But how comes it to pass, that a thing which has sweet air, is bitter in taste? The cause is because the feces of that thing is putrid and stinking in the elements, that is the choler or heat; for whatsoever is unnaturally hot, has a bitter taste; the air and the taste are one spirit, and as the spirit of the air presses outwards through a hot thing, so does the air embrace the taste about, and defends the subtle taste, that it should not be burnt by the vehement burning choler, as in the herbal is at large expressed.

But the cause why Saturn is sweet in taste is, that it is almost pure and clean, having scarce any unnatural heat in it, which can burn the subtle taste, therefore it has the taste externally, and the taste has the spirit of the air locked up in it.

My student, know what I said before, that a thing wherein is much burning heat, the air locks up the taste therein, because the taste shall not be corrupted by the unnatural heat. So the taste includes the air in it, when it issues forth from a thing which is externally cold; for the subtle spirits of the air or scent of a thing can endure no cold, as we see daily in herbs and flowers, that they yield no scent in the winter, as they do in the summer; but they hide themselves in the winter, and the spirit has the scent enclosed in it, and the spirit of scent or air.

Behold a man that has taken cold, immediately he loses his scent, and his tasting is diminished. Even so it is here with Saturn; it is quite cold, so that the taste manifests itself with the spirit of scent; for the spirit of the taste has the smell in it. Look upon sugar which is well clarified from its feces, how sweet it is in taste, yet it yields no scent, yet there is an extraordinary sweetness in sugar. What is the reason of this? Sugar is very cold externally, therefore is it as snow, and of a sweet taste; yet sugar internally is hot and moist, of the temper of gold, and of such great virtue that it is called the philosopher's stone, as it is approved, and very prevalent to cure all the distempers of a mans body, as appears by its operation. The reason why I say this my student, is that you should altogether understand its internal and external, and the spirits which are in these things, whereof we discourse; that thereby you should know God's wonderful works, and what wonders he works in these inferior things, which are all made for our use.

What has God in us, for whose sake he hath created all these wonders, and all these things? Wherefore, my student, believe in God, love him, and follow him, for he loves you, as he makes it appear, and manifests himself in all things, as well in their internals as in their externals. Oh how wonderful is our Lord and God, from whom all wonders proceed!

Now, my student, why is Saturn as malleable as Wax? By reason of its abounding sulfur, which is therein; for I find no malleability or fusibility in anything saving in sulfur, mercury and arsenic, and all these three are in Saturn; so that Saturn is quickly malleable, but all these three are cleansed with it from their uncleanness. And do you not know, that the philosophers call their stone arsenic, and a white thing; and they say their sulfur is incombustible; they call it likewise a red thing, all this is Saturn, in it is arsenic; for Luna is principally generated of a white sulfur, as is plainly taught in the book of sulfur, and all arsenic is internally red as blood, if its inward part be brought outwards, as is demonstrated in the book of colors.

Saturn stands almost in the degree of fixed Luna. So that in it there is a red sulfur, as you see, when its internal is placed outwards, it will be red as ruby; there are no colors but in the spirits, so that there is in it a red and a yellow sulfur. In it is Mercury, as may be seen, for Mercury is extracted out of Saturn in a short time, and with it little labor.

So that all three are in Saturn, but they are not fixed therein, but they are clean, pure, incombustible, malleable as wax; in it are all things which the philosophers have mentioned. They say, our stone is made of a stinking menstruate: What think you, is not Saturn dug out of a stinking earth? For miners are killed with the ill scents and vapors where Saturn is dug. And the philosophers say, our stone is of little value, being unprepared; they say, the poor have it as well as the rich, and they say true; for there are not poorer or more miserable people to be found than those which dig and work Saturn in the mine; and they say it is to be found in all towns and places, wheresoever you come Saturn is there. They say it is a black thing: What think you, is it not black? They say, it is a dry water, if gold and Luna are to be refined upon the test, must it not be done with Saturn? They must be washed and tried with it as a foul garment is made clean with soap. They say, in our stone are the four elements, and they say true; for the four elements must be separated out of Saturn. They say, our stone consists of soul, spirit and body, and these three become one. They say true; when it is made fixed for the white Mercury and sulfur with its earth, then these three are one.

Whereby is to be observed, that the philosophers have said true; they concealed its name for the sake of the ignorant, who are not their children, to keep them still in their ignorance. Thus my student, the ancients took care to conceal the name of the stone; now let us return to our purpose.

You have now Saturn washed and cleansed from all its impurity, and made as white as snow, fusible as wax, but it is not fixed yet; we will make it fix the Mercury and sulfur with its earth.

Take a glass vial, put half of your purified Saturn into it, reserve the other half till you have occasion to use it; lay a polished glass upon the mouth of the glass, set it in an urn with sifted ashes upon a furnace; or set it upon the tripod of secrets, or in the furnace wherein you calcine spirits; give it fire so hot as the heat of the sun at mid summer, and no hotter, either a very little hotter, or a very little cooler, as you can best obtain. But if you give it a greater heat, such as you may keep lead in flux, then your matter would melt as if it were oil; and having stood so, ten or twelve days, its sulfur would fly away, and your matter would be all spoiled, for the sulfur which is in your matter is not yet fixed, but is in the external.

Wherefore the matter melts presently, and though it be clean, yet it is most fixed; wherefore give so gentle fire to it, that it may not flux; so keep it six weeks, then take out a little of it, lay it on a glowing hot plate, if it immediately melts and fumes, it is not yet fixed, but if the matter remains unmelted, the sulfur is then fixed which is therein; then strengthen the fire somewhat, till the matter in the glass begins to look yellow, and continually more and more yellow, like to powdered saffron, then augment the fire yet stronger, till the matter begins to be red, then prosecute your fire from one degree to another, even as the powder becomes redder and redder by degrees, so hold on your fire, till the matter be red as a ruby, then augment the fire yet more, that the matter may be glowing hot, then is it fixed, and ready to pour the curious water of paradise upon it.

My student must know, that there are two ways of pouring on the water of paradise. I will teach you to make and prepare both, then you may take which you will; for the one is half as good again as the other.

My child, you may remember, that I ordered you to reserve the one half of the purified Saturn, which take and put into a stone pot, pour upon it a bottle or more of distilled wine vinegar, set a head on, distill the vinegar again from it in a bath, the head must have a hole at the top to pour fresh vinegar upon the matter, and extract the vinegar again from it, pour fresh vinegar again on, and again extract it; this pouring on again, and extracting or distilling off must continue so long, till the vinegar be drawn off as strong as it was when it was put in, then is it enough, and the matter has in it as much of the spirit of vinegar as it can contain; then take the pot out of the bath, take off the head, and take the matter out, and put it into a thick glass which can endure the fire, set a stopper on it, put it in an urn with ashes, which set on a furnace, first make a small fire, and so continually a little stronger, till your matter come over as red as blood, thick as oil, and sweet as sugar, with a celestial scent, then keep it in that heat so long as it distills, and when it begins to slack, then increase your fire till the glass begins to glow.

Now continue this heat till no more will distill, then let it cool of itself, take the receiver off, stop it very tightly with wax, take the matter out of the glass, beat it to powder in an iron mortar, with a steel pestle; and then grind it on a stone with good distilled vinegar, put this matter so ground into a pot, pour good distilled vinegar upon it, that two parts be full, set the pot into a bath with a head upon it, distill the vinegar off, pour fresh vinegar again upon it, distill it off again: thus do so long, that the vinegar be as strong as it was when it was first poured upon it, then let it cool, take the matter out of the bath, take the head off, take the matter out of the pot, put it into a stronger round glass which can endure the fire, as you did before, set it upon a furnace in an urn with sifted ashes, set a head, and a receiver luted to it, then distill it, first with a small fire, which augment by degrees, till a matter come over red as blood, and thick as oil, as aforesaid.

Give it fire till no more will distill, then let it cool of itself, take off the head, break the glass pot, and take the matter out, powder it again, and grind it on a stone with distilled vinegar, put it again into the stone pot, pour fresh vinegar upon it, set it into the bath, and its head on, distill the vinegar from it, pour it on again as has been taught, till the vinegar remain strong as it was.

Reiterate this distillation in the bath until the matter has no more spirit of the vinegar in it, then take it out, set it in a glass pot, distill all that will distill forth in ashes, till the matter becomes a red oil, then have you the most noble water of paradise, to pour upon all fixed stones, to perfect the stone; this is one way. This water of paradise thus distilled, the ancients called their sharp, clear vinegar, for they conceal its name.

My student, I will now teach you other ways to make the water of paradise; this is an easy way, but not so good, nor does it that high projection in humane medicines, yet it cures all diseases within and without, but the other cures miraculously in a short time.

THE SECOND WAY OF PREPARING THE WATER OF PARADISE

My student, if you would make it after this manner, you must take the half of your prepared Saturn which I ordered you to keep, upon which pour the half of your fixed and prepared water of paradise, take the half, put it into a stone pot, pour weak wine vinegar upon it, mix it well together, then take two pounds of calcined tartar, which is well clarified by solution and coagulation, so that it leaves no more feces behind it, sal ammoniac one pound, which is likewise so clearly sublimed, that no feces remain after its sublimation, pound both together to a powder, put them speedily into a pot, and stop it close immediately, or else it will run out; for so soon as the tartar and sal ammoniac come to the vinegar, they lift themselves up, and would immediately run out of the mouth of the pot, wherefore stop the pot presently, set the pot in a vessel of water, they will cool speedily, otherwise if the cold and hot matter should come together suddenly, they would contest together, rise up, and become so hot, that the pot would break for heat, if it were not set in cold water; therefore take heed, when you put the powders in, that you stop it immediately, and set it in cold water before you put the other powder to it, then they will unite, let them stand a day and a night in that vessel, then take them out, set them into a lukewarm bath two days and nights, let it cool off on its own, take the stopper off from the pot, and set a head on, set the pot in sifted ashes upon a furnace, distill with a small fire, and continually greater till all the vinegar be over, then augment your fire notably, till you see quick Mercury drop out of the pipe, when it ceases to drop, then augment the fire by little and little and drive it so long as it drops; you may observe when it will leave dropping, if in the space of one or two *Paternosters* one drop does fall, then augment the fire till the pot glows at the bottom, for twelve hours and when the Mercury is over, then should the sal ammoniac sublime up into the head, and the tartar remain with the body of Saturn at the bottom of the pot, which take out, put into a linen bag, hang it in a moist cellar, the tartar will dissolve, receive it in a glass, the body of Saturn remains in the bag.

Take it out and calcine it in a reverberating furnace three days and nights, with a great heat, as is taught elsewhere, then extract the salt out as is taught in the mineral book. You may make projection with the salt, and coagulate your tartar again, it will be as good or better than it was, likewise take your sal ammoniac out of the head, it is good again, and if you have no sal ammoniac, then take three pounds of calcined tartar, likewise so clarified that it leave no feces behind, you then need no sal ammoniac, therewith may you likewise extract the Mercury out of Luna and Jupiter, wherewith you may do wonders, as is taught in the mineral book, where is spoken of the quintessence of metals.

Now my student must know, that this Mercury or quintessence of Saturn is as good in all works as the Mercury of Sol, they are both alike good, and herein all the philosophers agree. My student, take this Mercury of Saturn, so drawn out of the receiver, put it into a glass box.

I have now taught you to make two sorts of the water of paradise; and know my student, that the first way is the best; though it be made with some danger, longer time, and more charge; for the vinegar is all good, yet the red oil is the best; its time is like unto the end, and though it be more tedious before you obtain the red oil, yet it fixes itself in a short time, if it come to the matter or fixed stone, into a simple essence in greater redness; but when the Mercury comes to the fixed stone, it holds on a long time in ascending and descending before it dies, and when it is quite dead, it makes the red fixed stone again into a fixed color, so covering the red stone with its coldness, that the red stone becomes white again, then you must boil it again gently with a small fire, till it begin to be yellow, prosecuting the fire from one degree to another, as the color is higher and stronger, and that so long till it attain to a perfect redness, which requires a long time before it be done, which is not requisite in the red oil; for the red oil dies or coagulates forthwith the stone, the one fixing itself with the other into a simple essence, in a short time.

Therefore I tell you, my child, that the time of the oil is alike long in the end, though it appear to be of a shorter time with the Mercury, but it is equally long at the end of the work, therefore I tell you the art of both works, that you may the better understand the art to make the oil from the innermost nature of the stone, which is found afterwards. The oil was unknown to the ancients, for my grandfather with his companions found it with great labor and length of time.

So there are two ways to dissolve the stone, and to pour upon it the clear water of paradise. Our ancestors called the oil their sharp vinegar; therefore, my student, keep the name private, and I will teach you first of all how you shall join the Mercury to your stone, which you extracted out of Saturn, to dissolve it; afterwards I will teach you to bring over the helm that red oil which you extracted out of your prepared Saturn, into a fixed stone, to dissolve your stone.

My student, weigh your fixed stone, take half as much of your Mercury, pour it upon the stone in the glass, cover the glass again with a polished stone which may just fit it, set it in an urn with sifted ashes, make a small fire like the sun's heat at midsummer, and give no more fire to it, until the water of paradise or Mercury become all a dead powder. And know, my student, that the red or fixed stone, which before was darkened, when it has drunk up the water of paradise, or Mercury, or how you will call it, that it be a powder between black and gray, then augment the fire from one degree to another, till the matter be perfect white, and when it is white, strengthen the fire yet more, from one degree to another, till it be of a dark yellow color, then make it yet stronger, till it be of a perfect red; then rejoice, for your stone is perfect, and malleable as wax. Praise God, who gives unto us part of his miracles; and do good to the poor, you may see it with your fleshly eyes, and use God's goodness miraculously in this corrupt life, for I tell you in good charity, that if anyone principally attain to this stone, that it is given, afforded, and lent to him from God.

Whosoever has this stone, may live in a healthful state, to the last term of his life, appointed him by God, and may have all whatsoever he desires on Earth.

He shall be loved and esteemed of all people, for he can cure them all internally and externally of all diseases which may befall them; but if the stone does not so, it is false, and deserves not the name of the vegetable stone, or philosopher's stone.

Therefore my student, if God give you this stone, look diligently to it, that you keep yourself from offending God, that you make not this stone on earth to be your Heaven; govern and rule yourself to God's glory and to the comfort of poor people, that God's praise may be augmented, to the defense of the Christian religion, and to the relief of poor and exiled Christians.

I tell you, my students, if you use it otherwise, God will leave you here a little while to your own will, but afterwards he will speedily send a punishment, either you shall be struck dead, or die by a fall, or die some other sudden death, and go body and soul to Hell, and be damned eternally, for your ingratitude to God, who so graciously vouchsafed you so precious and great a gift.

Therefore, my student, look carefully to it, so to govern yourself to God's glory, and the salvation of your soul, that the eternal curse may not fall upon you, and therefore I have left you this writing as my testament. Enough has been said to the wise, therefore look to yourself.

The multiplication of the stone is now perfected.

Now my student, you may take the half of your powder, put it into a glass and melt it, have in readiness a mold made hollow, of boxwood, great or small as you please, it must be made smooth and even within with an instrument, anoint it with olive oil, and when your red powder is fluxed, pour it into the mold, it will be a precious stone, red as a ruby, clear and transparent, take it out of the mold, and make projection upon the imperfect metals, and in the body of man.

Take ten times as much of prepared Saturn as I taught you before, by coagulation and solution, till it leave no feces behind, then take your precious red powder out of the glass, that two parts be full, set it into your warm bath, and let it dissolve: when any thing is dissolved, decant off that which is clear on the top into another glass, pour new vinegar upon it, let it dissolve again as before; decant and pour fresh vinegar upon it so often, till all be dissolved into a clear water, which is done usually in ten or twelve days, then set all that which is dissolved into a bath, and a head upon it, distill the vinegar, distill the vinegar from it again, and coagulate the matter so long till it be dry and shine, then put it into another glass, which set upon a furnace in an urn with sifted ashes, laying a polished glass upon the mouth of the glass.

My student, know that your matter is become fixed with the stone in the solution, make an indifferent hot fire in the furnace so hot as the heat of the sun in midsummer, or somewhat hotter, till the matter begins to be yellow, then go on with the fire from one degree to another, till you have a perfect yellow, then increase the fire from one degree to another, till you have a perfect redness, which is quickly done, in half the time for the color to come, and in the multiplication, but operate as before in the beginning, and pour paradise water upon the stone, as was taught you before in this work, boil and mortify it in every point to a perfect redness as hath been taught. Then may you again take half of it out, and make projection therewith, and multiply the other half again in all points as above said, so may you always continue working.

Now I will teach you the other way, and the best that is to water your red fixed stone or powder with the red oil, that it be fusible; you must know how much your red powder weighs, then take half the weight of your red oil, to the full weight of the stone, and pour it upon the red powder, and when the oil is poured into the glass, you may set a small head on, upon a furnace in sifted ashes, joining a receiver to the nose of the head, make a small fire under it, as the heat of the sun in March, and no hotter; for there is yet some moisture of the vinegar in the oil, that it may be abstracted, continue it in that heat, that you can perceive no moisture in the head, then augment the fire a little, as the heat of the sun at midsummer, and if there be yet more moisture in it, you will perceive it in the head, but it you perceive it not in six or eight days, then take the head off, and lay the polished glass again upon the mouth of your urn, increase the fire, that you can scarce endure your hand or finger in the ashes for the time of an *Ave Maria*, continue the fire in that heat till the red oil be all fixed with the powder in the glass, which you may know thus;

Take a little of the powder out of the glass, lay it on a glowing silver plate; if the powder malts as wax, and penetrates through the plate as oil does through a dry leather, and makes it gold throughout as far as the powder went, then is the stone finished, and if it does not do this, you must then let it stand in that heat till it do so without fuming.

Now, my student, when the stone is finished, take half of it out of the glass, put it into a glass melting pot, and melt the powder gently, which should be done presently, for it melts as wax; and being melted, pour it into the mold of boxwood as aforesaid, it will be a red stone, clear and transparent as crystal, red as a ruby, then make projection therewith, and set the other half again to multiply.

Then take in God's name twenty parts of Saturn, which is prepared by solution and coagulation, till it leave no more feces behind, as has been said at the beginning.

Dissolve these twenty parts of Saturn, dissolve it by itself in a glass with distilled vinegar; likewise dissolve the powder of your stone alone by itself in a glass with distilled vinegar, and when both are dissolved into clear water, pour both the solutions together into a great glass, set it into a bath, a head on, and a receiver to it, distill the vinegar from it in the boiling bath, till the matter be dry, then let it cool by itself, put it into a glass, lay a polished glass over the mouth of the vessel, and set it into a furnace in an urn with sifted ashes, make a fire under it like to the sun's heat in March, till the powder be perfect white, which is quickly done.

Then augment your fire from one degree to another, till the matter becomes yellower and yellower, to a perfect yellow, then increase it yet stronger, from one degree to another, till it be redder and redder, to a perfect redness; then pour your water upon the red powder with the red oil, or with the water of paradise, or with the clear sharp vinegar, or call it how you will, doing in all points as has been taught, till the red powder flux like wax upon a silver plate, without fuming, penetrating it as oil does a dry leather, that it become good gold within and without; then render thanks unto God, be obedient to him for his gifts and graces.

You may again take one half out of the glass, and make projection, setting the other half in again, as has been taught, so may you work all your lifetime for the poor, and perform other duties to God's glory, and the salvation of your soul, as I have said before; enough to the wise.

PROJECTION UPON METAL

Know, my student, how and in what manner you must use this stone, which makes projection upon Mercury, and all imperfect metals and bodies of Mars, Jupiter and Venus, whereof make plates glowing hot, whereon spread the stone, and lay coals on for a season, that the stone may penetrate, but the stones must be made quick with gold, and Jupiter also, which is very laborious, as is taught in the projection. But you must project upon Saturn or Luna, which need not be made quick, only flux them, and cast one part upon a thousand parts, it will be a medicine, cast one part of these thousand parts upon ten parts, it will be the best gold that ever was seen on Earth.

ITS USE IN MEDICINE

This stone cures all leprous people, plague, and all diseases which may reign upon Earth, or befall mankind; this is the true *Aurum potable*, and the true quintessence which the ancients sought; this is that thing whereof the whole troop of philosophers speak so wondrously, using all possible skill to conceal its name and operation, as aforesaid.

Take of this stone the quantity of a grain of wheat, lay it in a little good wine in a small glass, half full, or a quarter full, make the wine warm; the stone will melt like butter, and the wine will be red as blood, and very sweet in your mouth, as ever you tasted; for to speak comparatively, it is so sweet in taste that honey and sugar may be compared as gall to it; give this unto the patient to drink, lay him in bed, but lay not too many clothes upon him, the stone hastens forthwith to the heart, expelling thence all ill humors, thence dilating itself through all the arteries and veins of the whole body, rousing up all humors. The party will sweat, for the stone opens all the pores of the body, and drives forth all humors thereby, so that the patient will seem to have been in the water, yet will this sweating not make him sicker, for the stone expels only what is adverse to nature, preserving what is consonant unto it in it's being, therefore the patient is not sicker or weaker; but the more he sweats the stronger and lustier will he be, the veins will be lighter, and the sweat continues till all evil humors be driven out of the body, and then it ceases.

The next day you shall take of it the quantity of a grain of wheat, in warm wine again, you will go to stool immediately, and that will not cease so long as you have anything in your body which is contrary to nature, and the more stools the patient has, the stronger and lighter at heart will he be; for the stone drives nothing forth but what is adverse and prejudicial to nature.

The third day give the like quantity in warm wine, as aforesaid; it will so fortify the veins and heart, that the party will not think himself to be a man, but rather a spirit, all his members will be so light and lively, and if the party will take the like quantity of a grain of wheat every day for the space of nine days, I tell you, his body will be as spiritual as if he had been nine days in the terrestrial paradise, eating every day of the fruit, making him fair, lusty and young; therefore use this stone weekly, the quantity of a grain of wheat with warm wine, so shall you live in health unto the last hour of the time appointed for you by God.

What say you, my student, is not this the true *Aurum potabile*, and the true quintessence, and the thing which we seek? It is a spiritual thing, a gift which God bestows upon his friends, therefore, my student, do not undertake this divine work, if you find yourself in deadly sins, or that your intent be otherwise than to God's glory, and to perform those things which I have taught you before.

I tell you truly, you may see the work, or begin it, but I am certain you shall never accomplish it, nor see the stone; God will order it so, it will break, fall, or some one disaster or other will happen, that you shall never see the stone, or complete it. Therefore if you find yourself otherwise, do not begin the work, for I know assuredly, you will lose your labor; wherefore deceive not yourself.

Enough to the wise.

ITS USE IN EXTERNAL DISEASES

My student, there are some people who have external distempers on their bodies, as fistulas, cancers, injuries, or running sores, or pockmarks, be they what or how they will, and such, give him the weight of one grain of wheat to drink in warm wine for two days, as is taught before, the whole body within and without shall be freed from all which is adverse to nature, and you shall deal with the open sores thusly;

Take a drachma's weight of the stone, and set it in a pot of wine in a glass, the space of two or three *Pater-nosters*, that the stone may melt, and the wine will be as red as blood; therewith wash the sores morning and evening, laying a thin plate of lead over the same, and in a short time, as in twelve days, the sores will be whole; and give him every day the quantity of a grain of corn, in warm wine till he be well. If they be fistulas or other concave holes, that you cannot come at them to wash them, then take a syringe made of silver, and inject of that wine into them, and it will heal them as aforesaid.

And if one had a pound of the rankest poison in the world in his body, and immediately drank a drachma's weight thereof of the stone in warm wine, the poison shall forthwith evacuate by siege, together with all the evil humors in his body.

My student, here ends the most noble and precious work which is in the vegetable book; on whomsoever God bestows this stone, needs no other thing in this world, therefore keep it as close and well as you can, to God's glory, who grants that we may walk in his obedience.

Amen.

God is blessed in all his works.

TRACT ON THE TINCTURE AND OIL OF ANTIMONY

PREFACE TO THE ORIGINAL EDITION

Dear reader, at the end of his tract on vitriol, Roger Bacon mentions that because of the multiplication of the tincture that is made from vitriol, the lover of art should acquaint himself with the tract *De Oleo Stibii*. Therefore I believed that it would be good and useful that the tract *De Oleo Stibii* follows next. And if one thoroughly ponders and compares these tinctures with one another, then I have no doubt that one will not finish without exceptional profit.

Yet, every lover of art, should mind always to keep one eye on nature and the other on art and manual labor. For, when these two are not twain, then it is a purposeless work, as when someone thinks he can walk a long path on one leg only, which is easily seen to be impossible, Vale.

DE OLEO ANTIMONII TRACTATUS

ROGER BACON

Stibium, as the philosophers say, is composed from the noble mineral sulfur, and they have praised it as the black lead of the wise. The Arabs, in their language, have called it *Asinat vel Azinat*, the alchemists retain the name Antimonium. It will however lead to the consideration of high secrets, if we seek and recognize the nature in which the sun is exalted, as the Magi found that this mineral was attributed by God to the constellation Aries, which is the first heavenly sign in which the sun takes its exaltation or elevation to itself. Although such things are forsaken by common people, intelligent people ought to know and pay more attention to the fact that exactly at this point the infinitude of secrets may be partly contemplated with great profit and in part also explored. Many, but these are ignorant and unintelligent, are of the opinion that if they only had Stibium, they would get to it by calcination, others by sublimation, several by reverberation and extraction, and obtain its great secret, oil, and perfect medicine.

But I tell you, that here in this place nothing will help, whether calcination, sublimation, reverberation, nor extraction, so that subsequently a perfect extraction of metallic virtue that translates the inferior into the superior, may profitably come to pass or be accomplished. For such shall be impossible for you. Do not let yourselves be confused by several of the philosophers who have written of such things, like., Geber, Albertus Magnus, Rhasis, Rupecilla, Aristoteles, and many more of that kind. And this you should note. Yes, many say, that when one prepares Stibium to a glass, then the evil volatile sulfur will be gone, and the oil, which may be prepared from the glass, would be a very fixed oil, and would then truly give an ingress and medicine of imperfect metals to perfection.

These words and opinions are perhaps good and right, but that it should be thus in fact and prove itself, this will not be. For I say to you truly, without any hidden speech; if you were to lose some of the above mentioned sulfur by the preparation and the burning, as a small fire may easily damage it, so that you have lost the right penetrating spirit, which should make our whole antimonii corpus into a perfect red oil, so that it also can ascend over the helm with a sweet smell and very beautiful colors and the whole body of this mineral with all its members, without loss of any weight, except for the feces, shall be an oil and go over the helm. And note also this: How would it be possible for the body to go into an oil, or give off its sweet oil, if it is put into the last essence and degree? For glass is in all things the outermost and least essence. For you shall know that all creatures at the end of the world, or on the last and coming judgment of the last day, shall become glass or a lovely amethyst and this according to the families of the twelve patriarchs, as in the families of jewels which Hermes the Great describes in his book: As we have elaborately reported and taught in our book *de Cabala.*

You shall also know that you shall receive the perfect noble red oil, which serves for the translation of metals in vain, if you pour *acetum correctum* over the antimonium and extract the redness. Yes not even by reverberation, and even if its manifold beautiful colors show themselves, this will not make any difference and is not the right way. You may indeed obtain and make an oil out of it, but it has no perfect force and virtue for transmutation or translation of the imperfect metals into perfection itself. This you must certainly know.

AND NOW WE PROCEED TO THE MANUAL LABOUR, AND THUS THE PRACTICA FOLLOWS

Take in the name of God and the holy trinity, fine and well cleansed antimony ore, which looks nice, white, pure and internally full of yellow rivulets or veins. It may also be full of red and blue colors and veins, which will be the best. Pound and grind to a fine powder and dissolve in a water or *Aqua Regia*, which will be described below, finely so that the water may conquer it. And note that you should take it out quite soon after the solution so that the water may conquer it. And note that you should take it out quite soon after the solution so that the water will have no time to damage it, since it quickly dissolves the antimony tincture. For in its nature our water is like the ostrich, which by its heat digests and consumes all iron; for given time, the water would consume it and burn it to naught, so that it would only remain as an idle yellow earth, and then it would be quite spoiled.

Consider by comparison Luna, beautiful clean and pure, dissolved in this our water. And let it remain therein for no more than a single night when the water is still strong and full of spirit, And I tell you, that your good Luna has then been fundamentally consumed and destroyed and brought to naught in this our water.

And if you want to reduce it to a pure corpus again, then you will not succeed, but it will remain for you as a pale yellow earth, and occasionally it may run together in the shape of a horn or white horseshoe, which may not be brought to a corpus by any art.

Therefore you must remember to take the antimony out as soon as possible after the solution, and precipitate it and wash it after the custom of the alchemists, so that the matter with its perfect oil is not corroded and consumed by the water.

HOW THE WATER WHEREIN WE DISSOLVE THE ANTIMONY IS MADE

Take vitriol one and a half pounds, Sal ammoniac one pound, Arinat one half pound, Niter salt one and a half pounds, Rock salt one pound, Alum one half pound. These are the species that belong to and should be taken for the water to dissolve the antimony.

Take these species and mix them well among each other, and distill from this a water, at first rather slowly. For the spirit will go with great force, more than in other strong waters. And beware of its spirits, for they are subtle and harmful in their penetration.

When you now have the dissolved antimony, clean and well sweetened, and its sharp waters washed out, so that you do not notice any sharpness any more, then put into a clean vial and cover it with a good distilled vinegar.

Then put the vial in *Fimum Equinum*, or a Balneum Mariae, to putrefy for forty days and nights, and it will dissolve and be extracted red as blood. Then take it out and examine how much remains to be dissolved, and decant the clear and pure, which will have a red color, very cautiously into a glass flask. Then pour fresh vinegar onto it, and put it into digestion as before, so that that which may have remained with the feces, it should thus have ample time to become dissolved. Then the feces may be discarded, for it is no longer useful, except for being scattered over the earth and thrown away. Afterwards pour all the solutions together into a glass retort, put it into Balneum Mariae, and distill with sharp vinegar, rather a fresh one, since the former would be too weak, and the matter will very quickly become dissolved by the vinegar. Distill it off again, so that the matter remains quite dry. Then take common distilled water and wash away all sharpness, which has remained with the matter from the vinegar, and then dry the matter in the sun, or otherwise by a gentle fire, so that it becomes well dried. It will then be fair to behold, and have a bright red color. The philosophers, when they have thus prepared our antimony in secret, have remarked how its outermost nature and power has collapsed into its interior, and its interior has thrown out and has now become an oil that lies hidden in its innermost and depth, well prepared and ready.

And henceforth it cannot, unto the last judgment, be brought back to its first essence. And this is true, for it has become so subtle and volatile, that as soon as it senses the power of fire, it flies away as a smoke with all its parts because of its volatility.

Several poor and common Laborers, when they have prepared the antimony thus, have taken one part out, to take care of their expenses, so that they may more easily do the rest of the work and complete it, they then mixed it with one part Sal ammoniac, one part vitriol, one part Rebohat, to cleanse the corpus, and then proceeded to project this mixture onto a pure silver. And if the Luna was one mark, they found two and a half of good gold after separation; sometimes even more. And therewith they had accomplished a work providing for their expenses, so that they might even better expect to attain to the great work.

And the foolish called this a bringing into the Luna, but they are mistaken. For such gold is not brought in by the spiritus, but any Luna contains two mark of gold to the Loth, some even more. But this gold is united to the Lunar nature to such a degree that it may not be separated from it, neither by *aqua fortis*, nor by common antimony, as the goldsmiths know. When however the just mentioned mixture is thrown onto the Luna in flux, then such a separation takes place that the Luna quite readily gives away her implanted gold either in *aqua fortis* or in *aqua regia*, and lets herself separate from it, strikes it to the ground and precipitates it, which would or might otherwise not happen. Therefore it is not a bringing into the Luna, but a bringing out of the Luna.

But we are coming back to our proposition and purpose of our work, for we wish to have the oil, which has only been known and been acquainted with this magistery, and not by the foolish.

When you then have the antimony well rubified according to the above given teaching, then you shall take a well rectified *Spiritum vini*, and pour it over the red powder of antimony, put it in a gentle Balneum Mariae to dissolve for four days and nights, so that everything becomes well dissolved. If however something should remain behind, you cover the same with fresh *Spiritu vini*, and put it into the Balneum Mariae again, as said before, and everything should become well dissolved.

And in case there is some more feces there, but there should be very little, do it away, for it is not useful for anything. The solutions put into a glass retort, lute on a helm and connect it to a receiver, also well luted, to receive the Spiritus. Put it into

Balneum Mariae. Thereafter you begin, in the name of God, to distill very leisurely at a gentle heat, until all the *Spiritus Vini* has come over. You then pour the same Spiritum that you have drawn off, back onto the dry matter, and distill it over again as before. And this pouring on and distilling off again, you continue so often until you see the *Spiritum vini* ascends and goes over the helm in all kinds of colors. Then it is time to follow up with a strong fire, and a noble blood red oil will ascend, go through the tube of the helm and drip into the recipient.

Truly, this is the most secret way of the wise to distill the very highly praised oil of antimony, and it is a noble, powerful, fragrant oil of great virtue, as you will hear below in the following. But here I wish to teach and instruct you who are poor and without means to expect the great work in another manner; not the way the ancients did it by separating the gold from the Luna. Therefore take this oil, one lot, to eight lots of lead calcined according to art, and carefully imbibe the oil, drop by drop, while continuously stirring the *calx Saturni*. Then put it ten days and nights in the heat, in the furnace of secrets, and let the fire that this furnace contains, increase every other day by one degree. The first two days you give it the first degree of fire, the second two days you give it the second degree, and after four days and nights you put it into the third degree of fire and let it remain there for three days and nights. After these three days you open the window of the fourth degree, for which likewise three days and nights should be sufficient. Then take it out, and the top of the lead becomes very beautiful and of a reddish yellow color. This should be melted with Venetian Boreas. When this has been done, you will find that the power of our oil has changed it to good gold.

Thus you will again have subsistence, so that you may better expect the great work. We now come back to our purpose where we left it earlier. Above you have heard, and have been told to distill the *Spiritum vini* with the oil of antimony over the helm into the recipient as well as the work of changing the lead into gold. But now we wish to make haste and report about the second tincturing work. Here it will be necessary to separate the *Spiritum vini* from the oil again, and you shall know that it is done thus:

Take the mixture of oil and wine spirit put it into a retort, put on a helm, connect a receiver and place it all together into the Balneum Mariae. Then distill all the *Spiritum vini* from the oil, at a very gentle heat, until you are certain that no more *Spiritus vini* is to be found within this very precious oil. And this will be easy to check; for when you see several drops of *Spiritus vini* ascend over the helm and fall into the recipient, this is the sign that the *Spiritus vini* has become separated from the oil. Then remove the fire from the Balneum, though it was very small, so that it may cool all the sooner. Now remove the recipient containing the *Spiritus vini*, and keep it in a safe place, for it is full of Spiritus which it has extracted from the oil and retained. It also contains admirable virtues, as you will hear hereafter.

But in the Balneum you will find the blessed blood red oil of antimony in the retort, which should be taken out very carefully. The helm must be very slowly removed, taking care to soften and wash off the lute, so that no dirt falls down into the beautiful red oil and makes it turbid.

This oil you must store with all possible precaution so that it receives no damage. For you now have a heavenly oil that shines on a dark night and emits light as from a glowing coal. And the reason for this is that its innermost power and soul has become thrown out unto the outermost, and the hidden soul is now revealed and shines through the pure body as a light through a lantern: Just as on judgment day our present invisible and internal souls will manifest through our clarified bodies, that in this life are impure and dark, but the soul will then be revealed and seen unto the outermost of the body, and will shine as the bright sun.

Thus you now have two separate things: Both the spirit of wine full of force and wonder in the arts of the human body: And then the blessed red, noble, heavenly oil of antimony, to translate all diseases of the imperfect metals to the perfection of gold. And the power of the spiritual wine reaches very far and to great heights. For when it is rightly used according to the art of medicine: I tell you, you have a heavenly medicine to prevent and to cure all kinds of diseases and ailments of the human body. And its uses are thus, as follows:

AGAINST GOUT

In the case of gout one should let three drops of this *Spiritu vini*, that has received the power of the antimony, fall into a small glass of wine. This has to be taken by the patient on an empty stomach at the very moment in time when he sense the beginning or arrival of his trouble, bodily ailment and pain. On the next day and afterwards on the third day it should also be taken and used in the same way. On the first day it takes away all pain, however great it may be, and prevents swelling. On the second day it causes a sweat that is very inconstant, viscous and thick, that smells and tastes quite sour and offensive, and occurs mostly where the joints and limbs are attached. On the third day, regardless of whether any medicine has been taken, a purging takes place of the veins into the bowels, without any inconvenience, pain or grief. And this demonstrates a great power of nature.

AGAINST LEPROSY

To begin with the patient is given six drops on an empty stomach. And arrange it so that the unclean person is alone without the company of any healthy people, in a separate and convenient place. For his whole body will soon begin to smoke and steam with a stinking mist or vapor. And on the second day his skin will start to flake and much uncleanliness will detach itself from his body. He should then have three more drops of the medicine ready, which he should take and use in solitude on the fourth day. Then on the eighth or ninth day, by means of this medicine and through the bestowal of divine mercy and blessing, he will be completely cleansed and his health restored.

AGAINST APOPLEXY OR STROKE

In the case of stroke, let a drop of the unadulterated tincture fall onto the tongue of the person in need. At once it will raise itself and distribute itself like a mist or smoke, and rectify and dissolve the struck part. But if the stroke has hit the body or other members, he should be given three drops at the same time in a glass of good wine, as previously taught in the case of gout.

AGAINST HYDROPE OR DROPSY

In the case of dropsy give one drop each day for six days in a row, in *Aqua Melissae* or *Valerianae*. On the seventh day give three drops in good wine. Then it is enough.

AGAINST EPILEPSY, CATALEPSY, AND ANALEPSY

In case of the falling sickness, give him two drops at the beginning of the paroxysm in *Aqua Salviae*, and after three hours again two drops. This will suffice. But if further symptoms should occur, then give him two more drops as above.

AGAINST HECTIC

In case of consumption and dehydration, give him two drops in *Aqua Violarum* the first day. On the second day, give him two more drops in good wine.

AGAINST FEVER

In cases of all kinds of hot fevers, give him three drops in a well distilled St. Johns' wort water or chicory at the beginning of the illness. Early in the morning on the following day, again give him three drops in good wine on an empty stomach.

AGAINST PLAGUE

In the case of pestilence give the patient seven drops in a good wine, and see to it that the infected person is all by himself, and caused to sweat. Then this poison will, with divine assistance, do him no harm.

FOR THE PROLONGING AND MAINTENANCE OF A HEALTHY LIFE

Take and give at the beginning and entry of spring, when the sun has entered the sign of Aries, two drops; and at the beginning with God's help, be safe and protected against bad health and poisoned air, unless the incurred disease was predestined and fatally imposed upon man by the almighty God.

But we now wish to proceed to the oil of antimony and its power, and show how this oil may also help the diseased and imperfect metallic bodies. Take in the name of God, very pure refined gold, as much as you want and think will suffice. Dissolve it in a rectified wine, prepared the way one usually makes *aqua vitae*. And after the gold has become dissolved, let it digest for a month. Then put it into a Balneum, and distill off the *spiritum vini* very slowly and gently. Repeat this several times, as long and as often until you see that your gold remains behind congealed as a sap. And such is the manner and opinion of several of the ancients on how this oil may also help the diseased and imperfect metallic bodies.

And such is the manner and opinion of several of the ancients on how to prepare the gold. But I will show and teach you a much shorter, better and more useful way. Namely, that you instead of such prepared gold take one part *Mercurii Solis*, the preparation of which I have already taught in another place by its proper process. Draw off its airy water so that it becomes a subtle dust and calx. Then take two parts of our blessed oil, and pour the oil very slowly, drop by drop onto the dust of the *Mercurii Solis*, until everything has become absorbed. Put it in a vial, well sealed, into a heat of the first degree of the oven of secrets, and let it remain there for ten days and nights. You will then see your powder and oil quite dry, such that it has become a single piece of dust of a blackish gray color. After ten days give it the second degree of heat, and the gray and black color will slowly change into a whiteness so that it becomes more or less white. And at the end of these ten days, the matter will take on a beautiful rose white. But this may be ignored. For this color is only due to the *Mercurio Solis*, that has swallowed up our blessed oil, and now covers it with the innermost part of its body.

But by the power of the fire, our oil will again subdue such *Mercurium Solis*, and throw it into its innermost. And the oil with its very bright red color will rule over it and remain on the outside. Therefore it is time, when twenty days have passed, that you open the window of the third degree, the external white color and force will then completely recede inwardly, and the internal red color will, by the force of the fire, become external.

Keep also this degree of fire for ten days, without increase or decrease. You will then see your powder, that was previously white, now become very red. But for the time being this redness may be ignored (for it is of no consequence), for it is still unfixed and volatile; and at the end of these ten days, when the thirtieth day has passed, you should open the last window of the fourth degree of fire.

Let it stay in this degree for another ten days, and this very bright red powder will begin to melt. Let it stay in flux for these ten days. And when you take it out you will find on the bottom a very bright red and transparent stone, ruby colored, melted into the shape of the vial. This stone may be used for projection, as has been taught in the tract on vitriol. Praise God in eternity for this his high revelation, and thank him in eternity. Amen.

ON THE MULTIPLICATION OF LAPIDIS STIBII

The ancient sages, after they had discovered this stone and prepared it to perfect power and translation of the imperfect metals to gold, long sought to discover a way to increase the power and efficiency of this stone. And they found two ways to multiply it:

One is a multiplication of its power, such that the stone may be brought much further in its power of transmutation. And this multiplication is very subtle, the description of which may be found in the tract on gold. The second multiplication is an *Augmentum quantitatis* of the stone with its former power, in such a way that it neither loses any of its power, nor gains any, but in such a manner that its weight increases and keeps on increasing ever more, so that a single ounce grows and increases to many ounces. To achieve this increase or multiplication one has to proceed in the following manner:

Take in the name of God, your stone, and grind it to a subtle powder, and add as much *Mercurii Solis* as was taught before. Put these together into a round vial, seal with a Hermetic seal, and put it into the former oven exactly as taught, except that the time has to be shorter and less now. For where you previously used ten days, you may now not use more than four days. In other respects the work is exactly the same as before. Praise and thank God the almighty for his high revelation, and diligently continue your prayers fir his almighty mercy and divine blessings of this work and art as well as his granting you a good health and fortuitous welfare. And moreover, take care always to help and counsel the poor.

MEDICAL ASTROLOGY

As stated in the preface to this work, this is a verbatim replication of a full length work which I previously published, it having no real equivalent in antiquated medical lore. The mineral and herbal preparations listed in the second half of the work use frequent abbreviations.

MEDICAL ASTROLOGY

INTRODUCTION

Astrology has been practiced in all ages of the world, but like every other belief, it has its cycles; these cycles vary with the intellectual freedom of man, flourishes the human race becomes more enlightened, and as the human race rolls back into oblivion, Astrology and its devotees cease to exist, and the foundation of all science thus dies, temporarily, to await another tidal wave of advancement; again to rise and again to fall. Astrology has always been studied with a view of penetrating into the futurity of the human race, and the length of life, the diseases which one will be subject to, and the time of sickness has undoubtedly been studied more and is better understood at the present time that any other branch of the science, but so little has been written and handed down to the present generation that we are greatly in need of a more modern work of reference upon the subject. The rules laid down by Lilly and Ptolemy have been copied by all later writers and we may say with a good degree of accuracy that about all that is generally known of Astrology can be found in the works of these two men.

In the present treatise the authors do not claim every paragraph to be original with themselves, but they do claim that such as has been gleaned from ancient authors and all original ideas has been placed in such language that the merest tyro may read and understand. It has been our intention in the present treatise to give ail that is generally known and confirmed by facts, both old and new ideas concerning Medical Astrology, in order to form a ready reference work for the professional astrologer, and at the same time, to be interesting and instructing for the beginner.

Many drugs have been omitted for the lack of space and proof as to their proper place in the list, which we hope will be added to and the list largely increased in the future. The chapter on the "action of drugs" has been compiled from all sources, and the reader will find under this chapter the organs of the body acted upon principally, the time of action, and the principal characteristics of the different drugs most extensively used.

All drugs mentioned must be used in their homeopathic form, for he who believes in Astrology believes in the law of dynamic influence, therefore must believe in the dynamic force of chemicals. Should the present work prove of benefit to those who peruse its pages and assist them in gaining a broader knowledge of Astrology, and at the same time, broaden the field of astrological knowledge the authors desires will be accomplished.

W. & H.

RULER OF HEALTH

The ruler of health, commonly termed "Hyleg" is either the Sun, Moon or the Ascendant, and is found by the following method: After erecting the figure for the desired time, first, see if the Sun is located in the 1st, 7th, 10th or 11th houses of the figure, if so it must be taken for the ruler of health, but if the Sun is not located in these houses then look to the Moon, should it be in any of the above houses it will rule the health; but should neither Sun or Moon be found in any of the above houses, then the ascendant will rule the health. Again, should both the Sun and Moon be placed in the above houses we must judge by them both, but the most powerful one will have greater influence than the weaker. Should the Sun and Moon be of equal power, we then judge of the Sun in a male nativity and the Moon in a female nativity; but in the latter instance the afflictions of either the Sun or Moon will have a powerful influence in causing sickness, while the evil directions between the two are decidedly dangerous.

From an Astrological standpoint we look to the Sun, Moon and ascendant for indications of good or bad health, or as astrologers term it, the Hyleg- the giver of life. From the rules laid down by the ancient astrologer, and which are generally accepted by modern artists, we find that the 4th house rules the grave, or the end of life; the 6th house is termed the house of sickness; while the 8th house is the house of death. From the above we readily see that the 6th house and its ruler will assist in pointing out the kind of sickness which one will be affected by; therefore the 6th house and ruler are important factors and must not be overlooked in ascertaining the kind of disease one may be affected by. Should the ruler of the 6th house be posited in the 1st house, or rising at birth, and afflicting the ruler of health usually denotes a frail constitution and a great deal of tedious sickness during life, but does not necessarily indicate an early death unless other evil testimonies are found; should the ruler of health be located in the 6th house and afflicted we judge much the same.

The 8th house and ruler points out to us, according to their aspect with the ruler of health, what kind of a death a person will die; whether violent- by accident, drowning, by fire, water, hanging, etc., or a natural death- from old age, painless, etc., should we find the ruler of health afflicted by the 8th or its ruler; ruler of health in the 8th and afflicted, ruler of 8th in the 1st and afflicted, are testimonies of a violent death. The 4th house and its ruler represent the end of life, and point out the condition of man in his latter years of life, and not particularly referring to the grave. Should we find the cusp of the 4th house and its ruler well aspected and strong, we judge that the latter part of life will be fortunate and prosperous, but unfortunate and afflicted the reverse.

Thus we see that the 4th house and its ruler are of much smaller importance than the 6th and 8th in our treatise, but the afflictions of the 4th strongly assist in causing sickness to end fatally. We look to the 6th house and its ruler for the nature of sickness, and to the ruler of health and the 8th house and ruler at the time of such sickness, whether or not such disease will prove fatal.

CAUSE OF DISEASE

As before mentioned, either the Sun. Moon or the ascendant rule the health, and the aspects to the ruler of health by other planets indicate the time in life when one will suffer from ill health, and the 6th house and its ruler assists in pointing out the nature of such sickness. Therefore, when we find the ruler of health afflicted by evil directions at any time during life we conclude that when such direction culminates, the native will be troubled by ill health at that period, the nature of which we judge from rules given under "diseases of the planets, and signs." However bad the aspects may be between the rulers of the 2nd, 9th, 10th, 11th and other house, will not cause sickness but refer to the financial and other affairs of life. Hence, we often find a person coming into possession of a fortune, while perhaps they die at the same time with consumption; showing plainly that health and finances do not always travel hand in hand, and the Astrologer must not judge them so.

In the horoscope we find several causes of sickness, the first and principal causes are the primary, secondary, periodical and progressive directions of the planets. Of the directions, we find those of Saturn and Mars are the roost powerful in causing ill health, they cause mostly diseases of the body, (although Mars often affects the mind;) they cause measles, ague eruptive fevers, consumption contagious epidemics, asthma, gangrenous ulcers, etc., while Uranus, Mercury Moon (and to some extent the Sun) affect the mind, causing idiocy, insanity, inflammation of the brain, headache, etc., while Uranus afflicting the Moon by direction causes a desire to commit suicide, but the native usually lacks the courage.

The afflictions of the Sun or Moon usually causes measles, eruptive fevers, croup hurts and injuries, bleeding, broken bones and weakness in the eyes. Jupiter causes jaundice, billiousness, liver complaints, gangrene, and other ailments as given in "diseases of planets and signs." Venus causes gravel, female trouble and general disorders of the sexual system, and if in ill aspect to Saturn, Mars or Uranus, she causes venereal diseases.

Of the transits, we find those of Saturn and Uranus (and Mars if afflicting the ruler of health at birth) will cause ill health according to the sign such transits occur in; but the transits of Jupiter, Sun Venus, Mercury and the Moon do not affect the health unless evil directions are operating at the time, in this case transits of the Sun and Mercury over the ruler of health tend to aggravate sickness. The transits of Saturn over the ruler of health usually causes rheumatism, gout, lumbago and kindred ailments brought about by getting wet, over-lifting. Uranus transits over the ruler of health, much the same as Saturn, causes falls, sprains, hurts from machinery, etc., according to the sign the transit occurs, and the good or evil aspect of Saturn and Uranus at birth.

DISEASES OF THE PLANETS AND SIGNS

Each planet has a certain number of degrees in the zodiac of its particular nature; the planets nearest the Sun rule the greater number, thus; Mercury rules two, Venus two and Mars two; the remaining planets only one. We give below the signs and their ruling planets.

Aries is ruled by Mars
Taurus by Venus
Gemini by Mercury
Cancer by Moon
Leo by Sun
Virgo by Mercury
Libra by Venus
Scorpio by Mars
Sagittarius by Jupiter
Capricorn by Saturn
Aquarius by Uranus
Pisces by Neptune

Each sign of the zodiac also rules a part of the body, beginning at Aries, thus; Aries rules the head and face. Taurus the Ears, neck and throat. Gemini the arms chest and shoulders. Cancer, the Lungs and breast. Leo the heart and back. Virgo the bowels and stomach. Libra the Reins and abdomen. Scorpio the sexual system. Sagittarius the hips and thighs. Capricorn the knees. Aquarius the legs and ankles. Pisces the feet.

The signs all have diseases of their own nature and according to the part of the body they rule; although a planet weak and afflicting the ruler of health from Aries often produces weakness in Libra or in other words, the sign opposite the afflicting position is often affected, and sometimes the sign in square aspect is affected. For instance, Saturn and the Sun in conjunction in Capricorn causes weakness in the parts ruled by

Cancer, and sometimes in Aries and Libra, and so on with the other signs. We give below the diseases of each sign.

ARIES

Headache, toothache, fevers, both acute and chronic, Epilepsy, apoplexy, inflammation of the brain, catarrh, etc.

TAURUS

Croup, diphtheria, sore-throat, asthma, bronchitis, and other throat trouble.

GEMINI

Accidents in the arms, billiousness, flatulence, nervous diseases, pleurisy, rheumatism and inflammation in the arms and breast.

CANCER

Pulmonary Consumption, Dyspepsia, dropsy, cancer and false pleurisy.

LEO

Convulsions, fainting, palpitation and rheumatic affections of the heart, and eruptive fevers.

VIRGO

Diseases of the stomach, dyspepsia, colic, worms, diarrhea and dysentery.

LIBRA

Affections of the back, liver trouble, lumbago, sciatica,

FOLK MEDICINE

kidney trouble.

SCORPIO

Principally affections of the sexual system, venereal diseases, rupture gravel, piles and female diseases.

SAGITTARIUS

Injuries and broken limbs, rheumatism, intemperance, (a large majority of Sagittarius people have broken limbs some time in life.)

CAPRICORN

Affections of the knees, such as sprains broken bones, rheumatism, and supposed by some to produce leprosy.

AQUARIUS

Broken limbs, rheumatism in those parts, varicose veins, nervous twitching of the legs and feet, and blood diseases.

PISCES

Diseases and injuries of the feet, such as gout, chilblains, rheumatic pains and cramps in the feet and toes, corns, bunions and diseases caused by wet feet.

The fiery signs rule principally diseases accompanied by fever. Earthy signs produce croup, colic, diarrhea, etc. Airy signs, pleurisy, nervous and blood diseases. Watery signs, cancer, dropsy, gangrene, gout, cramps, rheumatism, scurvy, colds, etc.

FOLK MEDICINE

DISEASES OF THE PLANETS

Each planet produce diseases peculiar to their own nature, but a great deal depends upon the sign which a planet may be located in, but by referring to the diseases produced by each planet and then referring to the diseases of the sign which the afflicted planet is located in we can then form a pretty good opinion as to the nature of sickness.

THE SUN

Eruptive diseases, measles, smallpox, scarlet fever, diseases of the brain and heart, inflammation of the eyes, cramps putrid fevers, gangrene, fainting.

MOON

Apoplexy, insanity, diseases of the brain, bladder and urinary troubles, gout, rheumatism, scrofula, dyspepsia, colic, billiousness, diarrhea, gangrene.

MERCURY

Diseases principally of the brain, vertigo, inflammation and dropsy of the brain and defects in the memory, hallucinations, insanity, and also causes colds and catarrh.

VENUS

Diseases of the sexual system, venereal diseases, female diseases, diabetes, gravel, and kidney trouble.

MARS

Measles, scarlatina, shingles, erysipelas, itch, smallpox, chickenpox and other eruptive diseases, fevers, headaches, and hemorrhage of the lungs and sexual system, venereal diseases, abortions, etc.

JUPITER

Scurvy, cramps, pleurisy, diseases of liver, weakness in the back, colds and diseases caused by poor blood, and often causes constipation, piles, etc.

SATURN

Ague, malaria, tooth ache, neuralgia, earache, rheumatism, gout, lumbago, dropsy, constipation, consumption, etc.

URANUS

Complaints caused by bathing, sudden changes of weather, getting wet, such as croup, colds, asthma, rheumatism, gout, lumbago, cramps, diseases of the brain, insanity, and desire to commit suicide.

NEPTUNE

Similar to Uranus, rheumatism, gout, cramps in the feet, chilblains, and scurvy.

We notice from the above that some of the planets produce diseases similar to other planets. Thus: Mars causes eruptive diseases, while we find the same produced by the Sun and Moon. Venus causes ailments of the sexual system, we find the same under Moon diseases. Saturn causes gangrene and dropsy, while Jupiter and the Sun produce the same. Neptune, Moon and Saturn rheumatism.

JUDGMENT ON DISEASE

We now come to the reading of the horoscope or horary figure in order to form an opinion as to the nature of sickness, how long it will last, and whether or not it will result fatally, or leave the patient weak and debilitated. In judging of sickness from the horoscope we have only to erect a figure of the time of birth, and find the "ruler of health" and calculate the directions operating at the time, and give judgment by the rules given under "diseases of the planets and signs." If we find the ruler of health afflicted by the ruled of the 6th or 8th or other inimical testimonies, and this affliction passing from the ruler of the 6th to the 8th, and no good testimonies occurring, we judge that such disease will terminate fatally, but should the rulers of the 6th and 8th be fortunate planets, it will not end fatally unless the patient be very old and feeble; again, should Jupiter cast an aspect to the evil configuration, even a square or opposition to Saturn, or Venus cast any aspect when Mars is afflicting, such ailment seldom ends fatally unless the patient be old.

The most evil directions are those of Saturn to the Sun and ascendant, and those of Mars and Mercury to the Moon, such directions often end fatally; the afflictions of the Sun, Moon, Jupiter and Uranus to the ascendant (if the ascendant rules the health) are not so powerful in producing death. Regarding the age, the Moon and Mercury act most powerful under the age of 15, Venus and Mars from 15 to 25, Sun and Jupiter from 25 to 50, and Saturn and Uranus in old age. Although Saturn has a powerful influence at the age of 30, 45 and 60, while Mars and the Sun act very powerful at the age of 19, 27 and 38.

In judging from a Horary figure, we have a very stubborn matter to deal with. Judging of sickness, is quite different from giving judgment on finances, lawsuits, journeys and other affairs, and I would advise all astrologers to use a little care in giving their opinion from a horary figure. I have found the following rules almost indispensable in this respect.

1. It is best to only answer the question for the patient; should the patient be a child then we may judge from the parents questions.

2. If the question concerns accidents or poisoning take the time of their occurrence in preference to the time of asking the question.

3. If it be an attack of apoplexy, fits, cramps, delirium, etc., use the time of the first attack.

4. Don't give a hasty judgment, if you find Jupiter causing the ailment don't promise the patient relief as soon as the aspect is passed, but give the direction its full time; and if Jupiter be located in fixed signs the ailment will not be dangerous but tedious.

Sun, Mars and Mercury diseases are violent and governed by the motion of the Moon; at times the patient is given up and in 24 hours they may be greatly improved, and again to relapse. Diseases caused by Saturn, Venus and Neptune gradually get worse and get better gradually. In judging from a horary figure we find that Jupiter, Saturn or Neptune afflicting the ruler of the 1st or the Moon causes colds, rheumatism, grippe, and aggravates asthma, consumption, etc., while the Sun, Mercury or Mars afflict the ruler of the 1st or the Moon we find apoplexy, headaches, cramps, colic, etc., which are violent leaving the patient unconscious. Uranus afflicting the ruler of the 1st or Moon the mind is generally affected and the patient desires to commit suicide, imagines some one trying to poison them, symptoms rapidly flying from one part of the body to another, spasmodic.

Should we find the Sun ruling the ascendant and

afflicted by Mars we often find apoplexy, and other symptoms accompanied with high fever and violent pain abortions, bleeding to death, and loss of consciousness from pain, symptoms come on rather suddenly. The Moon rising and in opposition to Mercury we have noticed picking at the bed clothes, jumping spells, hallucinations, thinks some one trying to capture them, strikes, bites, and howls when any one comes near them; refuses to talk, at other times they talk continuously; spasmodic pains so violent as to drive the patient insane, and often causing them to make silly and out of the way remarks. Saturn and Mars afflicting each other often cause broken bones, sprains and falls from animals, but sometimes cause disease according to the signs they are located in. (people born with Saturn and Mars in conjunction seldom ever escape broken limbs some time in life, especially if located in Gemini, Sagittarius, Capricorn or Aquarius). Having shortly summed up the manner of giving judgment on the nature and length of disease, we would again warn every one against giving judgment from transits alone, consider well the position and strength of all the planets concerned in the sickness, and then calculate the directions and promise recovery or otherwise at time of their culmination. The following rule for judging of time in horary figures is given in "Simmonite's Horary Astrology," which we find to be the most accurate. "Should the aspects be cast from movable signs and angles of the figure we judge days for degrees; If from succeeding houses and angles, weeks; Cadent houses to angles, months; from common signs to angles, weeks; common signs to succeeding houses, months; fixed signs to angles, months; fixed signs to succeeding houses, and from common signs to cadent houses, years. Mixed aspects, say months for years; for months, say weeks; for weeks say days."

Note- Planets in north declination and and latitude act more powerful than when in south; and all are most powerful when rising.

DRUGS RULED BY THE PLANETS AND SIGNS

The rule usually followed by the great army of ancient and modern Astrologers in judging what each particle of matter, such as plant and animal life is ruled by is simply taken from the nature of such objects. For instance, nearly all birds and beasts of prey are placed under the dominion of Mars. But their rule does not hold good when they place the lion under the rule of the Sun, where some of them also place the horse. They have taught that all quiet and non-carnivorous birds and animals are under the rule of such planets as Venus and the Moon, etc.

Judging of plant life, they assumed that Mars ruled everything hot in taste, such as mustard, pepper, radish, etc,, and Venus ruling those sweet by nature and producing beautiful flowers, and so on through the list. In this manner they placed poppy under Saturn, and aconite under Mars. Common sense contradicts the greater part of this theory. Should we follow this rule we must place man under the rule of the Sun. Why? Because he assumes dominion over object which he comes into contact with. But broach such a theory to some of our Astrologers and they will make sport of you, and explain that man is ruled by different planets, according to the hour of birth, and should he have his choice of the hour in which to be born, he would be born under either of the nine planets. Now let us apply the same rule to the horse, lion and other animals; man is no more than the most intelligent of beasts, therefore has no more right to claim he may be ruled by any and all of the planets than the animal has; the same rule applies to plant life.

Does not Astrology teach us that seed sown when the Moon is in certain signs, and when some signs are rising are more fruitful and do better than those planted at other times? If such is the case, poppy would not grow if not planted under Saturn; pepper would die or be worthless if planted under the Moon or Venus. Such a doctrine is mere supposition and misleading, and should be forgotten as soon as learned. Let us investigate the influence of plants when their essence or tincture is taken into the human body, and pay no attention to their looks and taste in a state of nature, and we will find that many, if not the greater number of drugs are ruled by the signs.

It is true that each planet affects the body in a manner peculiar to itself, but even this is variable and uncertain, and much depends on where the planets are located. For instance, such planets as Mars and the Sun in Aries will produce different ailments than the same planets would if located in Virgo or Scorpio, and such ailments would require different chemicals to correct them. Should we accept this theory, we must look more to the signs than to the planets in choosing the remedy. Further investigation along this line may confirm the theory that the planets are most prominent in pointing out the cause of disease, while the nature and length lies more in the signs.

In giving the drugs ruled by the signs and planets many must necessarily be omitted for the lack of proof as to their respective places in the list. We must remember that two drugs made from almost the same substance do not act the same; viz, Nux Vomica and Ignatia are both forms of Strychnine, but their action is not alike by any means, Drugs which act best under...

ARIES

Aconite, Arsenic, Arnica, Chamomilla.

TAURUS

Kali Bichromate, Mercury, Lachesis and Capsicum.

GEMINI

Stramonium, Colocynthis, Sulfur and Ignatia.

FOLK MEDICINE

CANCER

Calcera Carbonica, Silicea, Alumina and Graphites.

LEO

Spigelia, Ferrum, Phosphorous, Coca and Digitalis.

VIRGO

Nux Vomica, Charcoal, Pepsin Aloes Ipecac and Podophyllum.

LIBRA

Pulsatilla, Conium, Lycopodium and Cocculus.

SCORPIO

Cantharis, Phosphoric Acid, China and Sepia.

SAGITTARIUS

Camphor, Ammonia, Coffee, Antimony and Hepar Sulfur.

CAPRICORN

Rhus Tox., Colchicum, Creosote and Helleborus.

AQUARIUS

Staphysagria, Opium, Natrum mur. And Iodine.

PISCES

Dulcamara, Drosera and Tartar Emetic.

Note- In the "diseases of planets and signs" we mentioned that afflictions occurring in one sign would affect the signs in square and opposition to it, and in many diseases the remedies mentioned in these signs is also useful. For instance, in diseases of Scorpio, the remedies mentioned under Taurus, Leo and Aquarius may prove useful, and so on with the other signs.

We find that the planets have a few remedies which invariably remain with the planet; such as Pulsatilla with the Moon; Sepia with Venus; Belladonna with Mercury; Aconite with Mars; Veratrum album with the Sun; Bryona with Jupiter; Rhus Tox., with Saturn; Opium with Uranus; and Dulcamara with Neptune. These drugs should be looked to in all afflictions.

WHEN TO GIVE MEDICINE

Very little has been written upon this subject from an Astrological standpoint, and the ordinary physician usually administers his chosen drug as soon as he can prepare it; in some instances the drug has the desired effect, while at other times the drug has no effect or is immediately vomited up by the patient. Many physicians have no doubt witnessed this phenomena, but wasted no time in learning of the cause of it.

The Homeopath usually believes in administering his drug between the paroxysms and not during the dangerous periods, in spasmodic affections; they have also, a favorite time of the day when to give medicine, at time of retiring, on rising, or between meals, bat not to be given within an hour before or after meals. We have learned that many of the drugs administered when certain planets and signs rise have little or no effect, and are often vomited up immediately after taken. Should you doubt this, give a patient Chamomilla when Jupiter is exactly on the ascendant, and also try it when Sagittarius ascends, or Jupiter in aspect to the ascendant. Simmonite says, medicine given when the ruler of the ascendant is retrograding will be vomited up again by the patient, we have not yet proved or or disproved this theory; but would prefer to administer all drugs when the signs ruling them, or the ruler of such sign is rising or in good aspect to the ascendant, or in other words, give drugs ruled by positive signs and planets when such planets and signs are rising, and negative drugs under negative planets and the signs, as homeopathic drugs work through sympathy and not by antipathy.

Many astrologers believe in the ancient theory that each hour of the day is ruled by one of the planets, independent of the rising sign, the hour beginning with sunrise. In this manner the Sun is supposed to rule the first hour of Sunday (from sunrise); Moon that of Monday; Mars , of Tuesday; Mercury of Wednesday; Jupiter on Thursday; Venus on Friday; and Saturn that of Saturday, each day beginning with sunrise. The order of the planets in this scheme is supposed to run thus; Sun, Venus, Mercury, Moon, Saturn, Jupiter, Mars, and beginning again at the Sun. We cannot imagine why this order is used, nor why Uranus and Neptune it not entitled to a place, and should advise all to test it before accepting it.

Dr. Reed, in a late work entitled, "Cyclic Law" advances the theory that the ebb and flow of the tides form the negative and positive parts of each day; the flow producing the positive period, while the ebb produces the negative. He claims to have verified this from considerable experience and observation. The tides may be calculated for Chicago as well as for New York (the influence) when it may be expected to act. However true the tide theory may be, such is not so powerful as the rising sign, but should we get a rising tide, with a sunrise on Sunday morning, with Leo rising, then the three would work in harmony, but the three occurring at different hours, prefer the rising sign; second the tidal wave, and last, the ruling hour.

By following the above rule when to give medicine, we may be may more in a position to administer drugs when they will act quickly and in a beneficial and curative manner.

DISEASES AND THEIR TREATMENT

In the following pages we give the treatment of the most common ailments which every one may meet and experience some time in life. Under each ailment we give the most useful remedies and following it in the same paragraph are the symptoms which point to the use of the remedy. But in choosing a remedy for an ailment sometimes two or more drugs, may seem to be indicated, but by referring to the chapter on "action of drugs" we may then be able to choose the proper remedy. Again, all the drugs mentioned here should be used only in their homeopathic form, and in the 3rd or 6th dilution, excepting such drugs as Charcoal, Lycopodium, Sepia and Dulcamara, which are supposed to be of little power below the 30th. Powders are the best form for family use. All the drugs mentioned herein can be had from any homeopathic pharmacy.

EMOTIONS

Bad effects from fright.

Aconite: Patient has palpitation of the heart and imagines they will die; fear remains after fright, anxiety, restless.

Belladonna: If fright has caused convulsions, especially in children; patient screams; twitching of the limbs, feverish.

Coffee: Great excitement, trembling, fainting, cannot sleep; fright from sudden pleasant surprises; very nervous.

Gelseminum: Diarrhea from fright.

Opium: Fright followed by twitching of the limbs; convulsions: unnatural sleep, delirium; involuntary evacuations.

GRIEF

Cocculus: Sadness, tendency to start, especially at night; headache from grief; watching over sick friends.

Ignatia: Patient is full of suppressed grief; weak, empty feeling in the stomach; spasmodic fits caused by grief.

Lachesis: Talks much, changing the subject often; tight pressure around the neck is unbearable; worse after sleep.

Phos. Acid: Great indifference to the affairs of life; dislikes to talk

Pulsatilla: Melancholy, with weeping sadness: disgusted with everything.

ANGER

Chamomilla: Children get into a rage, loose their breath and go into spasms.

Colic: Diarrhea from anger; refuses to talk or answer questions; indignant.

Nux vomica: Violent, ill tempered persons who are unwell after anger; irritable and wishes to be left alone.

VERTIGO

In this condition everything seems to be turning around, and the patient seems to be turning; the best remedies are;

Aconite: Vertigo when rising from a seat, looking up or stooping; cloudiness of the eyes and loss of consciousness.

Antim. Crud: Vertigo from overloading the stomach; tongue coated milk white.

Arnica: If caused from a blow or fall; dizziness; nausea; better when lying down.

Belladonna: Vertigo with vanishing sight; sparkling before the eyes when moving; rush of blood to the head.

Cocculus: Vertigo when sitting up in bed, or riding in a carriage.

Mercury sol: Vertigo and dimness of sight only in the evening; worse when lying on the back; objects turn black.

Nux vom: If caused from overwork mentally; constipation or the abuse of stimulants or patent nostrums.

Pulsatilla: Vertigo from disordered stomach; from grease and pastries; worse in the evening, and in rising from a seat.

HEADACHE

Aconite: Violent headache; fullness and heaviness in the forehead; vertigo when rising from a seat. Sun pains beginning in the morning, increasing till noon, and decreasing as the Sun goes down, ceasing during night; on left side principally.

Alumina: Throbbing pain; better when lying quiet; headache from constipation.

Arnica: Principally over the eyes; if caused from a blow or fall; darting pain; face and head hot, body cool; vomiting.

Arsenicum: Periodical headache; great weight in the forehead; beating pain; vomiting after eating of drinking;

constant thirst; anxiety and fear of death; worse during rest and better by motion.

Bryonia: Pains begin on waking in the morning; pain as if the head would split; worse from motion; wants to keep perfectly still; lips dry, parched and cracked.

Calc. Cars: Chronic headache: pain in the forehead; throbbing pain in the morning and continuing all day; feeling of coldness in the head: worse by motion.

Camphor: Pain in the cerebellum; after sunstroke; better when lying down; staggering; dizziness; worse on motion.

Chamomilla: Caused from catarrh or abuse of coffee; drawing pain in one side of the head; shooting or throbbing in the forehead; one cheek red and the other pale; pain almost drives the patient mad.

China: Ringing in the ears: weak, fainting spells; worse every other day; from loss of blood or animal fluids.

Cocculus: Headache from riding; throbbing headache, worse in the evening; worse from talking, noise, or bright light.

Coffee.: Nervous headache, sleeplessness, pain as if a nail was driven into the brain; worse from noise; head feels too small.

Ignatia: Boring pain in the forehead; pain as if a nail was driven out the side of head: after grief; better when quiet.

Ipecac: Vomiting most prominent feature; brain feels bruised; sick headache.

Nux. Vom: Stupefying headache: worse in the morning; stomach derangement.

Pulsatilla: From eating pastries; from sexual derangement; worse when lying down and in the evening; chilliness.

Sepia: Beating pain in the forehead.

Sulfur: Pain in the forehead and temples; heat on top of head.

Verat alb: Nervous headache; pain almost drives the patient mad; vomiting; cold sweat on head; top of head cold.

Headache from smoking requires, -acon-Ign-Nux vom.
From bathing: calc, pulsatilla.
From study: Nux v.-Sulfur.
From grief: Ign,-Phos acid.
From overheating: Acon,-Bell,-Bry.

SUNSTROKE

Aconite: See headache.

Antim. Crud: Fainting from overhead; ailment worse from exposure to the Sun.

Belladonna: Congestion of blood to the head; worse on stooping; great anguish; flushed face; violent fever.

Camphor: Severe headache; fainting; delirium; convulsions; skin is cold and covered with cold sweat, especially on the head; cramps in the muscles; debility.

Carb. Veg: Debility: vertigo; heaviness of the head; pulsing pains and pressure above the eyes.

TOOTHACHE

Aconite: Pains drive one almost frantic; stitching and throbbing pain; congestion of blood to the head; fear of death.

Arnica: Toothache after operation; the cheek swollen, red and hard; bruised pain.

Belladonna: Drawing, tearing pain, which comes on suddenly and leaves suddenly; worse when lying down and in the evening

Bryonia: Teeth feels to long; jerking, drawing pain; worse at night; jerking pain when smoking; cold water relieves.

Camphor: Cutting pain; slimy tenacious saliva in the mouth; relieved by drinking cold water; worse from warm food.

Carb. Veg: Teeth decay rapidly; gums recede from the teeth and bleed easily; tearing pain from hot, cold or salty food.

Chamomilla: Digging and gnawing pain after eating, and getting warm in bed; patient unable to point out the affected tooth; pain very violent.

Coffee: Violent pain; relieved by ice cold water; loss of taste; cannot sleep.

Dulc: Toothache from taking cold.

Ignatia: Jaws and teeth feel crushed; worse after coffee, smoking, and in the evening after lying down, and morning.

Mercury sol: Pain affecting a whole row of teeth; jumping pains, especially at night; teeth feels bruised and too long.

Nux vom.: Sore pain with stitching in the teeth and jaws; worse at night and morning; better in open air; irritable.

Phos: Toothache from having hands in cold water; gums bleed easily.

Pulsatilla: Drawing, stitching, jerking pain; worse from warmth; chilliness.

STIES

Hepar sulfur: Will usually correct the disposition to sties.

Pulsatilla: If given in the beginning is generally sufficient.

Staph: If they appear often, and leave hard spots; especially on the upper lid.

Other remedies are:

For sties on the upper lid,-caus.-ferrumm-merc.-sulfur.

On lower lid,-rhus tox.-phos.

Corners of eyes,-natr. mur.-sulf.

EARACHE

Aconite: Earache caused by exposure to cold wind; violent, jumping pain.

Belladonna: Digging, shooting pain; roaring and humming in the ears; great sensitivity to noise; pain in the head and eyes.

Chamomilla: Shooting pain as if a knife was thrust into the ear: from taking cold; pain drives the patient almost frantic; children want to be carried.

Dulc: Worse at night and from taking cold; worse while at rest.

Mercury sol: Tearing pain; suppuration seems eminent; worse at night and during damp, rainy weather.

Pulsatilla: Darting, tearing pain; ear feels stopped up; ear red and swollen.

COLDS

Aconite: In the beginning, with short, dry cough, and heat in the head and face.

Arsenic: Frequent sneezing; burning and soreness of the nostrils; chilliness after drinking; extreme thirst.

Bell: Sore throat with hoarseness; red, flushed face; dry hoarse cough; children cry when coughing; worse from motion.

Bryonia: Dry coryza; lips dry and cracked; dry cough, worse from drinking; stoppage of the nose in the evening.

Chamomilla: Fluent discharge from the nose; one cheek red and the other pale; dry cough; worse at night; when asleep.

Dulc: Dry colds; worse during cold, wet weather; better when moving about.

Hepar sulfur: Takes cold easily; stitches in the throat; hoarse, croupy cough; phlegm loose and choking.

Ipecacuanha: Fluent coryza; rattling of phlegm in chest

which does not yield to coughing; vomiting of mucus.

Lachesis: Fluent discharge from the nose and running from the eyes; dryness of the mouth; tight clothing excites coughing and suffocation; worse after sleep.

Mercury sol: Frequent sneezing and watery discharge from the nose; short, dry cough, worse at night.

Nux vom: Fluent discharge from the nose during the day, dry at night: the side of the nose which he lies on becomes stopped up; irritable and cranky.

Pulsatilla: Discharge of a yellowish, fetid mucus from the nose; takes cold easily: worse in evening and from warmth.

Sulfur: Discharge of clear water from the nose; loss of voice, taste and smell.

Loss of voice in the morning with paralysis of the tongue, requires, caus. Complete loss of voice, with roughness of the larnyx and windpipe, requires phos.

COUGH

Aconite: Short, dry cough; worse from smoking, drinking and at night.

Arsenicum: Dry cough, with a sense of suffocation; shortness of breath.

Bell: Dry, spasmodic cough; sensation of dust in the throat; redness and heat of the face; worse at night.

Bryonia: Dry cough, compelling one to sit up in bed at night; feels as though head and chest would fly to pieces in coughing.

Causticum: Short, dry cough; worse in the evening until midnight; relieved by drinking cold water; soreness of throat.

Hepar Sulfur: Croupy cough; rattling, choking cough; worse after midnight.

Hyos: Dry, spasmodic cough; worse at night, and when lying down; relieved by sitting up; bluish color of the face.

Ipecac: Dry cough; children almost suffocate when coughing; vomiting.

Mercury sol: Dry cough; spitting of blood; worse at night and in wet weather.

Phos: Dry cough; worse from talking and drinking; tightness in the chest.

Pulsatilla: Dry cough; worse at night, and when lying down; going off by sitting up.

Sulfur: Loose cough; expectoration of greenish lumps having a sweet taste; worse in the morning.

See Colds, and Croup also.

CROUP

Aconite: In the first stage; high fever and restlessness; after exposure to cold west wind; great pain on swallowing.

Belladonna: Flushed face: dry, barking, spasmodic cough: jumping during sleep.

Chamomilla: Croup with hoarseness; wheezing and rattling of mucus in the throat; short, dry cough, worse at night and during sleep

Cuprum: Violent, spasmodic coughing spells; short, dry cough, arresting the breathing; suffocating spells.

Dros: Short, hacking cough; sensation of a feather in the throat: patient places hand on stomach when coughing; voice has a deep base sound; spasmodic spells.

Hepar Sulfur: Rattling, choking cough; violent fits of coughing, as if the patient would suffocate; drowsiness.

Lachesis: In advanced cases; the slightest pressure on the throat and larynx causes spasmodic cough; worse after sleep.

Spongia: Crowing, barking cough; slow, wheezing respiration; suffocating fits; better with head bent back.

ASTHMA

Aconite: Shortness of breath; inability to breath deeply; worse when asleep.

Arsenic: Shortness of breath; suffocating attacks; worse at night, and when lying down; fear of suffocation.

Bryonia: Frequent, dry cough; stitches in the chest; worse on motion.

Hepar Sulfur: Attacks come on during the night, and with rattling, choking cough; worse during cold north-west winds.

Ipecac: Spasmodic asthma; short, panting breathing; worse on motion.

Phos: Loud and panting breathing; fatiguing cough; loss of voice.

Verat. Alb: Violent attacks in cold weather, and in the morning; cold sweat on the head and forehead.

Sulfur: Worse during sleep, and in the evening; tightness across the chest; constant heat on the top of head.

SORE THROAT

Belladonna: Inflammation, burning and dryness in the throat; sensation of a lump in the throat; principally on right side.

Lachesis: Sore throat; sensation of a lump in the throat, with a burning sensation; worse after sleep.

Mercury sol: Stitching pain on swallowing; worse at night and in wet weather

Phos: Sore throat from smoking.

PLEURISY

Sharp, cutting pains in the chest and side, usually continues from 3 to 7 days, and accompanied with fever.

Aconite: Piercing, sticking pains in the chest; inability to lie on the right side; high fever and great thirst; restless.

Arnica: After injures; stitching pain in the left side; patient complains of bed being to hard.

Bryonia: Stitching pain; great thirst; pains aggravated by breathing and from motion; splitting headache.

Mercury sol: Soreness, burning and stitching pain in the right side of chest; worse at night; when lying on right side.

Phos: Piercing pain, mostly on left side; tightness in the chest, with dry cough.

Rhus tox: If caused by getting wet, or over-lifting; shortness of breath, and worse during rest; better by motion.

Sulfur: When complicated with pneumonia; short, dry cough; stitches in the chest; worse on motion.

Verat. Alb: Painful constriction of the chest; cutting pain in the chest and side; bluish color of the face, with cold sweat.

FALSE PLEURISY

Similar to pleurisy, but more of a rheumatic affection, and often mistaken for pleurisy. Not generally accompanied by fever, while pleurisy is.

Arnica: Stitching pain, mostly in left breast; breathing is painful.

Nux vom: Sticking pain in the ribs; worse from breathing, and from motion.

Pulsatilla: Sticking pain in side, only when lying down; pains rapidly shifting from one part to another.

PALPITATION OF THE HEART

Aconite: Violent beating and palpitation of the heart, especially after fright.

Digitalis: Palpitation worse from motion, or on lying clown; sensation as if heart would stop beating if one moved.

Phos: Tightness across the chest; palpitation worse after eating and drinking.

FOLK MEDICINE

Spigelia: Unusually strong beating of the heart; the beating can be heard; increased by sitting down; by bending forward, and in the evening.

LOSS OF APPETITE

China: Loss of appetite; aversion to food everything tastes bitter; after sickness.

Hepar Sulfur: Stomach easily disordered; useful after abuse of mercury and quinine.

Nux vom: Bitter taste; aversion to food, coffee and tobacco; craves brandy.

Pulsatilla: Putrid, bitter taste; aversion to fat food, meat, bread or milk; loss of appetite from abuse of tobacco.

MORBID APPETITE

China: When troubled with worms; ravenous appetite; hungry soon after meals.

Silicea: Patient feels hungry but cannot eat when they try; constipation.

Staph: Ravenous hunger after eating, and when the stomach is full; desire for tobacco, wine, etc.

See under dyspepsia also.

DYSPEPSIA

Antim. Crud: If caused from overloading the stomach; tongue coated white.

Arnica: After injuries; eructations tasting like rotten

eggs: vomiting after eating.

Bryoxia: In hot weather; from drinking cold water when overheated; smell of food is intolerable.

Carbo veg: All food disagrees; sour belching, and burning in the stomach.

Calc. Carb: Weight in the stomach; cannot bear anything tight around the waist; everything tastes sour.

Cham: Bloatedness in the morning; aching pain in the stomach.

China: Stomach feels full and tight; aversion to food; weak and debilitated.

Lycopodium: Canine hunger; disgust of warm food; bloated after eating; heartburn; desire for oysters.

Nux vom: Bitter taste in the morning; cramp-like pain in the stomach, worse after meats; suitable after stimulants.

Pulsatilla: Tongue coated white or yellow; fatty food, pork, sweets and ice cream disagrees; nightly diarrhea.

Sulfur: Acidity of the stomach; feels weak and faint about 11 a.m.

For acidity of the stomach, give Sepia or Sulfur. For heartburn, Carbo veg, china and nux vom. For aching and burning in the stomach, arn.-ars.-bell.

HEARTBURN

Carbo veg: Water brash, especially at night; burning in the stomach.

China: Heartburn after every meal; great fullness after eating.

Nux vom: Belching of bitter fluids at night; vomiting after meals.

Sepia: Burning in the stomach.

Phos: Belching of bitter water; very sleepy after dinner.

COLIC

Bryonia: Pinching pain in the stomach; bilious vomiting after eating or drinking.

Chamomilla: Spasmodic pains in the stomach; caused principally from strong coffee.

Coloc: The principal remedy for cramp colic, particularly if patient bends themselves double, or lies down putting the entire weight on the stomach, which relieves; pain the stomach as though it were squeezed between stones.

Ipecac: Vomiting the principal symptom, horrible pain in the stomach.

Nux vom: Cutting, pinching pain; worse from motion; chronic constipation.

Pulsatilla: Gripping pain, with diarrhea; caused from eating fruits, ice cream, or slightly tainted meat, such as venison.

JAUNDICE

Chamomilla: Yellowness of face and white of eyes; green, watery stools.

Mercury: Skin very yellow; thickly coated tongue; bad smell from the mouth; loathing of food.

Nux vom: Pain in the region of the liver; sour or putrid taste; constipation.

DIARRHEA

Aloes: Yellow stools; pain in the bowels after eating: worse in warm weather, in the evening, after eating, while standing.

Antim. Crud: After bathing; overheat; cold water, or cold food.

Carbo veg: If caused by cold drinks, fat food, and after sickness.

Chamomilla: If caused from taking cold; from coffee, or tobacco; suitable for children.

Coloc: After eating cold, sour things; after anger; gripping pain; relieved by coffee, or smoking.

Dulc: From taking cold; during cold changes of the weather; worse at night.

Lycop: From milk; oysters; worse about 4 p.m., a little food seems to fill the stomach full; bloated; flatulence.

Mercury sol: In hot weather; sour smelling night sweats; dysentery.

Podoph: Greenish, watery stools; worse after eating or drinking; gripping colic.

Pulsatilla: If caused from meat, ice cream, fruit, or

tobacco; gripping pain in the bowels; chilliness; worse from warmth.

CONSTIPATION

Alumina: Stools dry and light colored; inactivity of the bowels.

Bryonia: Constipation in hot weather; stools hard and dry, look as if burnt.

Lycop: Loud rumbling in the bowels; stools voided with difficulty; abdomen bloated; passes much flatulence.

Nux vom: Stools large, hard and dry; frequent urging to stool, but nothing is passed; suitable after pills and stimulants.

Opium: Inactivity of the bowels; stools of small, black balls; after cantharis.

Phos: Stools long, narrow and hard like a dogs; alternate constipation and diarrhea of old people.

Pulsatilla: Constipation from eating rich, greasy food; more suitable for females.

Sulfur: If complicated with piles.

RHEUMATISM

Aconite: In the beginning; red, shining swelling of the affected parts.

Arnica: Bruised pain; feeling as though lame parts were resting on something hard

Belladonna: Red, shining swelling, with cutting, tearing

pain deep in the bones; pain changing from one place to another; pain comes on and leaves suddenly.

Bryonia: Stiffness, swelling, sticking pain; worse from motion.

Dulcamara: Caused from cold or getting wet; bruised pain; mostly in the back, joints of the arms and legs.

Sulfur: Chronic rheumatism; other remedies do not seem to have any effect; dull, aching pains.

SCIATICA

Aconite: Pain drives one almost desperate; anxiety and fear of death.

Coloc: Violent, rending and darting pains; worse from touch or motion; principally on the left side. See lumbago and rheumatism.

GOUT

Arsenic: Swelling of the feet; bummer pain; parts burn like fire; better from warmth and by motion.

Coloc: Little or no swelling; skin rose colored and leaves white spots from pressure of the finger; spasmodic pains.

LUMBAGO

Belladonna: Cramping pain in the back; sensation as if back would break.

Mercury sol: Symptoms all worse at night and during cold, wet weather.

Nux vom: Bruised pain in the small of the back; worse when turning in bed. See rheumatism and sciatica.

ACTION OF DRUGS

ACONITE

Duration of action, from 1 to 48 hours.

Antidotes: Nux vomica, Camphor.

Ailments are always accompanied by thirst, drinking little and often; fever with flushed face and rosy cheeks; great restlessness; imagines that they will die; predicts the time of death: hard, full pulse, useful only in the beginning of disease; suitable for acute inflammation; hemorrhages of bright-red blood; croup from suppressed sweat or getting wet; worse at night; lying on the left side; during west winds.

ALUMINA

Duration of action about 40 days.

Antidotes: Bryonia Chamomilla, Ipecac.

Scrofulous affections; complaints from the abuse of Mercury; bad effects from lead poisoning; painters colic; chronic constipation; all ailments worse on alternate days; from an empty stomach; in the evening, and at the Moon's changes.

ARNICA

Duration of action, about 6 days.

Antidotes: Camphor, Ignatia.

Will in most cases be found useful in ailments brought

about from injuries, falls etc., worse in the morning, and better in the evening and at night; patient restless and con plains of bed being too hard, and constantly shifting their position.

ARSENICUM

Duration of action, from 30 to 40 days in chronic affections.

Antidotes: Camphor, China, Ferrum.

Arsenic ailments are always accompanied by great anxiety, restlessness and fear of death; violent thirst, but drinking causes vomiting; sudden sinking of strength; pains are characterized by a burning sensation; worse after mid-night; after sleep; better from warmth.

BELLADONNA

Duration of action, from one day upward, and in some cases months.

Antidotes: Strong black Coffee, Opium.

Acts on the brain and nervous system. Congestion to the bead with flushed face and throbbing headache; violent thirst, drinking little and often; pains shifting from one part to another; affected parts have a red shiny appearance; sleepiness but cannot sleep; jumping while asleep; pains come on suddenly and disappear as suddenly; right side mostly affected; worse after midnight; in the sun; after drinking, from motion.

BRYONIA

Duration of action, from four or five days to three or four weeks.

Antidotes: Chamomilla, Nux vomica.

Ailments usually accompanied by a splitting headache; great thirst, drinking large quantities but at long intervals; bitter taste; abnormal appetite; rheumatic gouty pains of a stitching nature; worse from motion, during hot weather; better while at rest.

CALCERA CARBONICA

Duration of action, upwards of 50 days.

Antidotes: Camphor, Sulfur.

Great sensitiveness to cold air; takes cold easily; young people inclined to grow fat; more adapted to young people; ailments worse morning, evening; during increase of the Moon; in wet weather and from washing. Better when lying on the painful side.

CANTHARIS

Duration of action, several weeks.

Antidote: Camphor.

Principally adapted to ailments of the kidneys and sexual system; ailments usually accompanied by a burning stinging sensation; right side of the body mostly affected; worse from drinking coffee; when standing; in the morning; every seventh day, at the changes of the Moon.

CARBO VEGETABLIS

Duration of action, 1 to 2 months.

Antidotes: Arsenic, Camphor, Coffee.

Mostly adapted in chronic diseases; teeth loose, gums recede from the teeth and bleed easily; chronic cough; great fullness after eating or drinking; dyspepsia, the simplest food disagrees; useful for ailments remaining after chronic diseases; loss of animal fluids.

CAUSTICUM

Duration of action, 40 to 50 days.

Antidotes: Coffee, Coloc, Nux vomica.

Bites inside of cheek when chewing; greasy taste in the mouth; cough relieved by swallowing cold water; worse in dry weather, in the evening, from warm food; better from heat, during wet weather, lying on the painful side. More suitable for dark haired people, and those subject to warts, tetter; old injuries become sore.

CHAMOMILLA

Duration of action, 3 or 4 days.

Antidotes: Coffee, Ignatia, Pulsatilla.

Is mostly adapted for children; patient very irritable, everything makes them angry; does not wish to be looked at or spoken to; children want to be carried all the time; patient wants different things which they refuse when offered; great sensibility to pain; worse at night, while asleep, during sweat, from anger. Better from warmth, and when quiet.

CHINA

Duration of action, from 2 to 3 weeks.

Antidotes: Ars., Carboveg., Ferrum.

Ailments brought about from the loss of blood, animal fluids, debilitating disease; ailments worse at night, after drinking, by touching the parts, during wet weather, while lying on the right side. Better from bard pressure, in dry weather, after sleep, and when lying on the left side.

COCCULUS

Duration of action, 30 to 50 days.

Antidote: Coffee.

Vertigo when sitting up, when riding in a boat or carriage; violent vomiting when riding in a boat or carriage; sea sickness; disposition to tremble; hysterical spasms; worse after eating, drinking, or when riding.

COFFEE

Duration of action, 10 days.

Antidotes: Cham., Ign., Nux vomica.

Ailments accompanied by great sensibility of the nervous system; extremely sensitive to pain; all the senses are more acute; great hunger, eating very rapidly; bad effects of sudden surprises, from wine; worse at night, after eating, and from motion; cannot sleep.

COLOCYNTHIS

Duration of action, 30 to 40 days.

Antidotes: Caus., Cham., Coffee.

Irritable and does not wish to be talked to or bothered; bitter taste; violent colic compelling one to bend double;

gripping, pinching pains; ailments brought about from grief or anger; stiffness of the joints; beer intoxicates easily. All ailments worse from rest and in the afternoon.

CONIUM

Duration of action, 30 to 50 days.

Antidote: Coffee.

Especially adapted to the diseases of old people; bad effects of sexual excess; easily intoxicated; apoplexy with paralysis; swelling and induration of the glands.

DIGITALIS

Duration of action, 40 to 50 days.

Antidotes: Nux vomica, Opium.

Vertigo with trembling: various colors before the eyes; morning vomiting; diarrhea during jaundice; violent palpitation of the heart; swelling of the feet during the day, diminishing at night; ailments worse in the evening, at night, while standing, lying with the head bent back, from eating.

DULCAMARA

Duration of action, 1 to 2 months.

Antidotes: Ipecac, Mercury.

Complaints brought about from cold changes of the weather, taking cold, getting wet; dropsical swellings; rheumatic pains. Symptoms all worse in cold damp weather, at night, and when at rest; better from motion.

FERRUM

Duration of action, 10 to 20 days.

Antidotes: Arsen., China, Hepar sulf.

Pale, bloated face; bloated around the eyes; all food tastes bitter; can neither eat or drink anything hot; swelling of the feet; great debility from the loss of blood, or animal fluids; bad effects from tea, quinine, and alcoholic stimulants. Ailments worse in the evening, while at rest, periodically; rheumatic pains are relieved by slow motion.

HEPAR SULFUR

Duration of action, 8 weeks.

Antidotes: Belladonna, Chamomilla.

Unhealthy condition of the skin; suppurative diseases; slight injuries induce suppuration; ulcers in the mouth; salivation after the abuse of Mercury; choking cough; all ailments worse at night, from cold north-west winds, when stooping, from exercise, from moving the eyes; better from warmth, while at rest during perspiration.

IGNATIA

Duration of action 2 hours to 9 days.

Antidotes: Chamomilla, Pulsatilla.

Ailments caused from grief or fright; adapted to excitable, hysterical people; spasmodic complaints; twitching of the muscles; hiccough from smoking; empty feeling in the pit of the stomach; pains pressing from within to without; cutting pains as from a knife; worse after dinner, after lying down, after sleep, from tobacco coffee, brandy, or perspiration. Better when lying on the back, and from changing position.

IPECACUANHA

Duration of action, from 2 hours to several days.

Antidotes: Arnica, Nux vomica, China.

Ailments accompanied by nausea and vomiting; pale face; aversion to food; suffocating cough; loose rattling of phlegm in the throat; chilliness; is unable to bear the least warmth. Adapted to malarial disorders; worse at night and after eating or drinking.

LACHESIS

Duration of action, 4 or 5 weeks.

Antidotes: Arsenic, Belladonna.

Disposition to sadness; beating headache over the eyes; malignant diphtheria; tight clothing is unbearable; suitable for women at the change of life; gangrenous ulcers, having a bluish appearance; carbuncles surrounded by boils and purple spots; left side mostly affected; symptoms all worse after sleep. Bad effects from Mercury and China.

LYCOPODIUM

Duration of action, 40 to 50 days.

Antidotes: Camphor, Pulsatilla, Coffee.

Excessive hunger; desire for sweets; aversion to bread; the abdomen becomes bloated after eating ever so little:

constant rumbling in the abdomen; drowsiness during the day but cannot sleep at night. Ailments always worse about 4 p.m; on lying down, after eating, from pressure of clothing. Better from getting cold; coming to exercise; from eructation.

MERCURY SOLUBILUS

Antidote: Hepar sulfur.

Adapted to affections of the glandular system; affections of the mucous membrane and sexual system; the parts are swollen. with a raw sore feeling: perspiration accompanies most complaints but does not relieve. Worse at night; in damp and cold weather; from exercise.

NUX VOMICA

Duration of action, 15 to 21 days.

Antidotes: Coffee, Cham., Camphor.

Acts principally through the gastric system, and suitable for ailments caused from the abuse of tobacco, wine, coffee stimulants and patent medicines; complaints arising from mental exertion, sedentary life; hunger with aversion to food, desire for brandy and chalk; stomach sensitive to pressure; bruised pain in the back. Worse in the morning; after eating; from motion.

PHOSPHORUS

Antidotes: Camphor, Nux vomica.

Duration of action, unknown.

Acts on the respiratory system. Thirst for very cold drinks; hunger soon after eating; all food tastes bitter;

hoarseness with loss of voice; very sleepy after eating. Suitable after the loss of animal fluids; great debility, trembling; slight wounds bleed much; all ailments worse in the evening, from light. Better in the dark; after sleep.

PULSATILLA

Duration of action, 10 to 20 days.

Antidotes, Coffee, Ign., Nux vomica.

Acts on the stomach, bowels, brain and the nervous system. Vertigo when stooping; after eating; gastric disturbances from overloading the stomach with fruit, fat food, pastries. More adapted to females, pains accompanied by chilliness, and rapidly shifting from one part of the body to another. Worse in the evening; when lying on the left side; from heat. Better from motion; from cold.

RHUS TOXICODENDRON

Duration of action, 1 to 3 weeks.

Antidotes: Bryonia, Coffee, Sulfur.

Acts on the tendons, ligaments and skin. Ailments brought on by getting wet; taking cold; during cold, wet weather. Pains in the bones as if scraped with a knife. Worse at night, during rest and when first beginning to move. Better from continual motion; warmth relieves.

SEPIA

Antidotes: Aconite, Sulfur.

Principally adapted to ailments of the female sex; diseases of women with sudden sinking of strength; sour stomach; icy cold feet: everything tastes too salty; aversion to all food; burning in the abdomen. Ailments worse in the morning, in dry weather; after eating. Better from smoking; cold food and drinks, and after sleep.

SILICEA

Duration of action, indefinite.

Antidotes: Camphor, Hepar sulfur.

Feeling as if intoxicated; black spots before the eyes; suitable for scrofulous patients, and those having an unhealthy skin; limbs go to sleep easily; bad effects of vaccination; ulcers after the abuse of Mercury. Worse at night; during thunder storms; at the changes and increase of the Moon, and during changes of the weather.

SULPHUR

Duration of action, 1 to 6 weeks.

Antidotes: Nux vomica, Pulsatilla.

Acts on the skin, mucous membrane, and glandular system. Suitable for those having an unhealthy skin: subject to piles; constipation; weakness and trembling in the joints; stooping gait. Ailments worse every seventh day, at the changes of the Moon, in the evening; after washing periodically.

VERATRUM ALBUM

Duration of action, from one hour to six or eight days.

Antidotes: Arsen. Aconite, Ipecac.

Acts on the intestinal canal, brain and nervous system.

Crampy pains which will not bear the warmth of the bed; violent colic and vomiting, with coldness of the body; clammy, cold sweat, particularly on the head and forehead; violent thirst for cold drinks. All ailments are accompanied by violent pain, cold sweat and extreme coldness of the body. Worse in the morning; after midnight; from drinking; perspiration; from warmth of bed.

VARIOUS HERBAL LORE

For the purposes of this section I have included as much singular herbal lore as possible. In order to render the list of herbal species alphabetical I have merely appended, at the end of each little section, an abbreviation for the work which the entry comes from. The abbreviations follow:

The Canadian Herbal **C.H**

The Family Nurse **F.N**

Frays Golden Recipes **F.R**

The Indigenous Drugs of India **I.I**

The Occult Family Physician **O.P**

Acacia Arabica (Babula)

The gum obtained from Acacia Arabica, of the natural order Leguminosae. This tree is very common all over India, and yields abundance of gum of similar, though somewhat inferior, properties to those of the Acacia Vera. The bark is a powerful astringent, and its decoction is largely used as a substitute for that of Oak bark, with great success and efficacy. **I.I**

Aconitum Nepallus (Katbish)

The root of this plant, Aconitum Nepallus, of the natural order Ranunculaceae, grows in abundance in the Himalayan mountains, and is procurable at a very cheap cost in the Indian market. Besides its extensive use in Indian medicine, it is frequently resorted to as a poison for criminal purposes. All the species of Aconite, especially Perox and Nepallus, exercise a very deleterious influence on the animal economy, which is attributable to the presence of the alkaloid aconitina, and have, therefore, been fully treated in all works on toxicology. **I.I**

Agave Americana (Rukus)

The roots of the plant Agave Americana, of the natural order Amaryllidaceae. This plant has been long imported from America and naturalized in India. Its leaves yield fibers almost equal to the best Russian hemp, and manufactured at a very slight expense. From its root also is obtained a ligneous fiber much used in Madras. This is the common American aloe plant. The roots are used to adulterate sarsaparilla. Medicinal properties: Diuretic. The roots of this plant are employed as a diuretic, and are said to possess the anti-syphilitic virtue of sarsaparilla; but whether they really do so is doubtful. **I.I**

Agrimony

Agrimony, used freely in the manner of tea, will cure an ulcerated mouth, and is good for liver and kidney complaints. 1 ounce to a pint of boiling water. Dose, a wine glass full three times a day. **F.R**

All Heal (Woundwort)

This is a very useful herb. It grows in wet ground, has five or six pairs of winged leaves. The flowers are yellow and stand in clusters around the stalk at the joints, and bear light yellow fiat seeds, bitter in taste. The root is perennial, long, thick and a hot, biting taste. As its name implies, it is a good wound herb; the leaves being bruised, and applied to a fresh wound, will stop the bleeding and cure the wound. It relieves gout, cramps, and pains in the joints, vertigo, falling sickness, and made into an ointment cures the itch. **O.P**

Aloes

A warm, stimulating purgative. It quickens the circulation, and is particularly serviceable to persons of phlegmatic habits, weak stomachs, and sedentary life. Two or three grains operate as a laxative; ten grains is the medium dose; but it may be augmented to twenty, according to circumstances. It is injurious to bilious habits, and the piles, on account of its tendency to inflame the bowels. Considered improper during pregnancy, and for those troubled with bleeding at the lungs. It is recommended for thread-worms, and has been used as an emmenagogue. Soccatrine aloes are considered the best. **F.N**

Alum Root (Crane's Bill)

Grows from six to twelve inches high (on sandy soil)branches out, and from between its branches puts forth a purple flower succeeded by spikes which give it the name of Crane's Bill. The roots are astringent, used to cure dysentery, bleeding, flooding, whites; gargle for sore mouth. **C.H**

American Gensen

Grows by hill sides, and old pastures, two feet high in branches, leaves spear shaped, and surround the stalk like throughwort- on the upper side yellow flowers appear, succeeded by yellow berries around the stalk. It is better than imported Gensen. A tonic, which produces a healing effect upon the lungs and liver. It will also cure bots in horses. **C.H**

American Senna; Wild Senna (Cassia Marylandica)

The leaves and stems, in strong infusion or decoction, are a very good substitute for the imported senna. It is such a mild physic, that one third more of it is required. **F.N**

Aniseed

Aniseeds are the product of a small plant growing on the islands in the Mediterranean sea; they possess stimulating and carminative properties, useful in indigestion, flatulence and colic. The essential oil is extensively used in cough mixtures. Dose of powdered seed, 10 to 30 grains; infusion, a wine glassful; compound spirit, 1 to 4 drachms; essential oil, 5 to 20 drops on sugar. **O.P**

Apples

The free use of apples is a great assistant to brain work; children cannot use them too freely. **F.R**

Apple of Peru; Thorn Apple; Devil's Apple; Jamestown Weed (Datura Stramonium)

This plant when swallowed is a narcotic poison. The leaves, prepared like tobacco, and smoked, have given great relief in cases of pure spasmodic asthma. Applied to the part affected, or to the feet, they have been efficacious in removing spasms. **F.N**

Asparagus

The frequent use of asparagus is strongly recommended in affection of the lungs and chest; it is a very wholesome and agreeable vegetable. **F.R**

Asphodel

A drug of exceedingly disagreeable taste and smell. A powerful antispasmodic, much given in hysteria, and nervous debility, when not accompanied by inflammation. Taken as a pill, ten grains is the medium dose. One drachm of assafoetida in half a pint of pennyroyal water makes a white mixture, called milk of assafoetida, generally considered the best form for an antispasmodic; one or two table-spoonfuls may be frequently repeated. As an efficient expectorant assafoetida is given in whooping-cough, asthma, catarrh, and other pulmonary complaints, either in the form of pill, or an emulsion made by gradually adding and mixing two drachms of assafoetida with half a pint of water. **F.N**

Avens Root (Clove root)

Grows a foot high near fences, blossoms in July, on long spikes which are yellow. The seeds in the fall will stick to the clothes, root smells like cloves. Water Avens blossoms purplish-appears in May. They are astringent, good for canker and cleanse the blood; use them together. **C.H**

Balm (Melissa Officinalis)

An infusion of the herb is a cooling drink in fevers. When taken warm, it aids medicines given for perspiration. **F.N**

Balm of Gilead Tree (Populus Candicans)

The leaf-buds are very resinous and fragrant. They should be gathered when they are well swelled and just ready to expand. They remain thus but two or three days. Bottled in rum, they form a most excellent healing liniment for fresh cuts and wounds. **F.N**

Balsamodenrdon Mukul (Googul)

The tree Balsamodendron Mukul, also called the Commiphora Madagascarensis, of the natural order Terebinthaceae, is a native of East Bengal and Assam. This tree is said to yield the googul, the Indian Bedellium, but probably there are several species of the same genus which yield the same product such as B. Agallocha. It is collected in the cold season by making incisions in the tree and letting the resin fall on the ground. This accounts for the dirty condition in which it is found in the shops. It is a gum resin, and is sometimes used in place of myrrh. The odor of googul is more faint and agreeable than that of myrrh. It is largely used by the Hindus as an incense in their worship of gods and goddesses, before whose image they generally burn it, by which the whole of the surrounding atmosphere is impregnated with its agreeable smell. This gum resin is held by the Native practitioners as a purifier of blood; also alterative and pectoral. **I.I**

Barberry Bark

Is an excellent tonic, and a corrector of diseases of

the liver, beneficial in jaundice, slightly aperient. The bark used in connection with either cayenne or ginger, has always been found serviceable in indigestion. I have used the term tonic, because it is more frequently used among the public; but more properly speaking, the herbs so designated are correctives, and if you desire to be strengthened after the stomach has been previously prepared by such medicines; I would prefer that the butcher and baker have the credit of that. Pursue this course and you will need little of such medicines so designated by the faculty. **O.P**

Bath Root (White and Red)

Grows about a foot high, three oval leaves at the top of the stalk; and one flower, red, bell shaped, the root is bulbous and full of small fibers. It is tonic, astringent, and antiseptic. A teaspoon full of the powdered root three or four times a day is used in spitting blood, immoderate courses, and bloody urine. **C.H**

Bear Berry; Wild Cranberry; Mountain Cranberry (Airbutus Uva Ursi)

Astringent and diuretic. Very highly recommended for dropsy, paroxysms brought on by gravelly concretions, and other diseases of the kidneys. Of the powdered leaves from five to ten or more grains is a dose. A decoction is made by boiling an ounce of the plant ten minutes in a pint of water. A gill may be taken every hour. **F.N**

Bitter Sweet; Woody Nightshade; Nature's Wax Work (Solanum Dulcamara)

A decoction of the leaves and twigs is highly recommended for cancers, ring-worms, itch, and other cutaneous eruptions. Haifa gill may be taken morning, noon, and night, and increased to a pint a day according to its effects.

In delicate constitutions it sometimes occasions giddiness and vomiting. Such persons should try a quarter of a gill at first. The addition of cinnamon, or some aromatic, renders it less liable to offend the stomach. The good effects are seldom perceived under eight or ten days. Humors are often bathed with it, while it is taken internally; but when the surface is inflamed, this, and other external stimulants, are injurious. **F.N**

Black Oak (Quercus Tinctoria)

The bark is astringent and somewhat tonic. Given with advantage in intermittent fevers, and permanent diarrhea. A decoction is much recommended as a bath for children, when a combined tonic and astringent is desired, and the stomach does not receive medicines kindly. It has been used in this way for scrofula, chronic diarrhea, and the latter stages of cholera infantum. **F.N**

Bloodroot

Well known in large doses, it is a good emetic, in small doses of half a teaspoon full of the powdered root, it is good for ulcerated sore throat, croup, and hives. **C.H**

Blue and White Vervine

Blue and white vervine grows two or three feet high, by the roadside, the blue has small spindles on the top resembling a mouse tail, full of blue blossoms. The white has longer spangles with white blossoms. These are a powerful emetic alone or mixed with boneset. A tea of them is good for consumption, menstruation (root and top.) **C.H**

Bog Bean

Grows in the edge of marshy ponds with a green stalk. It rises a few inches having three leaves resembling bean leaves;

roots long, the size of a finger, green on the upper and yellow on the underside, spongy and porous, resembling a windpipe. It is very bitter and mixed with smartweed and Cordus Benedictus, or spotted thistle (which grows in gardens) equal parts; will cure the worst throat diseases; bronchitis, quinsy, etc. Make a tea of the root, gargle, bathe, and drink freely. **C.H**

Boneset (Thoroughwort)

Grows in marshes three feet high, the leaf surrounds the stalk at each joint, it has white blossoms. This is an emetic; good to act on the secretions of the liver in small doses. With vervine it forms the base of bilious emetic. **C.H**

Broad-leaved Dock; Butter Dock, (Rumex Obtusifolius)

The root has the same peculiar medicinal qualities as the curled species. Much recommended prepared as ointment for cutaneous eruptions. **F.N**

Bryony

Is a tall climbing wild plant, grows in bushes and slashings, leaves are somewhat like the vine; the flowers white, and the berries are red, and very showy. The root is large, rough, and whitish; stalks tough and about ten or twelve feet long, with tendrils at the joints to hold themselves. The root is a very strong purgative, even if a small dose be taken. Caution should be observed in taking it. It is used for dropsies, hysterics, etc., given in small doses. An electuary made of the root with honey, proves a powerful expectorant. The root, leaves, and fruit boiled, are good to cleanse old sores, canker, and gangrene; and the decoction frees the face from freckles, black and blue spots, etc. The root scraped, and laid on to a bruise, will draw the discoloration out in a few minutes. **O.P**

Buck Bean; Marsh Trefoil (Menyanthes Trifoliata)

Root used either in powder or decoction. Resembles thorough-wort in its effects. A tonic in small doses; but two or three gills of the strong warm decoction produce vomiting, purging, and perspiration. **F.N**

Burdock

Operates gently on the bowels, root and seed cleanses the blood. Good in rheumatism. Leaves, excellent draughts. **C.H**

Burnet (wild)

Found among grass three or four inches high with top like a pine burr. Great antiseptic. **C.H**

Butterfly Weed; Pleurisy Root; Archangel (Asclepias Tuberosa)

A strong decoction of the root, taken several times a day is highly recommended by physicians for pulmonary consumption, pleurisy, catarrh, and various diseases of the lungs. It produces expectoration, relieves the difficulty of breathing, and throws the patient into a gentle perspiration, without the heating tendency of some vegetable medicines. Large doses are somewhat cathartic. **F.N**

Butternut Tree (Juglans Cinerea)

The inner bark of the tree, and especially of the root, is a very mild and efficacious laxative. It is much employed in dysentery; and when the system is habitually restricted, it is better than more stimulating physic. Some drink a decoction, others make it into pills. Boil it with water enough to cover it.

Renew the water as it boils away, for an hour or two. Strain it, and simmer it down, till it becomes thick as molasses. Be careful not to burn it. When cool, make it into common-sized pills; of which two, three, or more, may be taken, according to circumstances. People troubled with weak or windy stomachs, sometimes shake in a little cinnamon, or pepper, before it is made into pills. An extract of butternut is sold, of which a teaspoonful operates gently, and twice as much actively. **F.N**

Caffea Arabica (Kuwa)

The albumen of the seeds of the plant Caffea Arabica, of the natural order Cinchonaceae, constitutes the aromatic coffee of commerce, which, when dried and roasted, is an agreeable tonic and stimulant. The cultivation of the staple has extended in a surprising manner, and very good samples can be obtained from Nuggur, Wyanand, the Pulney hills, and the virgin forest land of the western ghauts. Its use as an anti-hypnotic is well known. In cases of poisoning by opium, a strong decoction of coffee has been found to be of great use. It is also used occasionally in various other complaints of a nervous character. **I.I**

Calamint

It is good for pains in the head; it is also beneficial for gravel complaints, combined with rosemary and wood bettany; is good for water on the brain; it is a good female herb. **O.P**

Camphora Glandulifera (Nepal Sassafras)

The tree Camphora Glandulifera, of the natural order Lauraceae, is a native of Nepal. This article is identical in every respect with the American substance. It is used by the rich natives as a constituent of their favorite masticatory. It is, like the pharmacopoeial article, stimulant and diaphoretic, which virtues are generally attributed to the presence of an essential oil. **I.I**

Canada Thistle

Steeped and sweetened with honey, good for gravel and inflammation in the kidneys. **C.H**

Cannabis Indica (Gunjah, Churrus, Bhang)

The leaves and resin of the plant Cannabis Indica, of the natural order Cannabinaceae, are imported into Calcutta chiefly from Mirzapore, Bhurtpore, Nepal, and Ghazeepore. It is also cultivated in Jeypore and some parts of Bengal. The narcotic effects of this article are well-known in South Africa, South America, Egypt, Asia Minor, Turkey, India, and the adjacent territories of Burma, Siam, and Malacca. In all these countries it is used in various forms, as the ready agent of a pleasing intoxication. There are three different parts of the plant which all have narcotic properties:

(1) Churrus; a resinous juice, which exudes and concretes on the leaves, the stems, and flowers. It is collected either by coarse cloth, or leather being brushed against the plant. The resin, which adheres to the cloth or the leather, is afterwards scraped off, and kneaded into balls, which sell from 5 to 6 rupees a seer. It is smoked like tobacco to produce intoxication.

(2) Gunjah; This name is applied to the dried hemp plant which has flowered, and from which the resin has not been removed. A resinous extract composed of Churrus, with a green coloring matter chlorophyll, can be prepared by treating it with alcohol. It sells in the Calcutta bazaars from 5 to 7 rupees the seer, and is used for smoking chiefly.

(3) Bhang Subgee, or Sidhee, are the larger leaves and capsules without the stalks, which are used for making

intoxicating drinks, and a sort of intoxicating conserve or confection called majoom.

As a medicine, the Indian hemp is found to be narcotic, anodyne, and antispasmodic. It produces a peculiar kind of delirium, and that state of the nervous system which pathologists call catalepsy. Dr. O'Shaughnessy gave it a fair trial in tetanus, hydrophobia, painful neuralgic and rheumatic affections, cholera, etc. In tetanus it is still used by Indian practitioners with greater success than with any other remedy. It has a peculiar action on the uterus, and Dr. Churchill recommends it as a valuable medicine in some forms of amenorrhaea, dysmenorrhoea, and menorrhaegia. It increases appetite and excites aphrodisiac inclinations. Two preparations of this article are *officinal*- the tincture and the extract. **I.I**

Carica Papaya

The tree Carica Papaya, of the natural order Papavaceae, a native of America, has long been domesticated in India, and is now found common all over the Peninsula. A milky juice exudes from the rind of the fruit more copiously when it is unripe. It is supposed to possess powerful vermifuge properties, and resembles the white of an egg in its chemical composition. The seeds are also considered vermifuge. The unripe pepo is used in curries, and the ripe as a dessert in India. The milky juice is added to meat, with an idea that it removes its toughness, and makes it remarkably tender. **I.I**

Catnip

Good in fevers to promote perspiration. **C.H**

Cassia Elongata

The dried leaves of Cassia Elongata, of the natural order Leguminosae. Various other species of the genus Cassia are produced in this country in great abundance; their medicinal properties are very well known to native practitioners, who largely use the leaves, in combination with other drugs, for their purgative properties. Medicinal properties: Purgative. Used in the same way and on similar occasions as the official *senna*. It is rarely used alone, but as a vehicle or adjunct to other aperient drugs. **I.I**

Cayenne

A powerful rubefacient, that promptly stimulates the skin without blistering. Sprinkled on flannel wet with heated spirit, it is applied for violent pain in the bowels, and as a wash for rheumatism. When people apply such hot external remedies for the rheumatism, it is well to take something two or three times a day, to prevent its striking to the heart, or stomach; guaiacum, an infusion of Cayenne, or of prickly-ash, are suitable. Internally, Cayenne is a very strong stimulant, producing a general glow. It is applicable to palsy and lethargic affections, and useful to correct flatulence in languid stomachs. In powder, the dose is from five to ten grains; most convenient made into a pill. To make the infusion, pour half a pint of boiling water upon two drachms of the powder, steep it an hour, and strain it- three or four tea-spoonfuls taken at once. Cayenne may be made of the common red pepper, dried and powdered; but the process is troublesome to the eyes. **F.N**

Centaury Herb

Is an excellent general tonic, used extensively in jaundice, chronic liver complaint, and combined with agrimony and Colombo root invaluable for indigestion. **F.R**

Chamomile (Anthemis Nobilus)

An infusion of the blossoms is a mild tonic, good for enfeebled digestion and languid appetite. Recommended as an emmenagogue; likewise given for flatulence, and spasmodic diseases. It is administered between the paroxysms of intermittent fever, when Peruvian bark is considered too powerful. A luke-warm infusion is often taken to assist the operation of vegetable emetics. May weed, (Anthemis Cotula) is called wild chamomile, because it resembles this plant in appearance and medical qualities. **F.N**

Chequer Berry; Box Berry; Mountain Tea (Gaultheria Procumbens)

In much estimation as a warm aromatic stimulant. The oil, like that of peppermint, diminishes the sensibility of the nerve, when repeatedly applied to a decayed tooth. A strong infusion of the leaves is recommended as an emmenagogue, in cases attended with debility. A tea-spoonful of the essence, in a tumbler of sweetened water, is a pleasant and refreshing drink. **F.N**

Chickweed

The plant chopped and boiled in lard, makes a fine green cooling ointment, and is good for the piles, ulcers, sores, etc. The juice taken inwardly, is good for the scurvy. A cloth saturated with the juice and applied outwardly over the region of the liver, reduces inflammation; it is also good for inflammation of the eyes, when dropped into them. **O.P**

Cinnamomum Albiflorum

The tree Cinnamomum Albiflorum, of the natural order Lauraceae, grows in Malabar, Sumatra, Java, and several other parts of the Eastern Archipelago. The bark has an aromatic agreeable odor, but weaker than cinnamon. Its taste is sweetish, mucilaginous, rather acrid, bitterish, and tenacious; powder, of chamois leather color. The bark is much used for adulterating true cinnamon, but its mucilaginous character, when chewed, easily distinguishes it from the genuine variety. Its leaves (or those of the C. Tamala) are very much used as a condiment, and available at a nominal cost in all the Indian markets. Both bark and leaves possess carminative and stimulating stomachic properties. **I.I**

Clerodendron Viscosum (Bhant)

The Clerodendron Viscosum, of the natural order Verbenaceae, is a wild hedge plant, common all over Bengal, Malabar, and the S. Concans. The fresh juice of the leaves is used as a vermifuge, and also as a bitter tonic and febrifuge in malarious fevers, especially when they occur in infants. The root of this plant beaten up and mixed with wine or sour milk is given internally in colic; externally for drying up pustular eruptions on the skin. **I.I**

Cloves

Will stay a craving for drink, which use according to desire. **F.R**

Cocoa

Is a native of Southern countries, when genuine and properly prepared, is very wholesome and nutritious, containing a large quantity of oily or fatty matter, starch, etc. Cocoa does not effect the nervous system in the same manner as tea or coffee, and therefore it may be used where they are not proper. Cocoa can seldom be obtained in a perfectly pure state; the only way is to purchase the beans, crush and boil them over night, allowing it to stand and cool, and in the morning remove the fatty matter and reboil, it is then ready for use. The sick and weak, and those troubled with a weak stomach; will find that by adding a tea-spoonful of arrowroot, to the cup of cocoa, that it will not only increase its nutritive properties, but will make it easier to digest or assimilate. **O.P**

Colt's Foot

Colt's Foot shoots up a slender stalk with small yellowish flowers, the stalk being somewhat thick and hairy; these come before the leaves. The root is small and white, spreading much under ground. It grows in wet, sandy places, and flowers in May. It is a most valuable herb, and is not sufficiently appreciated. Its powerful expectorant qualities have rendered it celebrated as a remedy for coughs. It abounds with mucilage; it is slightly bitter and possesses tonic and demulcent properties. A decoction is made by boiling a handful of leaves in a quart of water till reduced to a pint, sweetened with rock candy, and acidified with a slice of lemon. A wineglass full to be taken three or four times per day. This is very useful in coughs and in all diseases of the lungs, shortness of breath, wheezing, etc. It thickens the expectoration when thin, and of course must allay inflammation. The syrup of Colt's Foot is one of the best known remedies for chronic bronchitis. Boiled in milk it is excellent for consumptive patients with distressing cough. It is a good remedy, combined with Wormwood, for calculous complaints; sweetened with honey, it is good for colds and asthma. The leaves of the Colt's Foot, combined with Eyebright, Buckbean, Betony, Rosemary, Thyme, Lavender and Chamomile Flowers make a first-class smoking tobacco. Persons troubled with asthma will find relief by using the above compound. Let the Colt's Foot preponderate. **O.P**

Columbo (American)

Grows about the Grand River and Lake Erie. Is better than the imported- as a stimulant it is much used. **C.H**

Comfrey Root

Is good boiled in milk for bowel complaints, immoderate courses, and flour albus. **C.H**

Common Juniper (Juniperus Communis)

On account of their diuretic effects, a decoction of the bruised berries is much used in stranguary, dropsy, etc. It is said to be good for old people with weak stomachs. European Juniper is stronger than American, if it retains the aromatic taste; but the virtue is often extracted before it is sold. **F.N**

Common Mustard (Sinapis Nigra)

The seed swallowed whole are a stimulating laxative much recommended for dyspepsia. A table-spoonful once or twice a day, soon after meals; they may be taken in molasses, or previously softened in hot water. For rheumatism and palsy, they are taken every few hours. White mustard is the kind generally preferred. Two or three tea-spoonfuls of common powdered mustard is a rapid emetic, and is often used to hasten the operation of other emetics. It is thought well suited to cases of great torpor of stomach; especially that produced by narcotic poisons. Native mustard is stronger than imported, and there is less liability to deception. **F.N**

Convulsion Root (Wild poppy)

Rises in rich soil in the woods, bunches of white stalks from four to six inches high, white buds, turning down like a poppy, roots resemble a mass of rotten wood full of small seed, the stalks bruised and steeped with beech drops equal parts- is a powerful remedy for fits in children or symptoms of fits in old or young. It may be freely drank with safety- it will always strengthen the system. **C.H**

Cow Parsnips

It grows with three or four large spread-winged, rough leaves, lying often on the ground, with long, round hairy foot-stalks under them, of a whitish green color, smelling strongly; from which springs, a round, crusted, hairy-stalk, two or three feet high, with a few joints and leaves thereon, and branched at the top, on which stand large white and sometimes reddish flowers, and often with white winged seeds, two together. It grows in moist places, and flowers in July or August. The seed is a good remedy in coughs and shortness of breath, falling-sickness and jaundice. The root is available for the same purpose, and boiled in sweet oil and the head rubbed therewith, will cure headache and drowsiness, lethargy, etc. The juice of the flowers dropped into the ears that run and are full of matter, cleanses and heals them. **O.P**

Crawly (Jewel Nerve Root)

Is generally found in the neighborhood of beach drops. It has no leaves, comes up with a single stalk about a foot high; with numerous pods hanging down like jewels, containing a fine seed, the root is brittle, not as large as a quill, growing as a bunch, the branches resemble fingers and toes- the powdered root two parts, skunk cabbage one part, wild turnip one part, mixed with molasses will cure the worst cough, or the root and top boiled with Indian Posey is extraordinary. **C.H**

Crowfoot (or Buttercup)

The common crowfoot is so well known it needs no description. They grow very common everywhere, especially in fields, and by the roadside. This fiery and hot spirited herb is not fit to be given inwardly but an ointment of the leaves or flowers will raise a blister, and may be applied to the nape of the neck to draw rheum from the eyes. The herb being bruised and mixed with a little mustard will raise a blister as perfectly as cantharides, and with far less danger. **O.P**

Cucumber

This makes a good wash for hot humors of the eyes. The usual course is to bruise the cucumbers and distill the water from them. It is also good for ulcers in the bladder, taken internally: The seed is good to provoke urine and cleanse the urinary passages. **O.P**

Curled Dock; Wild Rhubarb (Rumex Crispus)

The root is tonic and astringent, and at the same time laxative, like rhubarb. An ounce boiled in a pint of water; half a gill taken at once, as the stomach can bear it. Much used in decoction, for humors, and employed as a bath for the same purpose. The leaves boiled for greens are slightly laxative, and good for scorbutic disorders. **F.N**

Cydonia Vulgaris

The seed of Cydonia Vulgaris, of the natural order Pomaceae, produces the beheedana of Indian markets, where they are imported from Kabul, Bokhara, and Asia Minor. They are highly valued by the Mahomedans as a demulcent tonic and restorative remedy. From the presence of a mucilage, which they yield to water, they possess the demulcent and emollient properties of mucilage of accaciae. **I.I**

Dandelion

Grows in the dooryard or garden, with flat yellow blossoms near the ground, then rises a hollow stalk the size of a quill, on its top a white globe appears and is blown off by winds- the root will correct an unhealthy state of the stomach and liver, and procure an appetite. **C.H**

Dwarf Elder

This plant dies every year and rises afresh in the spring with a rough prickly stalk, two or three feet high, the root runs under the crust of the ground, as large as the finger; it tastes like sarsaparilla. It has bunches of dark colored berries, it colors the hair black, and is a powerful diuretic for curing dropsy. **C.H**

Elder Bush (Sambucus Canadensis)

Tea made of the blossoms, sweetened with W. I. molasses, or a syrup made of the berries, is safe and gentle physic for small children. A few tea-spoonfuls may be repeated according to circumstances. The young leaf-buds are too strongly purgative for little children. **F.N**

Elecampane (Inula Helenium)

Gently stimulant, tonic, diaphoretic, diuretic expectorant, and emmenagogue. Much used in chronic diseases of the lungs and chest, attended with general debility. Some take a teaspoonful of the powdered root every few hours; others drink half a gill of the strong decoction frequently. A syrup is made by slicing the fresh roots, covering them with sugar, and baking them an hour or two. **F.N**

Eryngo (Sea Holly)

Is a wild plant growing by the sea-side, and often cultivated for its medicinal virtues. The plant is prickly like the thistle, stalk firm, woody, round, straight and thick, leaves small, of a pale green, oblong, jagged and prickly. The plant is used for sexual apathy, and breeds seeds exceedingly; it is also good for yellow jaundice. The candid roots are most excellent for coughs, and general debility. They possess rare virtues as a diuretic. **O.P**

Erythrina Indica

The tree Erythrina Indica, of the natural order Leguminosae, is common in Bengal, Travancore, the Coromandel and the Concans, and is much used to support the black pepper vine, and to protect young coffee trees, and, from being armed with numerous prickles, it serves as an excellent hedge plant to keep off cattle from cultivated grounds. Leaves and bark are used in cases of fevers by the natives. The leaves are sometimes applied externally to disperse venereal buboes, and relieve pains on the joints. **I.I**

Featherfew

Is serviceable in female obstructions and hysteria. It makes a good drink for mothers before and after confinement. **O.P**

Fennel

One of the customs of boiling fennel with fish, is still adhered to by some, but to ask them why they do so is, because they don't know as a rule. Fennel boiled with fish consumes the phlegmatic humor, which fish copiously produce. Fennel is a good diuretic, hence a remedy for urinary diseases. The leaves or seeds boiled in barley water and drank, are good to increase the milk when suckling child. It will also remove nausea, etc. **O.P**

Fir Balsam Tree (Pinus Balsaniea)

The exuding balsam is called resin of Canada. Rubbed up with gum arabic, or sugar, and then dissolved in water, a few tea-spoonfuls may be taken as the system can bear it. It is laxative and diuretic, strengthening to the nervous system, good for chronic coughs not accompanied with inflammation. **F.N**

Foxglove

Properties: Invaluable, foxglove is such an active medicine that it will cure when all other remedies fail, and will completely restore beyond expectation (when the patient is not past cure); in the most hopeless case it will prolong life, and when death takes place whilst under its influence, it m often without pain or struggle. Hot more than half a tea-spoonful of the dried leaf rubbed to powder to be used in one day, to half a pint of boiling water. **F.R**

Friars' Balsam

No one should be without a small supply of Friars balsam. Lint soaked in it makes an excellent dressing for fractures and wounds, leading to rapid and satisfactory healing. Half an ounce of it to half-pint of rose water makes an excellent cosmetic for the removal of freckles or slight eruptions on the face. **F.R**

Garcinia Mangostana

This is the well-known fruit of Garcinia Mangostana, of the natural order Guttilera, brought into the Indian market from the Eastern Islands. The rind of this fruit chiefly imported from Singapore, has been used with much advantage in cases of chronic hemorrhagic dysentery. **I.I**

Garlic (Alium Sativum)

A general stimulant that quickens circulation and excites the nervous system. When the patient is kept warm, its effects are diaphoretic. Taken cool, it is used as a diuretic, for dropsies and calculous disorders. As an expectorant, it is given in chronic catarrh, humoral asthma, whooping-cough, and other pectoral affections, after inflammation has subsided. In moderate quantities, it is good for flatulence and enfeebled digestion. Recommended for worms. The bulbs may be swallowed in slices, in pills, or made into a syrup taken in milk. A grown person may take half a clove, or a whole one, several times a day. Of the juice, about a tea-spoonful may be taken at once. It renders the breath extremely offensive. Large doses, especially in excited states of the system, are apt to occasion irritation, flatulence, and fever. Bruised and applied to the feet, it is good for disorders of the head, quiets restlessness, and produces sleep. The bruised root steeped in spirit, or the juice mixed with oil, is used as a wash in infantile convulsions, and other spasmodic disorders of children. A single clove, or a few drops of the juice on cotton, introduced into the ear, has proved highly efficacious in some cases of deafness. **F.N**

Ginger

Stimulant and carminative. Good for dyspepsia and flatulence. If taken in powder, from ten grains to a scruple is a dose. An infusion made by steeping half an ounce of the powder, or bruised root, in a pint of boiling water; quarter or half a gill may be taken. Applied outwardly it is rubefacient. The powder, when snuffed, excites violent sneezing. Often added to bitter and tonic medicines to give them a warming and cordial effect. **F.N**

Ginseng

Grows in rich woodland a foot high, shooting out three branches, from the middle arises a pedestal, having on its top a bunch of kidney shaped berries- root, carrot shaped. It is good for nervous affections, to cleanse the blood, and to strengthen the spleen and kidneys. **C.H**

Gold Thread

Grows in cedar swamps and springy places. It has three

leaves like a strawberry, the root is the size of a thread, very yellow and bitter; a good tonic or gargle for sore mouth. **C.H**

Golden Seal

Grows about the Grand River and Bear Creek, from four to eight inches high, leaves like Alum Root, and like Mandrake, branches in two parts, frequently. Root as yellow as gold, size of a quill, with many fibers. Tonic, stimulant, and astringent. **C.H**

Hardhack (Spiraea Tomentosa)

Very astringent; but less apt to disagree with the stomach than most herbs of its kind. Used in advanced stages of diarrhea and cholera infantum, when there are no remaining signs of inflammation. Used as a tonic, in cases of debility. A decoction of leaves and flowers, dose about half a gill. Mixed with thorough-wort, in equal portions, it is recommended for chronic weakness of the bowels. **F.N**

Helleborus Niger

The root of the Hellehorus Niger, of the natural order Ranunculaceae. This and another species of the black Hellebore are produced in Nepal. Pure Kala-kootkee is scarcely procurable in the Calcutta market; but it comes adulterated with another species which is sold as genuine; but it has no purgative properties. Medicinal properties: A powerful cathartic, used in maniacal and dropsical cases; but its actions are so violent, and results so uncertain, that it has been discarded from ordinary practice, though in veterinary pharmacy it still holds a prominent place. **I.I**

Hemlock Spruce Tree (Pinus Canadensis)

The astringent bark, (used by tanners,) powdered and

sifted through muslin, dries the surface of the skin, when chafed behind the ears, etc. A decoction of the twigs and leaves much recommended as a sedative bath, in spotted or other malignant fevers. For rheumatic pain in the bones, it is good to soak the feet in very warm water, with hemlock branches steeped in it. Keep covered with blankets, and get into a hot bed. The pitch is used as a strengthening plaster. **F.N**

Hibiscus Abelmoschatus

The seeds of Hibiscus Abelmoschatus, of the natural order Malvaceae, are found in all the bazaars, and are much esteemed for their cordial, stomachic and antispasmodic virtues. Deduced to powder, the Arabs use them as an adjunct to coffee. This plant is also called Musk Hibiscus, and is very common all over India. **I.I**

Hog Thistle

Grows in new ground, summer flowers, the roots are sweet, let children eat them; they will destroy worms. **C.H**

Hop Vine, (Humulus Lupulus)

A decoction of half an ounce of the blossoms in a pint of boiling water is a useful tonic. On account of its anodyne qualities, it is sometimes taken to procure sleep. Hop beer invigorates the stomach, when oppressed with dyspepsia, or feelings of lassitude in the spring. A bag filled with hops and wet with hot rum, or vinegar, is a quieting application for pain in the bowels, cramp in the stomach, ague in the face, etc. They are often moistened with spirit, so as to prevent a rustling noise, and then made into pillows for nervous and wakeful people. In poultices and fomentations they are used to soothe painful swellings, etc. The very young shoots eaten as asparagus, are reckoned healthy. **F.N**

Horehound

Combined with boneset; good for a cough. **C.H**

Horse Radish, (Cochlearia Armoracia)

The root promotes appetite and digestion. As an active stimulant, it is used both externally and internally for palsy and chronic rheumatism. As a diuretic, it is employed in dropsical disorders, particularly when the digestive powers are weak. Highly esteemed in scorbutic affections. Half a drachm or more may be taken, grated or sliced. A syrup made of it is good for a hoarse cold. Boiled in milk, it is said to be a good wash to remove tan and freckles. The leaves are a good application for rheumatic pains. They often relieve the tooth-ache, but if kept on the face too long will produce a blister. Bound on the feet, they are excellent for the head-ache and for colds attended with feverish symptoms. The stems should be cut out, they should be slowly wilted before the fire, or dipped in hot vinegar, clapped in the hands till they become soft, and then applied warm. **F.N**

Hysoscyamus Niger

The plant Hyoscyamus Niger, of the natural order Solanaceae, is a native of Europe and Asia Minor, but now has been extensively cultivated in Sheharunpore, in the neighborhood of Agra and Ajmere, and also in the Botanic Garden of Calcutta. The seeds are sold in all the bazaars under the name of Khorasanee-ajowan. Its leaves and seeds are employed for their narcotic properties; the latter, however, being more active, are generally used. In its effects on the human system, this plant and its preparations stand mid-way between Opium and Belladonna, combining great soothing and anodyne power with the property of dilating the pupils. It can be used as a sedative in place of opium, when that drug is contra-indicated from its constipating and exciting properties. The leaves are sometimes used as cataplasms to allay pain and remove irritation. An excellent dry inspissated juice of the leaf has been prepared by Mr. Superintending Surgeon Ludlow at Agra and Ajmere, by exposing the juice in thin layers on a shallow earthen vessel to the intense heat of the sun in April and May. This extract has been used frequently, and considered far superior to any imported from Europe or prepared in this country by other processes. In three grain doses, its soporific and anodyne effects are most decisive, and its use, rarely, if ever, followed by any headache or other unpleasant symptom. **I.I**

Hyssop (Hyssopus Officinalis)

The bruised leaves are said to mitigate the pain of bruises and heal them without a scar. An infusion stimulates gently, and helps expectoration. Good for asthma, chronic catarrh, coughs, etc. especially in old, debilitated people. Elecampane, hyssop and horehound steeped together, and taken with warm flax-seed tea, when going to bed, is much praised as a cure for colds. **F.N**

Iceland Moss (Cetraria Islandica)

An ounce steeped in a pint of boiling water makes a drink demulcent, nutritious and tonic. Much recommended in chronic catarrhs, pulmonary complaints, and weakness occasioned by dysentery, or the copious discharge of external ulcers. Sometimes boiled into a jelly, strained and seasoned with lemon-juice and sugar. **F.N**

Indian Hemp

Grows in marshes and by the sides of streams, two or three feet high- purple blossoms on the top succeeded by silky pods pointing upwards, the stalk is covered by a tough bark-like hemp, the root is an excellent vermifuge and promotes menstruation. **C.H**

Indian Posie (Life Everlasting)

Is a balsamic herb growing on knolls in old pasture fields from one to two feet high, white blossoms on the top which continue throughout the winter; it has a beautiful smell, this herb boiled in milk and water is a popular remedy for the bloody flux, and inflammation in the bowels- it is invaluable as an expectorant. **C.H**

Indian Rhubarb (Water Dock)

Grows in marshes, in ponds, and stagnant water, from three to six feet high, resembling yellow dock. Several years ago at the Grand River an old Indian, Dr Hill, used the powdered root, in teaspoon full doses in hot water, for dropsy, rheumatism, liver complaints, and consumption; he said "if perspiration took place" after giving a dose of this medicine in a few hours he generally restored his patient with common remedies. It is the best agent I know for all scrofulous humors, for "venereal" a strong tea made of this root bruised with double the quantity of Adder's Tongue (the first leaf that appears in the spring, spotted and glossy) drank freely, and applied as a wash, will cure this loathsome disease. **C.H**

Ivy

A favorite popular remedy used in coughs, sore throat, and for promoting expectoration. Pick and wash twelve sound leaves, add a pint of cold water with a teaspoonful of ground licorice, boil, and strain off. A wineglass full twice a day. **F.R**

Jacob's Ladder

Jacob's Ladder is a vine that grows in old hedges and by fence sides, one stalk about breast high, then spreads off into small branches having curls like a grape vine clinging to other weeds, the fruit is a large bunch of black berries, and when ripe hung down under the leaves by a small stem; the root made into a tea and drank freely is a most certain remedy for gravel in the bladder or kidneys. **C.H**

Jalap

An active cathartic, operating briskly and often painfully. Given in most cases where physic is required particularly applicable in cases of dropsy, being an active diuretic. The aqueous extract, operates moderately, without much griping. The alcoholic extract, called resin of jalap, operates powerfully, and sometimes severely. From fifteen to thirty grains of the powder is a dose for a strong grown person, usually rubbed up with sugar. If taken in flax-seed tea, its effects are less irritating. Ten grains of powdered rhubarb, and ten grains of jalap powder, are a common cathartic, given in molasses, after an emetic has ceased operating, and the stomach needs to be more thoroughly cleansed. **F.N**

Kidneywort

Kidney-wort has many thick, flat and round leaves growing from the root, each having a long footstalk fastened underneath, about the middle of it. It is of a pale green color, and rather hollow on the upper side like a saucer; from which rise one or more smooth, hollow stalks, half a foot high, with two or three small leaves thereon, rather long, and divided at the edges; the tops are divided into long branches, bearing a number of flowers, round a long spike one above another, which are hollow like a little bell, of a whitish green color, after which come small heads, containing small brownish seeds. The root is round and smooth, grayish without, and white within. It may be frequently found growing among the rocks and stony places at the bottom of old trees, and on those that are decayed. It flowers in June in this latitude. Its medicinal virtues are greatly extolled by some medical writers. Some claim the juice and the extract will cure epilepsy. The juice allays inflammation of the liver and stomach and strengthens the bowels. The juice of the herb outwardly applied restrains erysipelas. It heals pimples, sores, etc., and taken inwardly it relieves inflamed kidneys, and combined with other diuretics will cure gravel and stone. Made into an ointment, it is good for the piles, sciatica and swelled testicles; the ointment or the juice alone is good for scrofula sores, chilblains and stops the bleeding of green wounds. **O.P**

Knapweed

It has many long and dark green leaves, dented about the edges, sometimes a little torn on both sides, and rather hairy, among which arises a long round stalk, four or five feet high, divided into many branches; at the tops stand great scaly green heads, enclosing a number of dark purplish red thrums or threads, which, after they are withered, come black seeds wrapped in down, resembling thistle-seed, but smaller. The root is white, hard and woody. It is found in fields and meadows and flowers in July and August. It is a good remedy for bloody flux, bleeding at the nose and inward bleeding. It is also good in catarrh affections, restraining distillations of thin and sharp humors from the head upon the stomach and lungs. It is used also for cuts and sores, as it soon dries them up and heals them gently. It may be made into an ointment for outward application. **O.P**

Lettuce

Water distilled from it is a mild sedative, without the constipating effects of opium. Grown people may take from half a gill to a gill. A tea made of the leaves, or milk squeezed from the plant, is a gentle opiate, to check chronic dysentery, allay coughs, and soothe nervous irritation. **F.N**

Licorice Root

Grows wild in many parts of this country, its virtues are great. Its demulcent properties render it very useful in coughs and bronchial irritation, and in some stomach complaints, arising from a deficiency of natural mucus which should defend the stomach against the acrimony of the food, and the fluids secreted in it. Licorice also works gently by urine, and is very soothing to ulcerated kidneys or urinary passages. **O.P**

Lobelia Inflata

This herb is a most valuable anti-poison. Much has been said and written as to the properties of lobelia; and instead of being a poison, practical experience- which is far better than theory- has proved that it is one of the most valuable herbs in the botanic practice. If medical men would divert themselves of theory, and give heed to facts, they would have discovered in the following analysis of its chemical properties truth from error: Lobelia, resin, chlorophyll, gum, lobelic acid, fixed oil, salts of lime and potassa, oxide of iron, and woody fiber. Many Indians who were troubled with shortness of breath, asthmatic affections, hooping cough, and in fact many diseases of the chest and lungs, have used this herb with striking success. I am satisfied that it is as kind and destitute of all hazard as boneset or any other herb, though it may be more efficient. It is already beginning to be appreciated by the medical world. It tends to remove obstructions from every part of the system, and is felt even to the ends of the toes; it cleanses the stomach, and exercises a beneficial influence over every part of the body; it is very diffusible, however, and requires to be used with ginger or some other stimulant. There is no medicine that is half so effective as lobelia in removing the tough, hard, and ropy phlegm from asthmatic and consumptive persons. It is an indispensable medicine in fevers, bilious, and long standing chronic complaints. It is useful in poultices to assist suppuration. The medicinal virtues of this herb are so multifarious that a large treatise might well be written on its curative powers. Suffice it, however, to say that it is a general corrector of the whole system, innocent in its nature, and moving with the general spirits. In healthy systems it will be silent and harmless. It is fully as well calculated to remove the cause of disease as food is to remove hunger, as it clears obstructions in the circulation, not regarding the name of the disease. In asthmatic attacks, take a tablespoonful of the acid tincture; in croup for children, one half the quantity. For deafness, take one drachm each: Tincture of lobelia, tincture gum myrrh, oil of sassafras, tincture of laudanum, olive oil, mix, and apply lint wet with the liniment in the ear, night and morning, then syringe out with warm water and soap. **O.P**

Loosestrife (Purple)

A very useful herb with woody square stalks full of joints, three feet high. The stalks branch into long stems of spiked flowers, about six inches long, growing in bundles, one above the other, out of small husks, like the spiked heads of lavender, with fine round pointed leaves of a purple or violet color. Seeds are small and brown. It grows in wet ground, and flowers in July. It is one of the best remedies for preserving the sight, and for the cure of sore eyes. It is fully as valuable as eyebright. It will cure blindness, provided the crystalline humor be not injured or destroyed. There are other species of this plant, the medical properties are much like the above. **O.P**

Low Mallows (Malva Rotundifolia)

An infusion of the plant sweetened with W. I. molasses is gently laxative. Very smooth and soothing medicine for piles, dysentery, and inflammation of the bowels. **F.N**

Low, Running Blackberry; Dewberry (Rubus Procumbens)

Properties similar to the high blackberry. Tea made of the leaves much used as an astringent wash, when the mouth is hot and sore, in fevers. **F.N**

Lungwort (Lichen)

Shell moss on maple and oak steeped, good for colds, coughs, and consumption. **C.H**

Mandrake

Given in chronic liver and bowel complaints. Its properties for exciting the liver to healthy action has few equals. It has been given successfully for incontinence of urine. A tea-spoonful of powder in treacle once or twice a day. **F.R**

Marsh Rosemary (Statice Caroliniana)

The root is astringent as galls. In dysentery, continuing from weakness, after inflammation has subsided. It has proved efficacious when other tonics and astringents have been tried in vain. For ulcers and sore mouths it is considered a much better wash than goldthread, with which it is often combined. Internally and externally it has been very successful in cases of malignant sore throat. A cold infusion is preferred, because some of the virtue evaporates by heat. Steep from twelve to twenty-four hours. **F.N**

May Apple; Wild Lemon (Podophyllum Peltatum)

A decoction of the root is a sure and active cathartic. Dr. Bigelow says: "We have hardly any native plant which answers better the common purposes of jalap, aloes, and rhubarb, and which is more safe and mild in its operation."

Some consider it a good medicine for dropsy, and it has been used in the southern states for curing intermittent fever. The Shakers prepare an extract of podophyllum much esteemed as a mild cathartic. A tea-spoonful of the powder usually operates with efficacy, without pain or inconvenience. **F.N**

Meadow Saffron

Colchinus Antumnale: It is a perennial bulbous rooted plant growing in wet meadows, flowering in September. It is a native of many parts of this country. It is poisonous to animals of all classes, but their instinct causes them to avoid the foliage in the fields. It is very useful in humeral asthma and for the cure of gout and rheumatism, in both of which it is a specific. **O.P**

Momordica Charantia

The Momordica Charantia and M. Muricata, of the natural order Cucurbitaceae, cultivated every where in the Peninsula, differ from each other in the forms of their fruit; the former having the fruit longer and more oblong, the latter smaller, more ovate, muricated, and tubercled. The fruits of both these species are bitter and wholesome, and eaten in curries by the natives, who value more the second variety, the Oochya of the Bengal bazaars. The juice of the fresh leaves, especially of M. Charantia, mixed with warm water, has been successfully used as an athelmintic. The whole plant pulverized is said to act as a good specific in leprosy and malignant ulcers, when applied externally. **I.I**

Motherwort

Good for nervous headache. **C.H**

Mountain Flax

This is a mild purgative, and very useful for children. It

is also very useful for dropsy of the bowels, rheumatic pains and catarrhal affections. It has also given relief in bilious disorders. It is very good for habitual costiveness taken in infusion. **O.P**

Mountain Mint (Oswego Butters)

Grows along the lake shored and on mountains and plains two or three feet high, its flowers resemble balm- its smell and taste is like summer savory, diaphoretic; good for colds, chill fever, and rheumatism. **C.H**

Mullein

Good mixed with celandine for piles. **C.H**

Nettle

It is common everywhere, and needs no description. It is a valuable plant, and not appreciated as it should be. The young shoots in spring, form a wholesome vegetable, boiled like other green table vegetables, and eaten. It is a good blood remedy, and removes the phlegmatic superfluity left in the body by winter. Cancer has often yielded to the juice of nettles, by taking the juice inwardly, and mixing a little oil of laudanum with the juice and rubbing the parts outwardly. The use of limbs, lost by rheumatism have been restored by the same preparation. Excessive corpulence may be reduced by taking a few of the seeds once a day for a few weeks. For Goiter take a few seeds night and morning, powdered; it makes a good gargle for it, as well as a poultice of the leaves. Nettle is anti-asthmatic; the juice of the roots or leaves made into an electuary with honey and sugar opens the bronchial tubes of the lungs, the stoppage of which causes wheezing, shortness of breath, etc. It stimulates expectoration of phlegm very freely. For retention of urine, and for gravel and stone. The flowers and seed should be made into a conserve. The decoction of the plant kills worms in children. The seeds serve to fatten fowls, good stimulant for horses. **O.P**

Nicotiana Tabacum

The plant Nicotiana Tabacum, of the natural order Solanaceae, is a native of the warmer parts of America, and extensively cultivated all over the world, for the leaves which, when dried, are variously manufactured, for the purposes of smoking and chewing. In India the leaves powdered, or sometimes cut into very small pieces, are mixed up with treacle and various other aromatics, according to the taste and means of the individual, and made into the consistence of a pill-mass, which constitutes the Tumak of Indian bazaars. Tobacco is a narcotic, emetic, and powerful sedative, especially affecting the heart, frequently causing great depression. Smoked, it is a sedative and expectorant in various cases of asthma. Occasionally used as snuff for affections of the head. It is dangerous on account of its poisonous properties, which are attributable to the presence of a volatile alkaloid, the nicotiana or nicotianin. **I.I**

Nigella Sativa

The plant Nigella Sativa, of the natural order Ranunculaceae, extensively cultivated in India, produces the triangular seeds, which resemble coarse gunpowder, and possess a strong aromatic odor and a flavor similar to that of Sassafras or Cubebs. The Nigella seeds have been long used in medicine, and are praised by Hippocrates as a tonic condiment. At present they are chiefly employed by native physicians as aromatic adjuncts to purgative or bitter remedies. In Bengal they are given to nurses in the belief that they increase the secretion of milk. Facts have been observed to corroborate the opinion. They are chiefly used as a condiment and stomachic. The seeds yield by expression 13 percent, of aromatic oil. **I.I**

Opium

A powerful narcotic, to be used with very great caution. In small quantities it quiets the nerves and induces drowsiness. The medium dose for a grown person is from one to two grains, but in some cases not more than one third or one fourth of a grain is administered. People who are so unwise as to use it frequently, become accustomed to considerable quantities; but the effects are ruinous. This drug is obtained from the common poppy. The Asiatic mode is to make lengthwise incisions in the green seed-vessels, the moment the flowers fall; a juice exudes, which is scraped off the next day when dry. This is opium. But a better mode is to cut off the stalk, about an inch below the seed vessel, as soon as the flowers begin to fall. Take off the milky juice that slowly exudes in drops, and put it upon an earthen plate to dry. Then cut the stalk about an inch lower, and proceed the same. **F.N**

Oxalis Corniculata

The Oxalis Corniculata, of the natural order Oxalidaceae, grows wild all over India, and resembles the European Sorrel in every respect. The small leaves, tender shoots, and flowers are given in electuaries by the Hindus as a cooling medicine in fevers, to the extent of two teaspoonful daily, and also used with efficacy in dysentery. **I.I**

Parsley

The roots are the parts used in medicine. A strong decoction is a good remedy in jaundice. It operates on the urine, and good for the expulsion of wind. It gently removes obstructions of the liver and spleen. It is good for dropsy, stone in the kidneys, and jaundice taken in connection with fennel, anise, caraway seeds, burnt saxifrage, in equal parts. **O.P**

Penny Royal (Iledeoma Pulegiodes)

An aromatic; good for flatulence, and checks sickness at the stomach. Half a pint of the strong infusion of the herb, taken hot when going to bed, is much used as an emmenagogue in common cases; and is likewise excellent to produce perspiration, when people have taken cold, with feverish symptoms. **F.N**

Peppermint

Valuable for the colic pain in the breast.

Petty Morel, Spikenard, Life of Man (Aralia Raccmosa)

A much-esteemed aromatic. An infusion of the berries is recommended for rheumatism. A decoction of the root is good for flatulence, and considered very salutary for humors. Mixed with dandelions, it forms a drink very beneficial for weakly people troubled with wind. **F.N**

Pimpernel

Is a very valuable plant to use for running ulcers, bites of venomous snakes, dogs and other animals, and wounds of all kinds. Poultice the wounds with the herb and drink half a tea-cupful of the boiled liquor three or four times a day. **F.R**

Piper Nigrum

The dried berry with pulp of Piper Nigrum, of the natural order Piperaceae, is the black pepper of commerce. The black pepper vine is a native of Malacca, Java, and Sumatra, and cultivated along the Malabar Coast. The black pepper deprived of its pericarp by macerating it in water, and allowing the pericarp to swell, burst, and separate, constitute the white pepper, the Sha-morich (Piper Alba). On analysis, pepper has been found to contain piperin, concrete acrid oil, volatile oil, gummy matter, extractive, malic and tartaric acids, starch and hassorin. The pungency and stimulant property of pepper resides in the acrid concrete matter. A powerful febrifuge action has been ascribed to piperin from 6 to 8 grain doses, but Sir William O'Shaughnessy adduces his own experience and that of Souberain in proving its inefficacy as such. It acts as a general stimulant, and is considered valuable as an external application in chronic piles in the form of Ward's paste. The pepper is extensively used by native practitioners both internally and externally, and largely consumed for culinary purposes, preference being given by some to the white variety for its less acridity. **I.I**

Pitch Pine Tree (Pinus Rigida)

Boil the knots till the pitch rises to the surface. Spread on leather, it is a very strengthening plaster for weak backs. Many prefer it to all other similar applications. A little nutmeg grated on the surface is an improvement. **F.N**

Plantago Ispaghula

The plant Plantago Ispaghula, of the natural order Plantaginaceae, is found common in many parts of India, especially in Assam. The seeds, available in all the Bazaars at a very cheap cost, are much valued for the peculiar mucilaginous matter which resides in their envelope or testa, and is readily imparted to cold or warm water. They are largely used in the preparation of a cooling drink. Medicinal properties: Demulcent and emollient. Employed with the greatest advantage in chronic diarrhea and dysentery, and in all inflammatory affections of the mucous membrane of the alimentary canal. It is also useful in gonorrhea. **I.I**

Pleurisy Root (Whiteroot, Butterfly Weed)

Grows in deep sand hills, about (Port Dover) two or three feet high, flowers on the top of bright orange color, succeeded by pods, silky, pointing upward like fingers; root carrot shaped, brittle, brown outside, white inside. This root is famed for curing pleurisy, inflammation of the lungs, liver, and dysentery. For any acute disease, cleanse the stomach and bowels, then steep a handful of this root in a quart of boiling water. Give a spoonful occasionally. **C.H**

Pogoostemon Patchouli

The dried flowering spikes and leaves of Pogostemon Patchouli, of the natural order Lamiaceae, are imported from Singapore, Sylhet, Penang, and the Malay Peninsula, and are sold in every Bazaar in Hindustan. Patchouli has a very powerful odor, and is extensively used by perfumers. When distilled, it yields an essential oil called Pachapatka-athur. The Cashmere shawl merchants use it in scenting their fabrics to distinguish them from the common manufactures of other places. **I.I**

Pokeroot (and berries)

Good for rheumatism. In poultice, good for different swellings. **C.H**

Prickly Ash (Xanthoxylum Fraxineum)

Very highly recommended for chronic rheumatism. Effects similar to gum guaiacum. A decoction is made with an ounce of the bark boiled in a quart of water; a pint may be taken in the course of the day. Sometimes given powdered; about a teaspoonful. **F.N**

Princess Pine

It is an excellent remedy for scrofula. It is also very useful in cancers, tumors and diseases of the urinary organs. Princess Pine and the roots of the Wild Lettuce dried out and powdered together are excellent to cure all bad humors. Take a teaspoonful of the powder in a glass of hot water and bathe the affected parts with it. It is also very useful to restore weak nerves. **O.P**

Privet

Legistrum Vulgare: A wild shrub, growing five or six feet high, The flowers are small and white. The fruit is a black berry. The tops are used, and are best when the flowers are in bud. A strong infusion in water, with the addition of a little honey and wine, make an excellent wash for the mouth, and throat when sore and inflamed, and when the gums are apt to bleed. It also makes a good wash for all sores. **O.P**

Purslane

This herb is so well known it requires no description. It is a superior remedy to allay heat in the liver, blood, and stomach, and in hot ague, there is nothing better. It restrains hot and choleric fluxes, the whites and gonorrhea, distillation from the head, and pains therein proceeding from heat, want of sleep, or frenzy. The seed is more effectual than the herb to cool the heat and sharpness of urine. The herb bruised and applied to any part, the seat of inflammation, will remove it. It is a good remedy for sore and inflamed mouth and throat. It will fasten loose teeth by rinsing the mouth with the juice. **O.P**

Queen of the Meadow (Gravel Root)

Grows in marshes about four feet high, the stalk is

reddish, flowers purple, leaves long, dark colored roots, full of oil which tastes like turpentine. For gravel, bloody urine, diabetes, dropsy. A strong tea of this root will always give relief. **C.H**

Red Cedar; American Savin (Juniperus Virginia na.)

A salve resembling the savin cerate is made of it. A decoction of the bruised leaves is taken for rheumatism, as a warm stimulant, producing perspiration. **F.N**

Rhubarb

At once a tonic and cathartic. From five to ten grains operate as a laxative and stomachic; from twenty to thirty as a purgative. Its medicinal properties are peculiar, being both cathartic and astringent. The latter effect follows the former; hence the stomach is left more braced and invigorated than with other physic. An infusion is much used for women, children, and people of delicate constitutions. In costive states of the body, its astringent qualities should be counteracted by mixing it with an equal proportion of soap. Roasting, or long boiling, diminishes its laxative qualities, while the astringent remain; this is sometimes done in cases of obstinate diarrhea. As a general rule, it is not a good medicine where inflammation exists. It is used in dyspepsia accompanied with costiveness, in chronic dysentery, and the secondary stages of cholera infantum. Equal portions of rhubarb and magnesia are very beneficial in bilious diarrhea, where there is any evidence of acidity. Rhubarb is second only to calomel in its power of changing to a natural color the very discolored evacuations common in such disorders; a result which is considered most desirable. Ten or twelve grains of rhubarb, mixed with eight or ten grains of super sulfate of potash is a mild and efficient purgative, that will generally remove ordinary disorders of the bowels. Two grains of powdered rhubarb, one grain of ipecacuanha, and two grains of soap, form an excellent tonic pill for dyspepsia; it is laxative, and leaves the stomach braced. One may be taken two or three times a day. The common infusion is made by steeping a drachm of sliced rhubarb an hour in half a pint of boiling water. Dose from a quarter of a gill to half a gill; taken every three or four hours till it operates. Caraway seed, or cinnamon, sometimes steeped with it, to diminish its griping effects. It is often taken in powder, or chewed. It is an expensive medicine. The Turkey rhubarb, specked with white, is less apt to excite vomiting, than that which is entirely deep yellow. **F.N**

Ricinus Communis (Castor oil plant)

The oil obtained from the seeds of Ricinus Communis, of the natural order Euphorbiaceae, growing wild in many parts of India, is extensively manufactured by expression. Seeds yield about 25 per cent, of pure oil (the cold-drawn), which is used as a cooling purgative. A larger quantity of the oil, about 35 per cent., may be extracted if the seeds are heated during expression, by which means much of the resinous principle of the seed is extracted. The oil thus procured can only be used for lighting purposes; if taken internally, it produces irritation and much griping. Medicinal properties: A gentle and quick cathartic. Its action is well known, and the oil is largely used by Native practitioners. When its action becomes violent, it can be best checked by administering lime juice. **I.I**

Rock Cress

It is a small wild plant, five or six inches long, the leaves, direct from the root are long, and deeply divided; those on the stalks are smaller, flowers small and white, standing among the leaves, at the top of the branches. The plant is a good diuretic, as well as a safe one. It is also good for jaundice, scurvy, and obstructions of the urine and kidneys. **O.P**

Rosemary

Rosemary is comforting to the stomach and brain; the oil mixed with spirits of wine forms what is called the oil of rosemary. A tea made from the leaves is good for pains in the head. It makes a good wash combined with yarrow leaves and southern-wood. The following ingredients make one of the most valuable preparations for preserving the hair: we know, viz: Two ounces rosemary leaves, three ounces southern wood and one ounce of yarrow leaves; simmer the whole in three pints of water, gently, down to one quart; when cool, strain through a cloth; then add four ounces of compound spirits of ammonia, and four ounces of olive oil. Apply with a sponge at bedtime. **O.P**

Rupture Wort

This herb spreads upon the ground, about ten or twelve inches long, divided into many small parts, full of small joints, very thick together; the leaves are very small, nearly oval, of a pale green; two at each joint, tinged with yellow. The flowers are very small and yellow, scarcely discernible from the stalks and leaves. The root is very long and small, and deep in the ground, it grows in dry, sandy and rocky places, and is cultivated in gardens. It has been found by experience that its name is what it implies, for it has cured many cases of rupture in children, and sometimes in adults, if the disease be not too inveterate, by taking a drachm of the powder of the dried herb every day for a week, or more in wine, or a decoction will often answer the same purpose. The juice or distilled water of the green herb, wall cure inward fluxes and gonorrhea. It will relieve stone and gravel, and an excellent remedy in stranguary. It is also a good outward remedy for wounds and sores, the green herb being bound on the wounds. **O.P**

Saffron (Crocus Sativus)

An infusion of the flowers is stimulant, antispasmodic, and tends to produce sleep. Mixed with snake-root it is given to keep out measles, and prevent eruptions from striking to the stomach, when outward applications are made; but some physicians doubt its efficacy in such cases. Large doses produce head-ache, stupor, and other disagreeable effects. It has been recommended as an emmenagogue. **F.N**

Sage (Salvia Officinalis)

Slightly tonic and astringent. A strong infusion of the plant relieves the head-ache, and is much used for that which accompanies measles and canker-rash. The exhausting night sweats attending hectic fevers have sometimes been cured by fasting morning and night, and drinking cold sage-tea constantly and freely. It checks nausea, invigorates a feeble appetite, and in small quantities is good for weak and windy stomachs. Mixed with honey and vinegar it is a good gargle for sore throats. A weak infusion, with a little lemon juice and sugar, is safe and pleasant drink in fevers. The powdered leaves taken freely in molasses are much recommended for worms. **F.N**

Sassafras

To cleanse the blood, a wash for sores. **C.H**

Saxifrage (White)

The common white saxifrage has a few small reddish kernels of roots covered with skin, lying among small blackish fibers, which send forth round, yellow green leaves, grayish underneath, lying above the ground, edges rough and hairy, each upon a little footstalk, from which rise brownish, hairy, green stalks, two or three feet high, with round leaves, rather branched at the top, on which stand pretty, large, white flowers, of five leaves each, with yellow threads in the center, standing in a brownish green husk, small black seeds follow the death of the flower. It grows in dry meadows, and grassy sandy places, and flowers in June and July. Its *officinale* name is *saxifraga alba*. It possesses superior diuretic properties, and is very useful for those troubled with gravel and stone in the bladder, and to relieve stranguary. Taken in strong decoction, it cleanses the stomach and lungs from thick tough phlegm. There are few better medicines for stone, than this. The saxifrage burnet, I have already spoken of in another part of this work. **O.P**

Scurvy Grass

This plant possesses anti-scorbutic and diuretic properties. It has superior powers as a blood cleanser. The juice or decoction taken in the spring every morning fasting, will answer this purpose. It removes obstructions in the liver and spleen, and restores the body to a more lively color. It makes a good wash for the mouth and gums in scurvy. It may be mixed with orange juice which makes it more agreeable. **O.P**

Sessamum Orientalus

The plant Sessamum Orientale, of the natural order Pedaliaceae, is extensively cultivated throughout India. The seeds are about the size of a white mustard seed. Three varieties are known, the white, the parti-colored, and the black. It is principally from the latter that the teel oil of commerce is obtained. The seeds contain about 40 per cent, of oil. According to Pereira, it may be used as a substitute for almond oil; it does not get rancid soon. It forms the basis of all Indian perfumed and medicinal oils. Specific gravity, 0.9253. Soluble in Ether, partially in Alcohol. **I.I**

Skullcap

This is a valuable nervine, and one so often used for nervous excitability; it is often used with good results in palsy of the limbs, more particularly when used in connection with some mild tonic. We have used it with good effect in delirium tremens, fits and convulsions. In any of the above complaints pour one pint of boiling water on one ounce of the powder and let it settle. Take a wineglass full three times a day. **O.P**

Skunk Cabbage

An expectorant and anti-spasmodic. **C.H**

Silk Weed; Milk Weed (Asclepias Syriaca)

A strong infusion of the root has anodyne qualities. Good for the same diseases as hyssop. **F.N**

Slippery Elm; Red Elm (Ulmus Fulva)

A decoction of the bark drank plentifully, is an excellent demulcent in lung fevers, and much recommended for piles, dysentery, and consumption. A healing wash for chilblains, eruptions, etc. **F.N**

Solanum Indicum

The Solanum Indicum, of the natural order Solanaceae, is common all over India. There are varieties of the plant differing from each other chiefly in the shape of the leaves. The root is used by Indian Doctors in dysuria and ischuria. It is considered as an exciting agent, and given in difficult parturition. Its infusion is also prescribed in fevers and coughs, and the juice of the leaves, with the fresh juice of ginger, is administered to stop vomiting. The leaves and fruit, rubbed up with sugar, are used as an external application to itch. **I.I**

Sorrel

It is so well known it requires little description. It is useful to cool the blood in all hot diseases, in ague, sickness, and fainting in fevers, and procure an appetite, in debility, and weak stomach. It destroys worms in children, it is cordial to the heart. The seed is the most powerful, it is astringent, and very useful in bloody flux. The decoction of the roots is good in jaundice, and the gravel, and other diseases of the kidneys and bladder. The decoction of the flowers made with wine, will cure the black jaundice, and ulcerated bowels. A syrup made with sorrel and fumitory, is a good remedy for the itch; the juice combined with a little vinegar, is a good remedy for the tetters, ringworms, etc. It removes kernels and sores in the throat; to gargle with the juice. The leaves wrapped in cabbage-leaf, and roasted; and applied to carbuncles, boils, or plague sore, soon ripen and break them. **O.P**

Spearmint (Mentha Viridis)

Qualities similar to peppermint, but less bracing. **F.N**

Spice Bush

Good in fevers to purify the blood. **C.H**

Spotted Plantain

Grows in the woods somewhat like plantain but the leaves are smaller, spotted green and white, and a single stalk runs up from the middle of the plant several inches, bearing near at the top small round buds. It has a certain cure for King's Evil. Make a poultice of the whole plant and apply it to the swelling and use a tea of the same for constant drink. **C.H**

Spruce Fir Tree (Pinus Abies)

The exuding gum, boiled and strained, forms a plaster, called Burgundy pitch, in very common use for weak backs, pain in the side, etc. **F.N**

St John's Wort

It grows a foot and a half high. The stalks are round, thick, firm, upright, and at the top divided into several branches. The leaves are narrow, short and obtuse at the end, and if held up against the light, they appear full of small round holes. Large and bright yellow flowers abundantly grow at the tops of the branches, full of yellow threads, which, when rubbed upon the hand, stain it red, like blood. The seed is black and smells like resin. It grows in meadows, woods and copses. A decoction of the flowers, is a powerful diuretic, promoting the flow of urine. It is also good for gravel, and inflammation of the ureters. It is also useful in intermittent fevers, dysentery, hemorrhages, chest complaints and jaundice. For wounds, the tops gathered fresh and bruised are used. Boiled in wine it is excellent for inward wounds and hurts. It is a good wound herb, made into an ointment. It soon closes cuts, wounds, etc. The decoction of the plant and flowers and especially of the seed, with the juice of knotgrass, relieves vomiting, spitting of blood, and obstructions of the urine. Two drachms of the powdered herb drank in a little broth, expels choler and congealed blood from the stomach. A warm decoction of the leaves and seeds taken before fits of ague, relieves, and, eventually drives them away. The decoction of the seed, frequently and continuously taken, will cure sciatica, falling sickness, and palsy. It will also cure St. Vitus dance. The blossom will remove film from the eye, simmered in sweet oil. **O.P**

St. Peters Wort

This herb is somewhat like St. John's wort. It grows with square upright stalks, brown, having two leaves at every joint, a little round pointed, with few or no spots in the leaves, and having some smaller leaves rising from the bosom of the greater, and a little hairy. The flowers are many and star-like, with yellow threads in the center, very like the St. John's wort, but larger. It grows in moist and damp places. Its medical virtues are much the same as St. John's wort. It is also a good wound herb. **O.P**

Stavesacre

This herb is a member of the crow-foot family, its *officinale* name is *delphinum staphisaqria*. Its seeds are violently emetic and cathartic. They are seldom given internally; though the powdered seeds have been given in dropsy, in very small quantities at first, and increased until the effect is produced. Dose at first should not exceed two or three grains. It is a vermin destroyer, and will kill lice and other parasites, by washing or bathing with the liquor. It will cure the itch. The seeds are merely boiled in water. **O.P**

Stone Root (Ox Balm)

Is found growing in rich soil two or three feet high, large oval leaves, blossoms pink colored, the whole plant has, when broken, a beautiful smell, the root shaped like a kidney or melt, covered with knobs resembling boils- and when dry as hard as a knot of wood. This root bruised and steeped is a certain cure for inward ulcers, enlargement of the spleen, and obstruction in the kidneys. **C.H**

Strawberry

Makes the breath sweet and agreeable, and removes all tartar from the teeth. **F.R**

Strychnos Nux-vomica

The tree Stryclmos Nux-vomica, of the natural order Loganiaceae, is a native of the Coromandel Coast, Ceylon, Concans, and the Bengal Jungles, especially near Midnapore. The wood is hard and durable. The bark is intensely bitter, and is given with success in intermittent and remittent fevers, preference being always given to that of the root. It is also employed as an antidote to snake-bites. In the Calcutta bazaars, the kuchila bark is commonly sold under the name of "Rohun," and substituted for the harmless bark of the Soymida Febrifuga. In Europe it is known as the false Angustura bark, and it is frequently used to adulterate the true variety. The seeds are employed in the distillation of country spirits to render them more intoxicating. Instances have been observed where people having accustomed themselves to the use of kuchila nut, can consume with impunity one entire nut in the course of a day. The pulp of the fruit seems perfectly innocent, as it is greedily eaten by many kinds of birds. The seeds of nux-vomica have been found, on analysis, to contain two vegetable alkaloids; Strychnine and brucine; besides an acid, the igasuric or strychnic, and yellow coloring matters, concrete oil, gum, starch, wax, and bassorin. To the presence of a larger quantity of Strychnine, can be attributed the active properties of the kuchila seeds. The exciting action of Strychnine on the Spinal motor nerves is well known. Its use in medicine as a tonic and laxative by stimulating the muscular coat of the bowel, is attended with great success. In cholera it has been used from an idea of its being able to check excessive purging, by restoring the relaxed capillaries from enervation, but its success is still doubtful. It has been lately advocated very much as one of the potent remedies for malarious fevers. It is said to be an adequate substitute for quinine, nay, in some cases it has been found to act with decidedly good effects. We used it in a large number of cases, and though able to bear testimony to its efficacy as a valuable tonic, we must acknowledge that as an anteperiodic, it cannot equal quinine. It is very valuable in many kinds of paralysis after the inflammatory actions in the nervous centers have subsided. **I.I**

Succory (Cichorum Intybus)

The same properties as low mallows. Consumptive people will do well to use it freely. **F.N**

Sumac; often called Shoemake (Rhus Glabrum)

The berries are astringent and refrigerant. An infusion of them is a pleasant drink in feverish complaints, and a good gargle for inflamed and ulcerated throats; likewise given to check the spitting of blood. **F.N**

Sweet Flag

It is an aromatic stimulant and tonic, and very useful in weakness of the digestive organs, loss of appetite and general weakness. Combined with peruvian bark, it has been of great service in the low stages of malignant fevers. The roots powdered and infused, or decocted, has cured the colic, flatulence and ague. The dose of the root is from 20 to 40 grains; of the infusion 1 to 2 ounces and the tincture 1 to drachms. **O.P**

Sweet-scented Golden Rod (Solidago Odora)

The oil obtained from the leaves is a gentle stimulant, tending to produce perspiration, possessing the qualities of peppermint, and other aromatics. From its spicy flavor, much used to cover the taste of laudanum and other disagreeable medicines, when rejected by the stomach. **F.N**

Tag Alder

The bark of the root boiled in cider is the best thing to cleanse the blood in the spring of the year. Take a teacup full every hour or two until it operates as a physic. **C.H**

Tall Blackberry (Rubus Villosus)

Decidedly astringent. A tea made of the roots and leaves, and a syrup made of the berries, are both in common use to check a relaxed state of the bowels. It should never be used in the first stages, or while there are any feverish symptoms. **F.N**

Tamarindus Indica

The pulp of the fruits of Tamarindus Indica, of the natural order Leguminosae, a native of the East and West Indies, is universally used by the Natives of India for various domestic purposes, especially to prepare tarts and pickles. It daily enters, in some form or other, into the composition of a Native dish. In famines, the poorer classes eat the seeds, after subjecting them to a certain preparation, to free them from their outer testa. Medicinal properties: The pulp of the fruit is a mild laxative and refrigerant, useful in simple costiveness; but it cannot be relied on where free purging is requisite. It promotes the action of sweet purgatives, as manna and cassia by combination, but weakens that of the resinous ones. The seeds are sometimes used by the Native practitioners as an antidysenteric and tonic. An infusion of the leaves is used as an anthelmintic. The pulp of the tamarind quenches thirst, and acts as an excellent stomachic. **I.I**

Tansy

This is a good medicine for stranguary, pains in the back and loins, useful in painful menstruation, and is a valuable herb for female weakness; and seldom fails to cure palpitation of the heart in a few days. The flowers dried and powdered are a cure for worms. **O.P**

Unicorn Root

Is good for female weakness, pains in the breast and sides, and nervous disorders. Dose a tea-spoonful of powder in half a tea-cupful of hot water three times a day. **F.R**

Valerian Root

Is useful in all cases of nervous debility, spasmodic complaints, and hysteria. Three gills of boiling water poured on an ounce of powder, clear. Dose a wine-glassful three times a day. **F.R**

Vine Maple (Sundial)

Is a green vine as large as a quill, running around small trees in swales. Ten or twelve feet high, large leaves with smooth edges, having sometimes bunches of black berries like grapes, root the size of a pipe-stem, very yellow and very bitter. It tastes like golden seal- it runs many yards underground, near the surface. It has cured scores of pain in the breast by chewing the root like tobacco. An excellent article in syrups- good for all bilious afflictions. **C.H**

Viola Odrata

The whole plant, Viola Odorata, of the natural order Violaceae, is sold in a dry state in all the bazaars of Bengal, and is given in infusion as a diaphoretic in fevers. In larger doses, it nauseates, and often produces vomiting. Its active properties have been ascribed to a principle which have been called Violina, similar in many respects to emetine, the active principle of Ipecacuanha. The powdered plant has also been employed in the preparation of Dover's Powder in place of Ipecacuanha, but its efficacy is less reliable than that of the other. **I.I**

Virginia Snake-Root (Aristolochia Serpentaria)

The roots are tonic and antispasmodic. Half an ounce may be well steeped in a pint of boiling water, and half a wineglass full taken repeatedly, according to circumstances. It checks vomiting, and tranquilizes the stomach, particularly in bilious cases. It is very good to allay the delirium, watchfulness, etc. that often attend febrile debility; but ought not to be used when the pulse is rapid. It is a popular diaphoretic to keep out measles, rash, and other eruptions, but physicians consider it too stimulating, when there are signs of inflammation. **F.N**

Water Mint

This herb is also used as a remedy for colic, pains in the stomach and bowels, and it promotes menstruation. A single dose will frequently cure colic. It removes obstructions and strengthens the system. Its virtues ought to be better known and more used. It has prevented more doctors bills among the poorer classes as it has prevented disease from taking a hold of the system, which means a great deal, since medic. Men have learned the art of making larger figures. **O.P**

White Pine Tree (Pinus Strobus)

Frequent morning walks in pine woods are very invigorating, particularly for consumptive people. It is even deemed healthy to have these trees in the vicinity of dwellings. The bark of the twigs, and young trees, is very mucilaginous. A decoction of it, when dried, is a gentle and soothing laxative. In its green state it cannot be too highly praised as a strengthening wash for weak joints, and healing and cleansing to inflamed wounds and sores. The gum taken as pills is very physical. **F.N**

White Pond Lily (Nymphea Odorata)

A poultice of the sliced roots has astringent properties, similar to alum-curds. It has sometimes been very injudiciously employed when it was desirable to bring swellings to a head. **F.N**

Whortleberry (Huckleberry)

Grows on mountains, plains, and in swamps. The fruit and root is strongly diuretic, many have been cured of gravel and dropsy by its use. **C.H**

Wild Cherry Tree, (Primus Virginiana)

The bitter aromatic bark is one of the most valuable of native remedies. It is atonic, at the same time that it calms irritation and nervous excitability; of course, it is very useful where debility is accompanied with inflammation. Often used in the hectic fever of scrofula and consumption, and applied to many cases of dyspepsia. Half an ounce of the bruised bark steeped twenty-four hours in a pint of cold water. Half a gill drunk three or four times a day, or oftener. Sometimes the powder is used, in doses of two or three teaspoonfuls. The bark of the root is more powerful than that of the trunk. A decoction is good to wash ill conditioned ulcers. **F.N**

Wild Carrot, (Daucus Carota)

An ounce and a half of the seed steeped in a pint of boiling water is a very efficacious emmenagogue, and a diuretic used in cases of dropsy, stranguary, etc. The seed of the common cultivated carrot answers a similar purpose; and a marmalade of the roots is recommended for sea-scurvy, on account of their antiseptic qualities. A strong tea made of them is said to have relieved people afflicted with tape-worms. **F.N**

Wild Sarsaparilla, (Aralia Kudicaxdis)

A strong decoction of the roots is recommended for scrofula and other humors. A gill may be taken frequently. The Spanish Sarsaparilla, if new and well preserved, is considered more efficacious than our native plant. **F.N**

Wild Turnip (Wake Robin)

Well known, is good for old people in cases of asthma, cough. It is good for women who are not regular, one teaspoon full of powdered root mixed with smartweed tea is also used for eye water. **C.H**

Willow Tree

The leaves and bark of this tree are used to staunch bleeding wounds, spitting of blood, and other fluxes, and will stay vomiting when boiled in wine and drank. The bark is good for inflammation of the eyes, and dimness of sight. A good wash is made from the leaves and bark in wine, it will cleanse the head of dandruff, and take away scurf from the head, by washing the part with it. **O.P**

Winter Evergreen; Pipsissiwa; Rheumatism Weed (Pyrola Umbellata)

This trailing plant has high reputation. It acts as a tonic in promoting strength and appetite. As a diuretic, it is much praised in cases of stranguary, dropsy, and various disorders of the kidneys. For humors, ulcers, and tumors, it is excellent; applied both externally and internally. Drank freely and perseveringly, it is said to have cured cancers. The wash is a stimulant, like bitter sweet. A strong decoction, or infusion, is made of the leaves and stems, sweetened with molasses, or syrup. Drank very often, and in any quantities. It is well to discontinue it occasionally, and renew it, lest the system become too much accustomed to it. It has been celebrated in cases of chronic rheumatism. **F.N**

Witch Hazel

A tea made of the leaves may be taken freely with advantage. "It is the best thing for bleeding of the stomach," and also in complaints of the bowels I have used it with good effect. **O.P**

Wormseed

Boiled in milk good for worms. **C.H**

Wormwood

Good for worms, it will cleanse the system. **C.H**

Yarrow

Yarrow is of great value to use in the manner of tea in the first stages of any disease; by its prompt use it will remove obstructions, colds, fevers, inflammation, pleurisy, spitting or vomiting of blood, piles, female weakness, bowel complaint, etc. **F.R**

Yellow Dock

Will purify the blood from humors. **C.H**

MEDICAL RECIPES

This section contains some actual recipes from several different medicinal works. Some of them come from the *botanical school* which advocated "simples" or herbal cures from "primitive" cultures as an alternative to the surgical "saw bones" of the day Europeans and Americans were typically used to. Here follow some works included:

I: *Primitive Physick*, 1743, by John Wesley. A long work which is mostly about simple cures for various ailments. I have included only the section of receipts here.

II. *The Canadian Herbal* of 1851 by Shuyler Stewart. As mentioned prior in the herbal section, these entries are just the tonics and cures listed, not the herbal entries.

III: *The Useful Family Herbal*, of 1829, by John Williams. This contains only the tonics and elixirs mentioned, not the herbal entries previously so.

IV: *The Family Companion and Physician*, which dates to 1862 and was previously mentioned in the herbal section. These entries are the medical preparations found at the end of the work.

FROM "PRIMITIVE PHYSICK"

Daffy's Elixir

Take of best senna, guaiacum, licorice sliced small, aniseeds, coriander-seeds, and elecampane root, of each half an ounce, raisins-of-the-sun stoned, a quarter of a-pound; let them all be bruised, and put into a quart of the best brandy. Let it stand by the fire for a few days, then strain it.

Another Receipt for Daffy's Elixir

Take of senna leaves two ounces; jalap powder one ounce; coriander seeds a quarter of an ounce; proof spirit or brandy three pints. Put all the ingredients into a bottle for four or five days, shaking it frequently. Strain off the tincture, and add three ounces of powdered sugar-candy. This medicine is more active than the preceding, and is calculated to remove obstructions in the bowels, in colics, and other complaints that require purging, especially when castor-oil has not had the desired effect. The dose, is one, two, or three tablespoonfuls, in a cup of chamomile tea, or water.

Tarlington's Balsam

Take balsam of Peru, and balsam of Tolu, of each half an ounce, gum storax in tears, and gum guaiacum, of each one ounce; gum benjamin, an ounce and a-half; hepatic aloes, and frankincense of each two drachms; let the gum be bruised, and put all the ingredients into a quart of rectified spirits of wine; shake the bottle frequently, and in eight days it is fit for use. This is indeed a most excellent medicine for man or beast, or any fresh wound. I know none like it.

Dr James's Powders

Instead of giving half-a-crown a packet for these powders, you may at any druggist's get Dr Hardwick's fever powder for a shilling an ounce, which if it be not the same, will answer just the same end.

Scotch Pills

Dissolve two ounces of hepatic aloes, with a small spoonful of sweet oil, and as much water, in a porringer, over a small fire. When it is of a proper consistence, make it into pills, with or without licorice powder.

Emetic Tartar Vomit

Dissolve four grains of emetic tartar, in half a pint of hot water. Stir it about well. When it is cold, it is fit for use. Take two tablespoonfuls every quarter of an hour till it operates, after which no more of the vomit must be taken. Drink a small cup of gruel, or weak chamomile tea, after every puke, to work it off. A pint, or a pint and a half of gruel and tea is generally sufficient. To settle the stomach, drink weak brandy and water, and lie down half an hour. One tablespoonful of the emetic tartar water, every quarter of an hour till it pukes, is sufficient for weak people. While others again require four times as much. A child of a mouth old may take a small teaspoonful every quarter of an hour; one of three month old will require two teaspoonfuls; and so on, in proportion to their age and strength. Children require nothing to work off a vomit; and a pint or a pint and a-half of gruel, or chamomile tea, is sufficient for adults. It is an absurd and pernicious practice to drink pint after pint of hot liquids to work off a vomit; it frequently leaves a very great relaxation of the stomach, which does not recover its tone for some months afterwards. The design of giving the vomit in the manner above described, is in order that it may work in the most gentle manner possible. If it operates two, three, or four times, it is sufficient. Violent vomits are often attended with dangerous consequences; whereas, gentle ones may be repeated two or three times a-week, if necessary. If a vomit works too violently, drink moderately of weak brandy and water, and apply a raw onion cut in two to the pit of the stomach. The best time for taking a vomit is in the morning fasting. But in cases where no time is to be lost, it may be taken at eleven o'clock, or in the evening. Persons who are constipated should not venture upon a vomit, till the constipation is removed, which must be done in an hour or two's time by a clyster, or a small dose of jalap powder, or any other opening medicine. In consumptive cases, and in the dysentery cases, Ipecac is the properest vomit. The Emetic Tartar is best calculated for removing acidity, bile, and putrid matter from the stomach. In the beginning of some nervous and putrid fevers, where the pulse is weak, and the stomach loaded with sour, fetid, yellow, or green matter, there is perhaps no medicine equal to it. The heaviness, listlessness, pains in the loins, and headache, are generally removed before next morning. Emetic Tartar, when it is prescribed with judgment, and taken properly, is one of the best medicines known at this day. I have given it to many thousands of patients with the utmost safety, and with the greatest advantage. I prefer it in every case to James's fever-powder, though a medicine composed of the same materials. The operations of Emetic Tartar may be directed to the stomach, the bowels, or the skin, as the case requires. Some of the quack doctors mix powdered ginger with Emetic Tartar, and call it the ginger vomit. I do not know that this is any injury to the medicine. But some of the low country druggists adulterate it with chalk or magnesia; these articles are only hurtful by preventing the purchasers knowing exactly the quantity they ought to take. It is therefore necessary to apply to apothecaries or druggists on whose veracity you can depend.

An Excellent Eye-Water

Take flowers of zinc and white copperas, of each a quarter of an ounce, water half a pint, mix them together. It is used in the same manner as the white copperas eye-water, but in most cases it is greatly preferable, particularly in the inflammations of the eyelids, and any external or internal excoriation. If it be too sharp, add a little more water to it.

FROM "THE CANADIAN HERBAL"

An Indian Cure for the Ague

Put three hen's eggs into a pint of vinegar, and when the shell is dissolved by the vinegar, the eggs are to be taken out whole, and half a gill of this vinegar is a dose three times a day.

An Indian Remedy (For Bloody Flux)

Take three pints of pine bark, three pints of water, let it simmer down to a quart, strain off, and add one pint west india molasses, the whole for a grown person, half for a child. This remedy is simple and effectual.

An Indian Remedy for Inflammation in the Head

Take red beet roots, pound them fine, press out some of the juice, let the patient snuff some up into the head, make a poultice of the beets, and lay it on the head. For the fever, make a strong tea of spice bush, and head betony, physic with mandrake two parts, blood root one part- make them into powder, roll into pills with flour and ginger. Dose, from four to six- keep strong drafts to the feet.

Anti-spasmodic Liniment

Take No. 6 (Thompson's) add to a half pint, half an ounce of camphor gum, one spoonful spirits of turpentine, one spoonful of Hartshorn, shaken together; for cramps, lockjaw- bathe. It is a most safe and powerful liniment.

Itch Ointment

Take fine sulfur, one ounce, turpentine one ounce, lard half a pound, melt the lard and turpentine; then add the sulfur, stir til cold- apply it two or three times a day. It soon cures the complaint without changing the clothes.

Celandine Ointment for Piles

Take wild or garden celandine, bruise and cover with any kind of spirits, and simmer a while; then add fresh butter, and let the whole remain over the fire til the leaves are crisped; strain and add one teaspoon full. Bees' wax for piles, and cutaneous eruptions- excellent.

Irritating Plaster

Take one pound of tea, half a pound of turpentine; Bees' wax half a pound, melt, strain, and boil a few minutes; then remove from the fire and stir in the following as it cools; finely pulverized mixed and sifted. Namely, pokeroot, mandrake, bloodroot, and wild turnip, three ounces each- keep stirring til the whole mass is well mixed- spread on a piece of soft leather and place over the part affected; keep it on as long as you can bear it; then remove and put it on again in a day or two; when removed wash the parts with salt and water, or comfrey. This plaster will bring out eruptions like the smallpox and cause a discharge of matter. It is superior to all other plasters for old ulcers, spinal diseases, pains in the side, etc.

Female Regulating Pills

Take beef gall (boil it in a kettle and when dry it will powder) one tablespoon full, gentian root one tablespoon full, vervine leaf tincture, ginger tincture, elder flowers or leaves tinctured, Indian Hemp root tincture, Tansey tincture, wet the whole mass with strong smartweed tea, work til thick enough, and then roll them in powder of bitter root and cayenne pepper. Powder all the above fine and sift before mixing. Bathe the feet in hot water and take from three to six at bedtime. An invaluable remedy.

Bilious Pills

Take half a bushel of butternut bark peeled in May or June, bruise and boil down half, strain and afterwards evaporate to the consistency of thick honey (be careful not to burn it.) It may be dried in a warm oven until it will pill, roll the pills in a powder of bloodroot and bitter root, equal parts- adding one spoonful of ginger to the mass before making into pills. Dose; from two to five pills the size of a pea at bedtime.

Emetic Pills

Boil boneset, vervine, and smartweed, equal parts, strain and boil down as thick as tar. Roll in cayenne and lobelia. Dose; from one to six, drink milk porridge or bran tea. Excellent.

Mandrake Pills (Anti-dyspeptic)

Take powdered mandrake root, four parts, gensen root powder, one part, cayenne pepper, two parts, wet the mass with smartweed tea and form into pills. Dose; from three to six at night, are sufficient to regulate the bowels. These pills are antidyspeptic, good for jaundice. They may be made with mandrake two parts, cayenne one part. Dose as above.

Vegetable Snuff

Take sassafras bark, colt's foot root, and bloodroot, equal parts. Dry and powder, sift and use- for catarrh and obstructions in the head.

Anti-spasmodic Mucilage

Pleurisy root, comfrey, dandelion, skunk cabbage (root), dried and powdered, equal parts, adding one spoonful of ginger to half a pint of the mixture. Dose; one teaspoon full in hot water night and morning.

Cough Powders

Take equal parts of horehound, wild turnip, skunk cabbage, bitter root; powder and mix one spoonful of cayenne to half a pint of the powdered mass. Dose; from half to one teaspoon full at bedtime, taken in smartweed tea. Excellent.

Indian Remedy for Jaundice

Take gold thread, steep it in vinegar, until it makes a strong bitter. Take a quarter of a gill three times a day.

FROM "THE USEFUL FAMILY HERBAL"

The Best Salve for Women's Sore Breasts ever Found

Take one pound of tobacco, one pound spikenard, half a pound comfrey, and boil them in three quarts chamber lye til almost dried; squeeze out the juice, add it to pitch and bees wax, and simmer it over a moderate heat to the consistency of salve. Apply it to the part affected.

An Ointment to Relax Stiff Joints and Shrunken Sinew

Take a pound of hog's lard, put into it a small handful of melolat green, stew it well together, strain it off, add it to one ounce rattlesnake grease, an ounce of olive oil, and ten drops of oil lavender. Mix them well together. Anoint three times a day and rub it in well with the hand.

Valuable Cure for Inveterate Old Sore Legs

Take the bark of cavron wood or shrub maple, boil it very strong, take part of the liquor and boil it down to a salve, and wash the part affected every time it is dressed. Apply new salve twice a day. Make a tea of the same, and drink it three times a day.

To Cure the Bite of a Rattlesnake

Take green horehound tops, pound them fine, press out the juice, let the patient drink a tablespoon full of the juice morning, noon, and night, or three times in twenty four hours. Apply the pounded herbs to the bite and change them twice a day. The patient may drink a spoonful of sweet olive oil. This seldom fails curing.

Cure for the Itch

Take half a pound of hogs' lard, four ounces spirits turpentine, two ounces flour sulfur, and mix them together cold; apply it to the ankles, knees, wrists, and elbows, and rub it on the palms of the hands, if there be any raw spots; apply a little three nights when going to bed.

The Red Salve for Swellings in Formation

Take linseed oil, one pound, sweet oil or fresh butter, half a pound, red lead, one pound, boil them all together, stir it boiling, then slack the heat and add to it two pounds of bees wax, one pound of rosin, and stir them together til cold.

Foote's Ointment

Take one pound of hog's lard, one pound of mutton tallow, half a pound oil spike, and heat them over a moderate fire until united; then add as much bees wax and rosin as will make it to a salve- the renowned Foote's Ointment. This cures all common sore where there is no inflammation.

An Excellent Family Bilious Pill

This pill, made frequent use of, prevents all kinds of fevers. Take one pound sweet rind aloes, four ounces jalap, four ounces pulverized blood root, two ounces cloves, and two ounces saffron, and beat them all to a fine powder. Pill them with molasses- mix them well in a mortar. The common way of using them is to take every night one, of the size of a pea, if you have a bilious habit. But if you wish them to act as a physic, take four or five on going to bed. They give no pain in the operation.

For the Toothache, if the Teeth Be Hollow

Take gum opium, gum camphor, and spirits of turpentine, equal parts, rub them in the mortar to a paste, dip lint in the paste and put it in the hollow of the tooth every time after eating. Make use of this three or four days, and it will generally cure the tooth from ever aching.

For the Bilious Colic

Take the above mentioned bilious pill, add it to half its weight in calomel, give four or five pills, and repeat the dose, and it is a certain cure for the bilious colic. Or take mandrake root, dried and pulverized; a large teaspoon full is a dose. This must be repeated several times.

A Sure Cure for Canker in the Mouth

Take one pound of fresh butter, put it into an earthen vessel well glazed, set it on the fire and let it boil; while boiling add to it four common green frogs- put them in alive, let them stew until the frogs are dry, then take them out and add to it a little chamomile and parsley; when cold stir in a little burned alum, pulverized, and if the fever is high, give a little rattlesnake gall, dried in chalk. This will cure the most inveterate canker in the mouth, throat, or stomach.

A Medicine to Cure Inward Ulcers

Take sassafras root bark, two ounces, coltsfoot root, two ounces, bloodroot one ounce, gum myrrh one ounce, winter bark one ounce, socotrine aloe one ounce, steep them all in two quarts of spirits and drink a small glass every morning, fasting.

For Cramp in the Stomach or Any Inward Part

Take ten drops of the oil of lavender on sugar or in wine. Repeat the dose once an hour if required.

A Cure for the Flying Rheumatism

Take princess pine tops, horseradish roots, elecampane roots, prickly ash bark, bitter-sweet bark off the root, wild cherry bark, and mustard seed- a small handful of each- one gill of tar water into one pint of brandy, or the same proportion. Drink a small glass before eating, three times a day.

Remarkable Plaster to Ease the Pain of Felons or Frog Felons, or Any Such Tumor, on the Hands or Feet or Elsewhere

Get a pitch pine knot from an old log, the side next to or in the ground. Split the knot fine, boil out half a pound of pitch; take four ounces of strong tobacco, boil it in water, strain out the tobacco, boil the resin until it is thick, then add the pitch to the resin, simmer it over a moderate heat, and stir all the time til it forms a salve altogether. If the swelling be on the hand or finger, lay the plaster on the wrist. If on the foot or toe, lay the plaster on the ankle. Or wherever it may be, lay it above the next joint, this will take out all the pain in a short time. Dress the sore with any other salve that is best. This cure is infallible.

An Excellent Remedy for Asthma

Take spikenard root, two ounces, sweet flag root two ounces, elecampane root two ounces, common chalk two ounces; beat very fine in a mortar, add to it a pound of honey, and beat it well together. A teaspoon full is a dose three times a day.

Excellent Pill for Hysteria

Take a quantity of white root, otherwise called Canada root- boil it in fair water- when it is boiled very soft, strain out the roots, and boil the liquor to the consistency of a thick paste, so that it may be pilled. Let the patient take two or three pills at a dose when the disorder is coming on.

Cure for Bleeding at the Stomach

Take a pound of yellow dock root, dry it thoroughly, pound it fine. Boil it in a quart of sweet milk, strain it off, and drink a gill three times a day. Take also a pill of white pine turpentine every day to heal the vessels that leak.

For the Dropsy

Take half a pound of blue flag root, half a pound of elecampane root, boiled in two gallons of fair water to one quart, sweetened with one pint of molasses. Let the patient take half a gill three times a day before eating.

For the Canker Rash

White birch root, pulverized very fine, given in small doses three or four times a day. Make a tea of the same, for constant drink. For the fever, give rattlesnake gall, three grains at a time.

For Rickets in Children (In the Bowels)

One ounce of rhubarb, powdered in one ounce of enceviniris, put into one quart of wine or brandy. If a child is a year old, it may take a tablespoon full at a time; if older take more, to half a gill for an adult. If any part of the body is affected with the disorder, bathe the part with brandy, and drink turkey root, steeped in wine, three or four times a day.

Sure Remedy for Women's Sore Nipples

When the infant stops sucking apply a plaster of balsam fir. It will cure in three or four days.

Cure for Itching Heels or Feet, or Ribbed Heels

Take any kind of tallow and tallow the part affected with it and rub it in by a hot fire, at night, on going to bed. Repeat it three or four times.

Preservative Against All Sorts of Bilious Fevers

The fullness of bile is the cause of all sorts of fevers, and jaundice, bilious colic, and cholera. Physic often with blood root and mandrake root mixed together, once a quarter, and make small beer with elder roots, spruce boughs, burdock roots, hops, white ash bark, sarsaparilla roots, and spikenard. Make a bitter with unicorn roots, and bark, white wild roots, and the yellow dust of hops. If a family will continue this method they will never be troubled with fevers.

For the Quinsy in the Throat

Sweat the throat with spotted carduus boiled in milk and water by holding a pot of it under the throat as hot as can be borne. Hold some of it in the mouth, and when the swelling has gone down, wear a piece of black silk about the neck constantly and it will prevent the quinsy from ever coming again.

For Swellings that Come of Themselves

An ointment of alder tags and sugar of lead simmered in hogs' lard, and melilot and saffron, simmered all together. Strain off and anoint the part affected; it will scatter the swelling if taken in time. Give the patient something to guard the stomach before anointing.

Excellent Poultice for Old Inveterate Sores

Scrape yellow carrots, wilt them on a pan or fire shovel, very soft. It takes out the inflammation and the swelling; and is an excellent poultice for a schirrous breast.

Excellent Medicine for Inward Pains or Ulcers

Take elecampane, comfrey, spikenard, masterwort, angelica, and ginseng roots, of each a pound, boughs of fir two pounds, chamomile one pound; put them into a still with a gallon of rum and two gallons of water; draw off six quarts, drink a small glass night and morning.

Another Excellent Essence, Good for All Sorts of Inward Weakness, Inward Fevers, Coughs, or Pain in the Side, Stomach, or Breast

Take twenty pounds of fir boughs, one pound of spikenard, four pounds of red clover; put them into a still with ten gallons of cider; draw off three gallons and drink half a gill night and morning.

For the Catarrh in the Head

Take yellow dock root, split it and dry it in an oven; bloodroot and scoke root four ounces of each; cinnamon one ounce, cloves half an ounce- pound them all very fine and let the patient use it as a snuff eight or ten times a day. Every night smoke a pipe full of cinnamon mixed with a little tobacco, and sweat the head with hemlock, brandy, and camphor. Pour a little camphorated spirits and brandy into the hot liquor to sweat.

For an Inflammation of the Head

Take red beets, pound them very fine, press out some of the juice, let the patient snuff some up into the head, and make a poultice of the beets, and lay it on the mould of the head. For the fever, use rattlesnake gall, cream tartar, and head bitney. Bleed as often as once a day. Physic with deerweed root, or wild mandrake root, with a little bloodroot. Keep strong drafts to the feet.

For a Nosebleed

Take common nettle roots, dry them, carry them in the pocket and chew them every day. Continue this three weeks.

FROM "THE FAMILY COMPANION AND PHYSICIAN"

Wine Bitters

2 drachms Wild Cherry Bark,
2 of Spignant Root,
2 of Solomons' Seal Root,
2 of Comfrey Root,
1 of Colombo Root,
1 of Gentian Root,
1 of Chamomile Flowers.

Bruise all, and add boiling water to cover. Let stand one hour; then add 1 quart Domestic or Port Wine.

Dose: 1/2 to 1 wine-glassful three times a day.

This is the best strengthening tonic I have ever found for weak and relaxed systems.

Sweating Powder

1/2 oz pulv. Opium,
1/2 oz pulv. Gum Camphor,
1/2 oz pulv. Ipecac,
1/4 lb. Cream Tartar.

Dose: from 1/4 to 1/2 a teaspoonful.

Mandrake Compound

Equal parts Pulv. Mandrake Root, Spearmint Herb, and Cream Tartar.

Sassafras Liniment

1/2 oz. Sassafras Oil,
1/4 oz Hemlock Oil,
1/2 oz Red Cedar Oil,
1/4 oz Camphor Gum,
1/4 oz Capsicum,
1/4 oz Turpentine Spirits,
1 pint Alcohol.

Mix all, and bathe the parts freely and frequently. For pain in the head, back, side, breast, or limbs.

Emetic Preparation

1 part pulv. Lobelia Seeds,
1 part Herbs,
2 parts Ipecac Roots,
1 part Blood Root.

Mix all thoroughly, and give one teaspoonful every twenty minutes, drinking freely lukewarm water, until the patient vomits freely. This will not only cleanse the stomach, but produce a lively action of the blood, and produce profuse perspiration, and often break up fever without the aid of other medicines, if taken in time.

Cough Drops, for Colds and Coughs

1/2 drachm Oil of Almonds,
1/2 drachm Balsam of Fir,
1/2 drachm Tinct. Balsam Tolu,
1/2 drachm Wine,
1/2 drachm Tinct. of Black Cohosh.

Mix all, and take from 25 to 30 drops three to live times

a day.

Rum Liniment

Take equal parts of good old Jamaica Rum, Laudanum, and Tinct. of Camphor. For inflammation. Warm and bathe tho parts, or apply a cloth wet in the same.

Cayenne Cough Powder

1/2 oz. pulv. Cayenne Pepper,
1/2 oz Skunk Cabbage,
1/2 oz Wild Turnip,
1/2 oz Ipecac,
1/2 oz Opium.

Dose: one eighth of a teaspoonful every four to six hours. For Colds, Coughs, Inflammation of the Lungs, and Difficulty of Breathing.

White Drops

1 oz. Oil of Sweet Almonds,
1 oz Sweet Spirits of Nitre,
1 oz Castile Soap, shaved fine,
1/2 oz Balsam Copaiba,
1/2 oz Spirits of Turpentine,
1 drachm Camphor Gum.

Sudorific Drops

2 oz. of Ipecac,
2 oz Saffron,
2 oz Camphor Gum,
2 oz Virginia Snake Root,
2 oz Opium,
2 oz Motherwort Extract,

3 quarts Holland Gin.

Mix all, and let stand two weeks. Strain or filter.

Dose: 1 tea-spoonful given in a cup of Catnip tea every hour or two, until it produces perspiration.

Cholera Compound

1 oz. Tinct. Camphor,
1 oz Rhubarb,
1 oz Opium.

Mix all.

Dose: from 20 to 30 drops every fifteen minutes. For Dysentery, Cramp of the Stomach, Pain of tho Bowels, Bilious Colic. Etc.

Compound Tincture of Spearmint

Take the best old Holland Gin and apply to the green herb. Bruise and press out the juice, and add equal parts Sweet Spirits of Niter and Tincture of Blue Flag. Dose must be regulated by the urgency, of the case as well as the habits of the patient, say from 1 tca-spoonful to 1 table-spoonful every thirty to sixty minutes. For Stoppage of Urine and Disease of the Kidneys and Prostate Glands, Etc.

Red Ointment

3 oz. of Fresh Butter,
2 1/2 drachms of Red Precipitate,
1 oz Prepared Tutty,
1 oz Camphor Gum, dissolved in 1 oz Olive Oil.
1/2 oz. of white Wax.

Melt the Wax in the Oil, and while cooling, stir in the other ingredients, and continue to stir until cold. For Sore Eyes, Eruptions, etc.

Neutralizing Powder

1 oz. pulv. Turkey Rhubarb,
1 oz Saleratus,
1 oz Peppermint Herb.

Dose: 1 large tea-spoonful. Add 1 pint of boiling Water. When cold, strain, sweeten, and add 1 tablespoon full of brandy, and take from 1 to 2 tablespoons full every thirty to sixty minutes.

No. 4 Powder

1/2 oz. pulv. Dandelion Root,
1/2 Mandrake Root,
1/4 oz Blood Root.

Mix all, and add a few drops of Peppermint Oil, and mix well.

Dose: every morning the amount that will lay on a five cent piece.

Camphor Compound

Take Whiskey, Camphor and Water, warm wet cloths and apply to the parts inflamed.

Sarsaparilla Syrup

1 lb. American Sarsaparilla,
1/2 lb. Guaicum Shavings,
1/4 lb. Elder Blows,

1/4 lb. Burdock Root,
1/4 lb. Bark of Sassafras Root.

Add water; boil well; turn off; add more; boil and turn off; and so continue until the roots are boiled soft; then strain and simmer down to one gallon. Add a little spirits, and sweeten to taste. For impurities of the blood.

Dose: from a half to one wine-glassful, three times a day.

Caustic Potash

You will take Hickory, hard Maple, or white Elm, and burn into ashes; then leach and strain the lye free from ashes, and simmer down until dry; then stir until cold and fine.

Fire Oil Ointment

Take 1 oz. of pure Fire Weed Oil and 1 lb. of hog's Lard. Mix all cold and it is fit for use.

Gargle

To cure common Sore Throat, take 1 Sumac Bob and add a pint of boiling water, and gargle the throat three to five times a
day.

To Remove Warts and Corns

Take 1 lb. of common Potash, and half a pint of water; add half an oz. of Extract of Belladonna, 1 oz. of Gum Arabic, and a little Wheat Flour, so as to form a paste. Keep well corked. Apply a little to the parts affected, and let it remain about live minutes. Then loosen the edges with a sharp knife, and presently you can take it out by the roots. Then add a little

Sweet Oil and Vinegar, and keep the parts warm and dry until healed.

Strengthening Plaster

Take 3 parts Hemlock Gum, and 1 of White Pine Gum. Melt and strain. Spread on a thin piece of leather, and apply while moderately warm.

Hair Dye

Preparation No. 1:

Take 2 drachms Gallic Acid, 1 oz. Alcohol, 3 oz. soft Water. Mix all. After cleansing the hair well, and drying, apply it with a tooth-brush. Let it dry well.

Preparation No. 2:

Take 2 drachms Nitrate of Silver, 1 of Spirits Ammonia FFFF, 1 oz. soft Water. Mix. After applying No. 1 as directed, then apply No. 2 in like manner.

Katharion

To restore Hair in the head; also to give it gloss and beauty.

Take 1 pint of Alcohol,
1 oz. Cantharides Spirits,
4 oz. Castor Oil,
1/2 oz. Bergamot.

Pain Extracting Plaster

For Colds, Coughs, and Spinal Affections. Take transparent Burgundy Pitch, and add Beeswax for consistency.

Melt, spread, and apply.

Anti-Spasmodic Drops

1/2 oz. Fluid Extract of Ladies' Slipper.
1/2 oz Catnip,
1/2 oz Skull Cap.

Mix all.

Dose: from 5 to 15 drops once in two hours. This is a valuable medicine for Headache, Neuralgia, Nervousness, etc.

Fire Ointment

Pulverized Charcoal mixed with hog's Lard, spread on cloth, and applied, will extract the fire in a few minutes and relieve the pain.

Balm of Gilead Ointment

Take the Balm Buds and the inner Bark of Sweet Elder, equal parts. Add fresh Butter to cover. Simmer slowly four or five hours, until crisped. Then press out, and when cold it is fit for use. This is a valuable medicine for Cuts, Burns, Scalds, Frosted Limbs, Ulcers, etc. It may be used on any eruption where the skin is broken.

White Liniment

For Chilblains, Rheumatism, Sprains, and Bruises, on man or beast. Take 1 pint of Olive Oil and 8 pints of Ammonia-Hartshorn. Mix and shake well before using. Keep well corked, and apply freely and frequently.

Soothing Syrup

Take Motherwort Herb, 4 parts, and Poppy Blows, I part; extract the substance, sweeten well, and give the child a few drops according to age and strength.

Worm Powder

Take 1/2 oz of Senna, 1/2 oz Carolina Pink, 1/2 oz Manna.

Add 1 quart of boiling water; let stand six hours; strain and sweeten, and give the child half a tea-spoonful three or four times a day, say a child six years old. Vary according to age.

Inflammatory Liniment

Take equal parts good old Jamaica Rum, Laudanum, and Tinct. of Camphor. Warm, and bathe the parts freely and frequently.

SOME OLD MEDICAL TERMINOLOGY

Here I have compiled a few terms related to weights and measurements, as well as to types of diseases and symptoms or merely medical terms generally. Some terms are still informally used regionally or regularly.

Ague: Chronic malarial infection.

Animalculae: Early term roughly equating to "germs."

Aperient: Laxative, normally a mild one.

Apoplexy: Paralysis, normally related to a stroke.

Bilious Fever: Fever associated with intestinal difficulties. Often typhus.

Carminative: Any herbal substance thought to support digestion.

Catarrh: Inflammation and stuffiness associated with various diseases such as influenza.

Change of Life: Menopause in women.

Chillblain: Swelling due to excess cold.

Colic: Abdominal cramps and pains.

Costiveness: Constipation.

Croup: Often streptococcus. Sometimes laryngitis.

Debility: Weakness.

Decoction: A concentrated result from boiling plant materials.

Dyspepsia: Indigestion.

Drachm: Sixty grains. About 1/8 ounce.

Electuary: A Sweetened medicine.

Emetic: Substance causing vomiting.

Expectorant: Anything which causes mucus to loosen.

Erysipelas: Streptococcus infection.

Falling Sickness: Epilepsy.

Febrifuge: Anything reducing feverishness.

Felon: Fingertip abscess. Staph infection of the area.

Female complaints: Menstruation, whether due to heaviness of flow, irregularity, or excessive pain.

Flux: Diarrhea, usually severe.

Goiter: Thyroid swelling due to iodine deficiency.

Grain: About 60 milligrams. Still used as a weight measurement for the purposes of bullets.

Gravel: Kidney stones or similar complaints.

Grippe: Flu, especially a severe one.

Hysterics: Mania or panic.

King's Evil: Scrofula, lymphatic swelling.

Lockjaw: Usually a symptom of tetanus.

Marasmus: Wasting disease, normally the term used for children.

Nervous Debility: Nervous breakdown.

Paroxysm: Convulsion.

Piles: Hemorrhoids.

Phthisic: Tuberculosis. Sometimes other lung disorders leading to wasting.

Quinsy: Throat inflammation.

Remittent Fever: Any fever in which temperature remains elevated at all times despite variance.

Rickets: Symptomatic effects of vitamin D deficiency.

Saleratus: Sodium Bicarbonate

Stranguary: Various urinary disorders causing difficult flow and pain.

St. Vitus Dance: A syndrome following streptococcus infection and some other diseases, which causes spasmodic jerking of the body.

Sudorific: A compound which causes sweating.

The Itch: When not general, usually refers to a sexually transmitted disease, often Chlamydia or Gonnorhea.

Tincture: An extract, into alcohol, glycerin, water, etc.

Vermifuge: Substance which is used to kill parasites.

Water: When not used in the context of actual water, this term refers to urine.

Wen: A cyst or other growth in the skin.

Winds/windy: Gassy.

BIBLIOGRAPHY

This short bibliography is meant as a suggested reading list for those who want more materials to peruse on the subject of folk medicine.

Anshutz, E.P, *New, Old, and Forgotten Remedies*, 1900

Biddle, John, Materia Medica and Therapeutics for Physicians and Students, 1889

Bryan, W.S Plumer, *Prayer and the Healing of Disease*, 1896

Budge, E.A Wallis, *The Divine Origin of the Craft of the Herbalist*, 1928

Clarke, J.H, *Gunpowder as a War Remedy*, 1915

Cullen, William, *A Treatise of the Medica Materia* (Two Volumes), 1802

Fernie, W.T, *Meals Medicinal with 'Herbal Simples'*, 1905

Foreman, Richard, *The Cherokee Physician*, 1849

Harding, A.R, *Ginseng and Other Medicinal Plants*, 1908

Henkel, Alice, *American Root Drugs*, 1907

Henkel, Alice, *Wild Medicinal Plants of the United States*, 1906

Hooker, William Jackson, *Medical Botany* (Five

Volumes), 1832

Lewis, Charles A, *The Only Osteopractic Method of Treating Diseases at Home*, 1902

Lindley, John, *A Natural System of Botany*, 1836

Pechey, John, *The Compleat Herbal of Physical Plants*, 1707

Reid, Hugo, *Outlines of Medical Botany*, 1839

Renouard, P.V, *History of Medicine From its Origin to the Nineteenth Century*, 1867

Ringer, Sydney, *A Handbook of Therapeutics*, 1888

Slack, George, *Slacks Herbal*, 1892

Stout, H.R, *Our Family Physician*, 1885

Thomson, Samuel, *New Guide to Health*, 1825

Withington, Edward Theodore, *Medical History from the Earliest Times*, 1894

THE END

9 798567 631072